War and Media

The Emergence of Diffused War

Andrew Hoskins and Ben O'Loughlin

polity

The right of Andrew Hoskins and Ben O'Loughlin to be identified as Authors of this Work has been asserted in accordance with the UK Copyright, Designs and Patents Act 1988.

First published in 2010 by Polity Press

Polity Press
65 Bridge Street
Cambridge CB2 1UR, UK

Polity Press
350 Main Street
Malden, MA 02148, USA

ISBN-13: 978-0-7456-3849-2
ISBN-13: 978-0-7456-3850-8(pb)

A catalogue record for this book is available from the British Library.

Typeset in 10.5 on 12pt Plantin
by Servis Filmsetting Ltd, Stockport, Cheshire
Printed and bound in Great Britain by
MPG Books Group Limited, Bodmin, Cornwall

The publisher has used its best endeavours to ensure that the URLs for external websites referred to in this book are correct and active at the time of going to press. However, the publisher has no responsibility for the websites and can make no guarantee that a site will remain live or that the content is or will remain appropriate.

Every effort has been made to trace all copyright holders, but if any have been inadvertently overlooked the publisher will be pleased to include any necessary credits in any subsequent reprint or edition.

For further information on Polity, visit our website: www.politybooks.com

WAR AND MEDIA

For Philip Seib

CONTENTS

ACKNOWLEDGEMENTS

The emergence of *War and Media* has been richly aided through a range of collaborations we have enjoyed over the past five years. We had the benefit of working on two projects funded by the Economic and Social Research Council (ESRC) New Security Challenges Programme over this time, with Mina Al-Lami, Akil Awan, Carole Boudeau, Mark Carrigan, Stuart Croft, Marie Gillespie, James Gow and Chris Perkins.

Our ideas were also shaped through our participation in the excellent ESRC seminar series, 'Ethics and the War on Terror: Politics, Multiculturalism, and Media', headed by Gillian Youngs, who has long been an inspiration to us. Input of another kind came through the journal *Media, War & Conflict*, which is a constant source of cutting-edge work in the field, and through our collaboration with Barry Richards and Philip Seib.

We are very grateful to two anonymous reviewers and especially to Oliver Boyd-Barrett for their close reading of our draft manuscript and for their insightful advice.

Our ideas have also benefited from debate and feedback from our participation in more than 100 workshops, symposia and conferences over the past few years, including input from Lance Bennett, Philip Bobbitt, Antoine Bousquet, Angharad Closs Stephens, Bill Durodie, Sarah Maltby, Laura Roselle, Chris Rumford, Martin Shaw, Annabelle Sreberny and Phil Taylor. We are also indebted to the ongoing support for our work provided by Steve Brown, Andrew Chadwick, Rachel Hendrick, Nuria Lorenzo-Dus, Sarah Maltby, William Merrin, Anna Reading and David Smith.

We are indebted to Andrea Drugan at Polity for her vision, professionalism and enthusiasm. We are also grateful to Neil de Cort and Sarah Dancy for their assistance in moving the book through production.

TABLES AND FIGURES

1

INTRODUCTION

Roger Silverstone writes:

> I have a memory of an interview broadcast on BBC Radio 4 on *The World at One* during the height of the war in Afghanistan which followed hard on the heels of the attack on the World Trade Center. It was with an Afghani blacksmith who, having apparently failed to hear or understand the US airplane based, supposedly blanket, propaganda coverage of his country, offered his own account of why so many bombs were falling around his village. It was because, his translated voice explained, Al-Qaeda had killed many Americans and their donkeys and had destroyed some of their castles. He was not, of course, entirely wrong. (2007: 1)

The world imploded in the twentieth century. Once news could be transferred electronically, rather than via printed paper or newsreels on trains and boats, information about war, conflict and catastrophe could traverse distances almost instantaneously. The potential for global awareness, for a global village, meant danger and suffering could be brought closer to us. And as our fields of perceptions continue to change, conflict and the people involved in it become visible in new ways, affecting our relations to war. Whether through live broadcast or interactive media, we can now connect to war in a manner that was not possible before; we can read and respond to the blog of the soldier in the field of operations, download the PDF terror-training manual, click and donate to the humanitarian worker, or listen to the live translated voice of the Afghani blacksmith as we have our lunch.

Just what these transformations mean for our world is hardly understood. The difficulty that governments, militaries, media organizations and other big institutions have had adapting to this world in the first years of the twenty-first century is hard to overstate. Images and stories have emerged, been debated and reacted to by populations around the world even before these big institutions have decided on their understanding of them, let alone their strategy. All that can be done, some argue, is to have narratives in place for any and every eventuality, just in case.

Human society no longer works according to mechanical principles, if it ever did. Thanks to media technologies, we live in a new media ecology marked by – terrorized by – 'effects without causes', to borrow a term from Faisal Devji' (2005). Things just seem to happen 'out of nowhere', such as the 9/11 attacks in the United States. Of course, this is not strictly the case. Actions are planned and executed, whether by occupying powers, terrorist cells or humanitarian rescue groups. But instant recording, archiving and distribution of images and stories add a chaotic element to any action. Nobody knows *who* will see an event, *where* and *when* they will see it or *how* they will interpret it. Nobody knows how the reactions of people locally or around the world will feed back into the event, setting off a chain of other events, anywhere, in which anybody may get caught up. The Danish cartoons of the Prophet Muhammad, images of abuse from Abu Ghraib prison, and 9/11 itself all demonstrate that the effects of events cannot be foreseen by those who originally record them.

Nothing can be gained from reproducing the conventional academic approaches to war and media, be these constructed historically, specifically to a particular conflict, or comparatively, focusing on basic themes. Such an account would be significantly blinkered to the genuinely paradigmatic shift occurring in modern media and in modern warfare – the emergence of diffused war. Providing an intervention adequate to the dynamics of the flux of the post-broadcast era is difficult. Unfortunately, in the study of warfare, the disciplinary boundaries that regulate what is relevant and what is not – in terms of traditions, theories and methods – are not so malleable. This book attempts to overcome these limitations. If we recognize that it is the media surround itself – the new media ecology – that constitutes the very condition of terror for all of us, how can we analyse and understand its dynamics? Media enable a perpetual connectivity that appears to be the key modulator of insecurity and security today, amplifying our awareness of distant conflicts or close-to-home threats, yet containing these insecurities in comforting news packages. This connectivity is the principal mechanism through which media is weaponized, made a tool of warfare. It is not simply that media perpetuate a residual awareness of ongoing distant conflicts and the possibility of terror near or far, but that this connectivity is what enables a world of 'effects without causes' in which risk and danger seem impossible to calculate. Such a context makes order and security less easy to achieve. It is this connectivity by all participants and witnesses, in this emergent environment, which anchors and begins our account. It is in the new media ecology that established theories and assumptions about audiences, propaganda and warfare are, at the very least, significantly challenged (Der Derian, 2009: 252).

This book seeks to find intelligibility, not order. Our intention is to provide the concepts and tools for the reader to acquire greater literacy of war and media. For some, this will not be easy. For those used to thinking of military strategy, propaganda and political communications in conventional terms, our presentation of the relation of war and media may jar. But, as Philip Bobbitt writes, 'almost every widely held idea we currently entertain about twenty-first century terrorism and its relationship to the wars against terror is wrong and must be thoroughly rethought' (2008: 5). So it is for war and media in general. It is to that challenge that we respond.

1. Diffused War

Our account of diffused war refers to a new paradigm of war in which (i) the mediatization of war (ii) makes possible more diffuse causal relations between action and effect, (iii) creating greater uncertainty for policymakers in the conduct of war. In this section we shall unpack this definition and show how its three axes – mediatization, causality and decision-making – can shape and reinforce one another in ways that make diffused war a coherent and intelligible paradigm. It is significant that we have chosen the term 'axes', since each is a matter of degree rather than being simply present or absent. Not all war is mediatized; not all actions have unforeseen effects; and uncertainty rarely paralyses policymakers absolutely. Rather, there is a modulation of each; policymakers' certainty oscillates over time, for instance. It is our contention that these three axes capture the dynamics of an emerging paradigm of war.

We have not developed the concept of diffused war to explain *why* war occurs in the first place, but to describe and explain the changing character of war – the what, how, when and where. The causes of war may be relatively stable, a matter of political and economic interests for state and non-state actors. The opening decade of the twenty-first century was marked by wars for control of resources and territory, and the development of private markets for security forces and surveillance technologies, amongst other things. There is little novelty there. However, the way war proceeds – its justification, conduct, reconstruction, remembrance – is changing markedly, and it is these changes that the concept 'diffused war' seeks to capture.

It is easier to discern the distinctiveness of diffused war by setting it in a historical context. The 'first media war in history' was the Crimean War of 1853 to 1856, according to Ulrich Keller (2001: 251).[1] This appears to be a remarkable claim, given the volume of the news, literary and photographic record of the Great Wars, the TV 'living-room' war of Vietnam, and the opening of the global satellite era with the spectacle of the 1991 Gulf War. However, for Keller, the Crimean War marked a significant shift from war as a show at which some civilian 'spectators' were there, co-present to the event, to something more organized for commercial mass consumption. It was 'the first historical instance when modern institutions such as picture journalism, lithographic presses and metropolitan show business combined to create a war in their own image' (ibid.: ix). Aspects of the war were deliberately organized as a mass spectacle. For instance, some phases of the war were highly visible to crowds, who had to be contained by the British cavalry in their fascination to view the colourful uniforms of the advancing regiments prior to a major attack on Sebastopol (ibid.: 251).

Yet, Keller argues, the eyewitnessing of certain historical events has traditionally been the privilege of elite audiences, and it was not until the Victorian era that war became more significantly 'mediated', including through 'theatrically structured performances':

Even if performed almost simultaneously with the actual events, often by invalids just returned from the theatre of *war*, these were *mediated* stage presentations, made possible by the availability of a group of professional eyewitnesses who formed, with their cameras and communication lines, a fully-fledged apparatus of front-line observation. The verbal and pictorial reports of these lieutenants of the urban crowds, together with the art works and show attractions, made the Crimean War the first *media* war in history. (Ibid.: 251; original emphasis)

Keller's visual history of the Crimean War illuminates a significant phase in the history of shifting *representations* of warfare, along with the shifting *perceptions* of warfare by those whose collective name wars are often fought or claimed to be fought in. Keller's work usefully questions the notion of 'media war' as principally a product of the mass media of the late twentieth and early twenty-first century.

This is an interesting observation for a number of reasons. For instance, in chapter 6, we suggest that the presence (or absence) of an event in collective or social memory is often related to the mechanism through which a person originally experienced it (usually through media), and the 'fit' of its original representations with the media of the day that reproduce or perpetuate a certain history of warfare. The neglect (or amnesia) concerning the Crimean War in modern media accounts has not occurred for any particularly conspiratorial reasons, but, rather, because it did not provide any moving images that would later make good television. And it is the medium of television that has utterly defined the vicarious experience of modern warfare, as well as shaping the way in which war is an object of study, which even historians may take note of.

Keller's work in detailing the significance of the role of the visual media in mid-nineteenth century warfare raises the important question: how would war proceed in isolation, if our media did not exist? Keller is explicit: 'Media-generated images precede that which they represent; more crudely put, reality nowadays conforms to the pictures, not the other way around (ibid.: ix). Thus, the legitimizing, the contesting and the waging of warfare have become shaped much more by the media 'production' of warfare than any discernible 'original' or 'authentic' experience. But as we move forward through this book, it becomes clear that there are also unmediated aspects of war, either deliberately hidden or taking place in areas where media technology does not reach. The emergence of diffused war is not instant and completed.

We shall now unpack the three axes of diffused war, defined as an emerging paradigm of war in which (i) the mediatization of war (ii) makes possible more diffuse causal relations between action and effect, (iii) creating greater uncertainty for policymakers in the conduct of war.

The mediatization of war

As a result of changes in the communications technologies available to news media, citizen media and to militaries themselves, media are becoming part of the practices of warfare to the point that the conduct of war cannot be understood unless one carefully accounts for the role of media in it. This is what it means to speak of war as media*tized*. Stig Hjarvard makes a clear distinction between the terms 'mediation' and 'mediatization': 'Mediation describes the concrete act of communication by means of a medium in a specific social context. By contrast, mediatization refers to a more long-lasting process, whereby social and cultural institutions and modes of interaction are changed as a consequence of the growth of the media's influence' (2008b: 114). Sonia Livingstone, in her article 'On the Mediation of Everything', describes this mediatization of institutions and relations:

> [W]e have moved from a social analysis in which the mass media comprise one among many influential but independent institutions whose relations with the media can be usefully analyzed, to a social analysis in which everything is mediated, the consequence being that all influential institutions in society have themselves been transformed, reconstituted, by contemporary processes of mediation (2009: 2).

In other words, they have been mediatized.[2] War is 'transformed' and 'reconstituted' in precisely this way; the planning, waging and consequences of warfare do not reside outside of the media. If we probe the connections between humans, technology and media to interrogate the emergent character of war and terrorism, we find that they all inhabit the same and unavoidable knowledge environment, what we have called our new media ecology. To write of the mediatization of the conduct of war is to refer to the manner in which media are integral to those practices in which actual coercive or kinetic force is exercised, such as the guiding of troops and vehicles, the use of drones, the symbolic acts of violence central to terrorism, insurgency and, indeed, major military operations. And rather than mediation and mediatization being processes exclusive to different eras, the two modulate together, although we have seen greater mediatization occurring as time has passed and digital media has become more ubiquitous.

The mediatization of war matters because perceptions are vital to war – the perceptions of a public who can offer support to a war, of government trying to justify a war, and of those in the military themselves, who are trying to perceive and understand exactly what is happening as war is waged. It is through media that perceptions are created, sustained or challenged. For example, Paul Virilio, writing on the emergence of a new 'logistics of military perception', argues: '*[T]he history of battle is primarily the history of radically changing fields of perception.* In other words, war consists not so much in scoring territorial, economic or other material victories as in appropriating the "immateriality" of perceptual fields' (1989: 7; original emphasis). In other words, the battle is for how things are seen and perceived. This means both a battle of symbols and representations, and also a battle to construct how perception operates in the first place.

Let us start with battles of symbols and representations. In war and conflict today, making visible and public the capture of large armies or cities may often be of limited symbolic value. For instance, in Afghanistan in January 2008 a Taliban assassin managed to enter and began firing a weapon in the Serena Hotel, perhaps the only hotel in Kabul with a gym in which international women can exercise. The hotel was a purely symbolic target. The act was a message with three audiences. To international people, the message was that you are not safe in Kabul. To local Afghans, the message was that we are still operating and you may want to side with us. And to the Taliban itself, the assassin's action said: we are still effective, whatever NATO says about its success against us. The Taliban did not need to regain control of Kabul itself or entirely defeat the NATO forces in order to make its point. A few months later, in April, Taliban members infiltrated a military parade and nearly assassinated the Afghani President, Hamid Karzai (Gul, 2008). The Taliban again showed they could access the most secure space that Afghani or NATO troops could provide. Whether or not the President was killed, a symbolic act was achieved. Indeed, the asymmetry of much of the contemporary so-called 'war on terror' is related to the high visibility of terrorist targets – presidents, skyscrapers, tourist hotels or nightclubs – versus the diffused form of the propagators of terror. These diffused, 'small-time' terrorists are able to shape how we perceive security locally and globally. In traditional war too, such as the 2003 Iraq War, it is snapshot images such as the fall of Saddam's statue or the abuse of prisoners at Abu Ghraib that came to stand for, or represent, the entire war. To fight a war is to fight to construct and fill in fields of perception.

The interaction of media and war also entails a battle for how perception operates at all. How we perceive war is not just a matter of the content of news, of the images and stories presented to us, but also a matter of how we relate to media. The operations of a terrorist organization such as Al-Qaeda shape how the Internet is constructed and regulated, for instance. Attempts by governments and security services to prevent the diffusion of jihadist materials online may alter use of the Internet more broadly. War and conflict are drivers of the form media take, of how media are controlled and of what information reaches whom. Robots and drones – unmanned aerial vehicles (UAVs) – have been developed for warfare, enabling a new scope to the perception of war zones and the ability to control affairs remotely (cf Chow, 2006). At the time of writing, more than 40 countries produce, market or use battlefield robots or drones, from major powers to Belarus, Colombia, Sri Lanka and Georgia (BBC World Service, 2009; *The Economist*, 2009). Commanders based in the US can see what their soldiers see in Afghanistan thanks to real-time streaming devices. Indeed, this creates problems: instead of network-enabled, decentralized 'swarming' units, tensions emerge about whether it is the distant commander or the local, mediatized soldier who controls the crosshairs and decides who is shot at (Singer, 2009). As these tensions are worked out by militaries, and new perceptual technologies developed, so these tools will spread into domestic, civilian life, shaping how we can engage with each other, with states and with companies. Looking to the future, just as the identity of soldiers as warriors is complicated if they themselves become mere robots controlled remotely by distant commanders thanks to mediatization, so our identity as voters, protestors or even as political leaders may be rewritten by new perceptual technologies.

It is crucial to recognize that the absolute interpenetration of media and warfare has produced an emergent set of far more immediate and unpredictable relationships between the trinity of government, military and publics. These are significantly engaged in an emergent kind of conflict – which we are calling 'diffused war' – that is *immersed in* and *produced through* a new 'media ecology' (Cottle, 2006). War is diffused through a complex mesh of our everyday media: news, movies, podcasts, blogs, video games, documentaries and so on. Paradoxically, this both facilitates and contains the presence and power of enemies near and far. Media bring war closer in some ways, but keep it distant in others. Media bring the voice of the Afghani blacksmith or Osama bin Laden to our eyes and ears, but do not necessarily help us understand them. The conventions of so-called 'traditional' warfare have been splintered by the availability and connectivity of the principal site of war today: the electronic and digital media.

For those engaged in combat and those wishing to observe, communications technologies have diminished the proximity and the unmediated visibility of warfare. Whether one is fighting in the war or watching it as an audience member, these technologies create a distance from what has conventionally been considered the stuff of warfare: human bodies being injured, land being secured. This might seem counterintuitive: surely nothing is more immediate than war? 'Like hanging, war concentrates the mind', writes Mirzoeff (2005: 2). That pain and injury are inflicted on bodies is the fact. As Clausewitz argued, a soldier's goal is to inflict damage and suffering (1976: 91, 93). For those involved, nothing could be more immediate, and nothing could be more absolute. Elaine Scarry writes:

> It is commonplace that at the moment when a dentist's drill hits and holds an exposed nerve, a person sees stars. What is meant by 'seeing stars' is that the contents of consciousness are, during those moments, obliterated, that the name of one's child, the memory of a friend's face, are all absent. (Scarry, 1985: 30)

The perceptions of a person suffering pain in war are obliterated. In the most extreme situation – being killed – the defeated party in a war loses its world. But there are many layers to perception in war. Not all are killed. Most of the time, in contemporary warfare, the experience of war is mediated. Here is a reporter's snapshot of British military operations in Afghanistan in May 2008 under NATO auspices:

> Britain's war in Helmand is being fought in real time on six big plasma screens, which dominate a dark room at a base in the desert town of Lashkar Gah in southern Afghanistan. It is a digital response to a primitive insurgency, as if a city trading floor had landed to govern a medieval land. Soldiers, sent out among adobe-walled compounds and poppy fields, report by text to a military chatroom about the explosive devices that destroy limbs. Commanders watch the combat from the skies, filmed by unmanned drones and shown in black-and-white. The reality of war is disguised by the watch keeper's jargon; his talk of what happens 'if it ends up going kinetic'. That means bullets are being fired and bombs are exploding and it is not what the army wants. (Glover, 2008)

The very culture of warfare (and the relationship between war and media) pivots around changing fields of perception. We shall explore later in this introduction and throughout the book how these changing fields of perception, enabled by the mediatization of war, alter war in significant ways. Mediatization alters the form of military organization possible. It challenges the notion of an enemy with a clear 'centre of gravity' to be targeted, and notions of war as a linear process leading to a clear outcome, allowing for clear aims and objectives. Those directing war, reporting on war and trying to keep informed about war as a citizen are faced with the possibility that their conceptions of time and space, progress and proximity, need reconsideration. And this takes us to the next axis of diffused war, the complication of cause-and-effect relations and the challenge that mediatized war poses to the exercise of power in war.

Diffuse causal relations between action and effect

The mediatization of war makes possible more diffuse causal relations between action and effect. The pervasive delivery of connectivity and visibility disrupts notions of intentionality and control. Modernity is conventionally understood as a period in which individual actors used their reason and productive abilities to transform nature and the world around them in order to create industry, technology and social order. People, companies, governments and, indeed, military forces could act and be reasonably sure of what would be the consequence. Actor A could have power over actor B or the environment they inhabit in order to control what ends would be reached. It was clear who each actor was, and that their behaviour was the cause of whatever happened. But such an account of the world seems inadequate today.[3] For example, as Devji (2005) argues, Al-Qaeda is an organization virtually without causal power or capacity yet it has global effects. Al-Qaeda ultimately has no control over the many individuals and networks that act in its name (Rid and Hecker, 2009: 217). Anybody could commit a terrorist act and claim it was on behalf of Al-Qaeda. Nor could Al-Qaeda predict or control the effects of the 9/11 attacks. Not only is it impossible to draw the boundaries of Al-Qaeda and say who is in or outside the organization, but it is also not clear that those acting in its name even have specific effects they wish to achieve. The act in itself is enough. Devji writes: '[T]he actions of this jihad, while they are indeed meant to accomplish certain ends, have become more ethical than political, since they have resigned control over their own effects, thus becoming gestures of duty or risk' (2005: 3). The Mumbai terrorist attacks of 2008 are an example of this. Durodie (2009) writes:

> At the height of the Mumbai siege . . . one of the perpetrators, Fahad Ullah, used the mobile phone of one of the victims to call India TV and conducted a live interview with two journalists there.
> About a minute into their four minute conversation, the two journalists, one male, one female, asked him in turn 'What are your demands?'. At this point Fahed Ullah answered 'Wait one minute' and he was heard consulting someone else as to their demands.
> . . . to this day, over six months since the attack, no-one has come forward to claim responsibility for it, or to identify their demands and purposes.

Politics and political violence conventionally imply an act for a cause such as defending territory, interests or a people's pride; one acts to have an effect, and takes responsibility for that act and effect. However, this is not so simply the case with Al-Qaeda and those inspired by it. It is not an actor with a locus of decision-making (Burke, 2004; cf. Bobbitt, 2008). The units and lines of political action are further complicated by the blurring of domestic and global aspects of the jihad, and the invocation by Al-Qaeda of 'universal complicity' of all those who have witnessed, we can infer, acts of US 'imperialism' or aggression against Muslims. Potentially, anyone is drawn into relations with the jihadists. Finally, it seems nothing determines the 'cause' and effect of any particular Al-Qaeda attack: it seems purely contingent. It depends on the presence of local agents, who could be anyone, anywhere, and the victims equally could be random. And it is this model of action, 'effects without causes', that is enabled only through the new media ecology.

Causal relations are thus increasingly difficult to predict, given the underdetermined character of social and political relations. Military headquarters and major media organizations cannot guarantee the success of their framing or narrative because of a key phenomena, 'emergence': namely the massively increased potential for media data literally to 'emerge'; to be 'discovered' and/ or disseminated – instantaneously – at an unprescribed and unpredictable time after the moment of recording, and so to transcend and transform that which is known, or thought to be known, about an event. The global spread of online video clips or images such as Abu Ghraib or the execution of Saddam Hussein exemplify this (see chapter 2).

As we explore in chapter 6, the rapid development of digital media, its availability and portability, and the supreme accessibility, transferability and circulation of digital content, has thus potentially profound effects in shaping current and future events and also in transforming those considered 'settled' in collective memory. Both the unintentional and the intentional recording of events by the ubiquitous electronic/digital media (CCTV, mobile phone cameras, etc.) contribute to an archive of unpredictability that unsettles past, present and future.

For instance, the proliferation of remote and mobile audiovisual recording devices includes the mass availability of amateur or 'bystander' photographs and video, which adds to a growing 'surveillance culture' and which shapes news narratives in sometimes unpredictable and random ways. To take two examples: the amateur footage of the police capture of the suspects of the attempted 21 July 2005 London bombings on a West London balcony, and the mobile video of the police raid in Forest Gate, East London, in the summer of 2006 (both scooped by ITV News) were used to shape the news narratives of 'reasonable' and 'excessive' force deployed by the police, respectively. The police could not control how such images would be interpreted, however, particularly following the shooting of the Brazilian plumber Jean Charles de Menezes by police on 22 July 2005. Mobile phone photographs and video recorded by members of the public are now routinely requested by news organizations at times of the breaking of catastrophic news stories and other events, but could emerge much later to unsettle news narratives.

The mediatization of war does not necessarily result in the immediate end of Big Media institutions such as the BBC, CNN, *New York Times* or *Le Monde*, but it has lead to their transformation. They are not old or new media, but *renewed* media (Hoskins and O'Loughlin, 2007). It heralds a struggle between the established and relatively ordered regime of mainstream news – particularly television news – and an 'ordered disorder' of information that is potentially much more diffused. For example, as William Merrin (2008) observes: 'In place of a top-down, one-to-many vertical cascade from centralised industry sources we discover today bottom-up, many-to-many, horizontal, peer-to-peer communication' (see also Bennett, 2003). So, the broadcast model of Big Media is being unravelled through a set of more diffused and less predictable relations with the 'producers' of that which becomes its (and 'their') content. If the notion of a linear flow of news content (or propaganda) from elites to ordinary citizens ever did have validity, it is certainly challenged now.

One significant aspect of this shift (from what we call below the first to the second phase of mediatization) is the very extent and potential of the media archive, that is, the store of images, clips and stories available for retrieval and use. If, once, Big Media organizations had relatively large archives of stock images and reports to call upon, the emergence of digital media has not only resulted in a 'long tail' (Anderson, 2007) of the past (images, video, audio) whose 'emergence' into future presents is contingent in terms of the when, but also unsettled the terms of who has control over and access to such archives. David Weinberger (2007) calls this the 'third order' of information, involving the removal of the limitations previously assumed inevitable in the ways information is organized. (The 'first order' is the actual physical placing or storage of an item and the 'second order' is that which separates information about the first order objects from the objects themselves – such as the card catalogue). In *Everything is Miscellaneous*, Weinberger argues that 'the 'miscellanizing' of information not only breaks it out of its traditional organizational categories, but also removes the implicit authority granted by being published in the paper world (ibid.: 22).[4] Now, with potentially infinite archives and unpredictable emergence of images, challenges loom for both Big Media and audiences about which information and news are authoritative and credible, and even about what authority and credibility actually mean.

We must be careful not to discard notions of linear communication and causality altogether, however. In the first axis we noted that some of the conduct of war is unmediated, accidentally or deliberately. The dynamics of emergence, the proliferation of digital archives and the possibility for disrupted memories and narratives are not absolute and universal. As we have described, major news organizations have not been wiped out in the increasing shift to a post-broadcast, participatory media ecology. As we turn next to the third axis of diffused war, the exercise of power, we must keep in mind that these shifts are uneven and require continued, careful study.

Greater uncertainty in decision-making in war

The third axis of diffused war concerns the ability of military and media organizations to make decisions with any degree of certainty about the outcome. The mediatization of warfare creates the condition for violence and conflict characterized at times as 'effects without causes', but at other times as well controlled and legitimized. Policymakers and editors cannot know in advance which it will be. Here we set out some of the key concepts for understanding the difficulties of decision-making, including chaos, complexity, risk and effects or impact. Discussion of these concepts illustrates the contingency of attempts to wage or justify war today.

Brian McNair (2006: 3) characterizes the nature and the scale of the transformations in journalism and news as a move from a 'control' to a 'chaos' paradigm. The former (control) for McNair emphasizes the role of the relations and power that we have here attributed to 'Big Media'. These are based upon the determination of media content according to the political and economic interests of an elite holding 'control of the cultural apparatuses of media', enabling them to create 'planned and predictable outcomes' (ibid.), such as the theory that media can 'manufacture consent' (Herman and Chomsky, 1994). The latter (chaos), while still accounting for the 'desire' for power and control by the same elites, suggests that 'the performance, or exercise of control, is increasingly interrupted and disrupted by unpredictable eruptions and bifurcations arising from the impact of economic, political, ideological and technological factors on communication processes' (McNair, 2006: 3).

As we have described above, because of emergence, it is no longer possible to explain social phenomena as the outcome of, or accumulation of, individual acts (Lash, 2005; Urry, 2007). From a policy perspective this is problematic: individual acts could be isolated and made the object of intervention. The problem for government and military policymakers is conceiving of policy and strategy in a time of 'complexity'. The latter term is preferred over 'chaos' in the work of Urry (2007), for example, who points to the rapid and unexpected movement of people, things and images which make order contingent, not given. For Urry, the result is neither chaos nor order, but 'metastability'.

Alongside complexity, a key term in military policymaking since the 1990s has been 'risk'. Transnational security threats such as terrorism, pandemics and environmental catastrophe, alongside patterns of global migration, have triggered new paradigms of governance based on the regulation of flows – flows of money, people, microbes and nuclear materials (Bauman, 2000, 2006; Cooper, 2006; Sassen, 2006). However, Bauman argues that the increasing focus in Western political cultures on personal safety from assorted threats (terrorists, paedophiles, local gangs) is a manifestation of 'a sense of impotence: we seem no longer to be in control, whether singly, severally or collectively' (2007: 26). This condition is stabilized by a separation of politics from power, of tools to order and direct the economic, social and political forces that bear upon our lives: David Held describes the resulting condition as one of 'global structural vulnerability' (Held, 2006). Governance has increasingly been based on pre-emption and precaution as means to manage threats which might not even materialize, but whose consequences would be catastrophic and unknowable. Conceptions of risk have been reconceived.

This sense of connection, complexity and emergent change is captured in a quote from Sir David Omand in 2005, at that time Security and Intelligence

Officer at the Home Office with responsibility for national 'resilience' in case of emergency:

> There are certain obvious characteristics we need to take into account in our planning. The speed and penetration of global communications. The tightly coupled markets that can transmit shocks instantly around the globe. The known vulnerabilities of complex information infrastructure, for instance controlling logistic systems or power grids. More fundamentally the commercially competitive pressures on the Boardrooms that now control most of our critical national infrastructure that in years gone by would have been in public sector control or at the least subject to influence in the public interest. Just in Time value chains, leanness and speed to market all can introduce greater fragility in the face of unexpected disruption. Our knowledge of these inter-relationships is far from complete. I know of no full mapping of an advanced economy anywhere in the world, or even of a manageable methodology for obtaining one. (Cited in Dillon, 2007: 14)

National political, social and economic infrastructures are too complex to know, Omand suggests. He infers, it seems, that this makes such infrastructures more fragile, 'in the face of unexpected disruption'.

Since the 1990s in particular, Martin Shaw (2005) argues, Western powers have engaged in 'risk-transfer war' in which each war generates its own 'economy of risk', where particular risks to particular people have particular value. There is an inequality between those who define risks, who set the terms of the war, and those exposed to the risks – the soldiers and civilians in the war zone whose lives are at risk, and politicians and military leaders whose political capital is at risk. But today, feedback effects mean risk cannot confidently be transferred. There is a continual risk of 'stray' images emerging from the battlefield, which may shape public opinion both at home and among the population in the war zone. In the case of the 2003 Iraq War, there is also the risk of terrorists using such images to justify attacks on the 'homeland' of countries involved in the war, such as the 2004 Madrid bombings and the July 2005 London bombings. In this way, it can be said that military and security agencies can only live with risk, and not eliminate it. Thus, fighting diffused war requires learning, adaptation and managing feedback, and not a fixed doctrine. The result is permanent war against contingency itself, a diffused war without end.

There is a tension – a dialectic of technological development and social relations – which is producing 'complex intersections' that may appear as 'flows' but are more flux-like (Urry, 2007: 25). Despite talk of flows (of people, capital, goods, images, germs, weapons), this is not a helpful metaphor; it is more accurate to speak of flux, i.e. continuous change and a parallel continuous potential for media users/audiences to participate in the production and distribution of media commentaries *about* these changes. In media studies during the age of mass communication, Raymond Williams (1977) wrote of 'flows' as a constant stream of communications which the audience member could turn on or off; like electricity, television, radio or the daily newspaper, which will always arrive, always be on-tap, but which people could decide whether or not to tune into. Today, however, communication is less uniformly linear. Flows can go from broadcaster to audience, and also back again; communication can begin with the soldier in the field producing a blog that leaks important information that military leaders would prefer remained not to be broadcast. We explore these patterns in more detail in chapter 7.

Instead of steady flows, then, can communication be characterized as more disordered and unpredictable, feeding into events themselves? It is important to situate such flux in relations of war and media within broader conditions of globalization. In his analysis of the latter, Arjun Appadurai writes of 'crises of circulation' insofar as the disorder of circuits of communication lead to tensions and, potentially, conflict:

> [A] crisis of circulation . . . may be seen as a crisis produced by what in my earlier work I called the 'disjunctures' between various kinds of flows – of images, ideologies, goods, people, and wealth – that seem to mark the era of globalization. These disjunctures are largely produced by modes and means of circulation which operate with different rhythms in their negotiation of space and time. Sometimes discussed as disjunct global flows, they produce local contradictions and tensions of many kinds. Since all these tensions have something to do with processes of global flow that are not coherently synchronized, they may be termed crises of circulation. (2006: 29–30)

Flows of people create disjunctures, for instance, when a war creates refugees who migrate to an unprepared or unwelcoming society, creating conflict and possibly forcing the migrants to move on again or even move back to the zone from which they were displaced originally. The steady, predictable flows are disrupted. Or flows of money hit disjunctures during a liquidity crisis when suddenly banks and other financial institutions lack the capital to fund loans to businesses and consumers, which slows down economic activity. A crisis in one country can rapidly affect others, given the degree of financial interdependence of national economies – witness the 'contagion' that followed the East Asian financial crisis of 1997–8. So it is with war and media: the leaking of an image or a misplaced quote can spark international unrest, as a range of perspectives, opinions and interests are suddenly brought into collision. In addition, decision-making is affected by the speed of flux. It is not simply that real-time or close to real-time reporting by journalists and bloggers can problematize the conduct of war as it happens, but that decision-makers conducting war (and news editors) will have to account for immediate communication feedback and build this in to their planning. Nevertheless, we must be cautious too: the Bush Administration managed to elicit support from major US news organizations and US publics for the 2003 Iraq War and sustain this support for a considerable length of time, even in the context of communicative flux, Abu Ghraib images and international dissent. This book will survey a range of examples across the spectrum of control and chaos and suggest how to bring precision to analysis of these dynamics.

Thus, the conduct of war and conflict today – the exercise of kinetic and symbolic power to defeat an enemy – involves the difficulty of the management of such flux amid complex systems that make the 'cause' and 'effect' of any conduct (by 'us' or by 'them') as diffuse.

A critical research question, which we address in chapter 10, is how we conceive and measure the effect of communication on audiences, who are the ultimate arbiters of the legitimacy of a war. Here, is it important to note our original source of the term 'diffused', namely in its use by Abercrombie and Longhurst (1998). They define a new 'diffused audience', that is, the nature of the audience–media relationship in our 'media drenched society' is one in which 'everyone becomes an audience all the time' (ibid.: 68–9). To be precise, we could all be an audience. Spontaneity is the essence of diffusion: Whether or not an audience forms around a story, and who is in the audience, cannot be known beforehand. It can no longer be assumed that there is a stable audience who all watch X programme at Y time in Z context (e.g. working families watch TV news at 6 o'clock in their living rooms every weekday evening). Of course, this still happens to a certain extent – there are still mass audiences for certain news programmes and publications – but such audiences are also diffuse at other times. Consumption of news, as with a great deal of media content today, is increasingly atomized in relation to the capacity of individuals to assemble a personal diet of news feeds through RSS on the web which aggregates and delivers self-selected content (such as news headlines, blogs, podcasts, etc.) There may indeed be mass audiences consuming the same content at the same or at different times, although as part of a new personal and often more mobile 'media mix' (Jansson and Lagerkvist, 2009). At the same time, the opportunities for those possessing even basic media literacy to contribute to this media content are unprecedented. From DIY blogs, through journalist and other 'professional commentators' on news organization sites such as the British *Guardian*'s 'Comment is Free' (and of course the responses of their readers) and attempts by the BBC World Service to host a 'global conversation' on its forums (Anderson, 2008), to government and even military e-engagements with their perceived constituencies, there is a diffused mass of media and mediatized traffic. In this new media ecology then, does it make any sense to think about and conceptualize its diffused participants in terms of an 'audience'?

One way authorities have sought to bring certainty to decision-making is through automated surveillance of both online and offline behaviour. Already companies acquire and trawl data from social media such as Facebook for information on consumer preferences, recommending music, books and other products to users based on their profiles and previous purchases (Beer, 2009). In the search for potential terrorists, authorities harness similar tools, allowing them to move away from racial profiling of targets based on supposed dangerous identity groups to looking for unusual *behaviour*. Automated searching is enabled by technologies that sift through people's travel, financial and consumer transactions (Amoore and de Goede, 2008), which use algorithms to generate patterns of what counts as potentially deviant and dangerous behaviour. These surveillance technologies 'screen out' the normal but bring into focus the unusual. The logic of such visual calculation is for authorities to identify terrorists before they commit a violent act, enabling pre-emptive intervention. Amoore quotes Michael Chertoff, US Secretary for Homeland Security, speaking in 2007 about one of the 9/11 terrorists: 'Ideally I would like to know did Mohamed Atta get his ticket paid on the same credit card. That would be a huge thing. And I really would like to know in advance, because that would allow us to identify an *unknown terrorist*" (2008: 135; emphasis added).

The figure of the 'unknown terrorist' is problematic: if a person's behaviour fits the pattern of previous behaviour characteristic of terrorists in the recent past, does that make the person a terrorist-to-be, even if they do not know it? Technologies that visualize and identify such figures pose ethical problems. Is it the case, as Amoore suggests, that 'the response before the event can never be a responsible response' (ibid.: 136)? She argues that we are witnessing automated calculations based on probabilities, for which nobody is responsible, only the programme's algorithm. What seems an apolitical technology masks an extremely political system, she argues:

> The algorithmic mode of attentiveness becomes the 'multicultural' society's technology of choice precisely because it gives the appearance of living alongside difference, of deciding without prejudice – 'we are interested in behaviour not background'; 'this is not racial profiling' . . . in fact it categorizes, isolates and annexes [people] in ways that conceal the violence inside the glossy wrapper of techno-science. (Ibid.: 137)

Authorities can increasingly call upon these automated technologies to identify potentially dangerous people rather than rely exclusively on the 'vigilant visualities' of ordinary citizens (Amoore, 2007). Each leads to a moment of decision for security services of whether to act, but the mechanism by which the information is generated enables particular modes of decision-making: in this case, an automated one. The result is that despite the considerable volume of data and communications on the Internet, our very use of these technologies enhances authorities' control by rendering more of life transparent, archived and searchable.

Alongside decision-making concerning counterterrorism, such automation is present in conventional warfare too. Due to online news and users' participation in media, debates about the justification of war can be monitored and guided by authorities; in chapter 7, we see how this occurs in public diplomacy. The conduct of war involves automated devices such as drones, which can be pre-programmed to carry out specific tasks. But might the use of these technologies to enhance control create resentment and resistance? How do people in Afghanistan or Pakistan feel about being targeted by flying robots?

The significance of the emergence of the three axes that constitute diffused war can be further understood by looking at how war and media have shifted from a first to a second phase of mediatization.

2. The Two Phases of Mediatization

The strategizing, fighting and legitimizing of contemporary warfare were oriented around a 'mass' media, particularly in the late twentieth century. Television, be it mythologized in relation to its impact in determining the outcome of the Vietnam War, or pivotal to the propaganda in the wars over

Kosovo and the Gulf, for example, became the pre-eminent medium over this period in 'information' war. More broadly, the 'broadcast era' was seen as characterized by the dominance of Big Media (Gillmor, 2006) such as the BBC, CNN or national newspapers, with news-making being entirely the province of journalists and the economics of publishing and broadcasting creating large, powerful institutions and news networks. The rhetoric of traditional warfare sits easily with Big Media in its institutionalization and top-down hierarchy of management and organization. Unwieldy, yet highly tangible and easily scalable and quantifiable, Big Media's success is instantly measurable in ratings and audience-share, and its propaganda value, be it through military-management or via the courting of politicians, is well documented (see, e.g., Taylor, 1998/1992; Connelly and Welch, 2004; Kamalipour and Snow, 2004).

Once satellite news-gathering[5] replaced the electronic news-gathering of the 1970s, the impact of Big Media upon the very character and the waging of warfare went global. It is at this time that there occurred what we are calling the 'first phase' of mediatization and, indeed, what we have characterized as 'mediatization of warfare': situations in which those conducting war are aware of themselves as involved in a process being recorded and disseminated via media, and media consider their coverage as part of the war itself. Mediatization is part of a long historical transformation in which institutions and practices assume a 'media form' (Hjarvard, 2004, 2008a, 2008b). Mediatization, at this first stage in the late twentieth century, was not just a question of the advent of real-time (or near real-time) global media that reflexively fed back into and shaped events being reported on,[6] for one could argue that this occurred to a limited extent in the Crimean War (see above) and any other war in which aspects of conflict were designed to be covered by media. What defined this stage as mediatized was that the very knowledge of the phenomenon developed into a self-reflexive enterprise: media knew and advertised the fact that they offered a 'front row seat' as they 'brought us history' as it unfolded. An awareness of the perceived impact of the reporting on and the presentational stylizing of warfare feeds back to affirm and to develop the orientation of Big Media to future news events.

A key example of this phase of the mediatization of warfare is evident in CNN's successful monopolization of the 1991 Gulf War, notably, an object created through the practices of television; that is, in parallel with the military's conduct of the actual war, CNN's rolling 24-hour news coverage helped constitute the conflict as an object for viewers and citizens. The 'pleasure, style, and commodity' of what has been labelled television's 'televisuality' (Caldwell 1995: 30) are significant factors in the mediatization of warfare of this period. This included CNN's televisual reconsumption of its own coverage – a 'celebration' by network news of what it has already delivered ('remember when we brought you . . .'), and authentically connected with the audiovisually supported witness testimony of its journalists, embedded in the original media event. Thus, CNN clung to its self-produced mediatized memory of the 1991 Gulf War throughout the 1990s and beyond, and, across all Big Media this (and other Big Media productions) were extensively employed as key arbiters of later conflicts and particularly as 'blueprints of illegitimacy' to both promote and to contest the 2003 Iraq War (Hoskins, 2004a).

Following the 1991 Gulf War, the social sciences, including media, communication and cultural studies, were energized in an assessment of the mediatized transformations in time and/or space that this global television event heralded (Virilio, 1994; Wark, 1994; Shapiro, 1997). The 'indexical wham' of the war is partly attributable to the apparent centrality of CNN with its 'news strategy of pure speed' (Wark, 1994: 38) enveloping the multiple times and places that comprised the event. Television news' capacity to vision a simultaneous 'paradoxical presence' (Virilio, 1994: 63), so that the essential 'participants' in an ongoing event appear intimately connected (and not least to their audiences), has been credited to the network. The impact of the immediate and intensive connectedness of events, key participants in those events, and audiences, where mediatized responses can be seen to feed and shape reflexively the trajectory of an event defined as news subject, has been called the 'CNN effect' (Boden and Hoskins, 1995; Livingston, 1997; Volkmer, 1999; Robinson, 2002). The apparent dominance of a single shared global perspective was partly due to the fact that CNN (first launched in 1980) was the only available worldwide 24-hour news satellite channel at the time. But television often tracked the Gulf War in real-time, all-of-the-time, and it is this that established the event as a benchmark for a new mediatization of time and space.

The mediatized continuous connectivity of the Gulf War – the intensive and extensive flows and counterflows of information about this event – forged an 'event time' (Gitlin, 1980: 234) of broadcast and other news during which period the time horizon of mediatized expectations and orientations shrunk to the event itself. The war was on TV all the time. During these times, audiences' experience of the here-and-now lost their immediate spatiotemporal referents (Friedland and Boden, 1994: 6) as times and distances became 'plugged in' to the present-time system of television news, with the studio as centre and hub. In one way, the usual 'compression' of events in scheduled and punctuated television news programmes was reversed, and time itself seemed to slow down as there was no 'time out' from the coverage (and even the usual advertising 'breaks' were suspended in the opening hours of the war). For instance, an instructive and accessible account indicative of approaches to this era is that of McKenzie Wark, whose account of media 'vectors' we return to in chapter 7:

> We live every day also in . . . the terrain created by the television, the telephone, the telecommunications networks crisscrossing the globe. These 'vectors' produce in us a new kind of experience, the experience of telesthesia – perception at a distance. This is our 'virtual geography', the experience of which doubles, troubles, and generally permeates our experience of the space we experience firsthand. (1994: vii)

So, our experience of television and other mass media has gone from a 1970s *flow* (Williams, 1974) through the *event time* of the Gulf War, to a twenty-first century 'torrent' (Gitlin, 2001), or, rather, as we come on to explore below: *flux*. However, the second phase of mediatization we identify is the broader impact of the media upon processes of social change so that everyday life is increasingly embedded in the mediascape. It is not so much that events are straightforwardly *mediated* by media to audiences; rather, media have entered into the production of events to such an unprecedented extent those events are *mediatized* (Cottle, 2006).

The second phase of mediatization requires a shift in how we approach and formulate the very relationship we have with media, and with the events, near and far, on which our experience is so dependent. We are not outside media, separate from it, as independent entities 'decoding' what is sent to us (Lash, 2005). The proliferation of new media technologies renders more of life matter to be recorded, disseminated and debated on near-instantaneous and deterritorialized scales. Hence, we now live in a 'new media ecology' in which people, events and news media have become increasingly connected and interpenetrated through the technological compressions of time–space. We are moving towards an 'age of universal comparison' in which we can compare media, compare ourselves, and compare others more easily and instantly than before (Deuze, 2007: 14). This increased visibility and publicity of life has economic, political, cultural and social implications that social theorists attempt to capture and characterize as, for instance, a 'liquid life' in which we are immersed (Bauman, 2006). These trends are, of course, partial and uneven, and people enjoy very different degrees and experiences of this 'immersion'. But there is a need in fact to grasp the nature and potential consequences of this second phase of mediatization on a whole range of phenomena; in this book we focus on war.

The two phases of mediatization are important to understanding the emergence of diffused war documented in this book, and we summarize them in table 1.1.

3. Conclusion

The relationship between war and media today is characterized by the emergence of diffused war. Diffused war creates immediate and unpredictable connections between the trinity of government, military and publics, forcing each to find new ways to manage information about war. There are three axes to diffused war, which work together, to varying degrees, across the situations of war and conflict that we face today. The emergence of diffused war has happened in the historical context of a shift from a first to a second phase of mediatization. Having established these conceptual frameworks, this book addresses key themes and dilemmas in contemporary war and media. Along the way we offer a comprehensive introduction to some of the major thinkers of our times on these matters. We survey the latest studies, we point to areas where knowledge is thin and new research is required, and we end the book by suggesting a series of significant challenges and questions for those wishing to understand war and media in the years to come.

Table 1.1 The Two Phases of Mediatization

Phase of mediatization	Characteristics	Central questions in this phase
First	Discrete, large organizations, mass media, mass audiences, international news coverage dominated by a small number of Western media organizations and driven by satellite television. Mass warfare enabled by mostly distanciated and temporally limited military strikes. Actions and effects largely predictable and measurable.	How do media make war visible? How do media deliver war to audiences? How does media shape public opinion, and how does public opinion shape how war is conducted?
Second	Intense international competition for provision of news beyond and onto the West. Continuous connectivity creates diffuse audiences and messages and media themselves are weaponized. Temporal horizons and geopolitics of warfare transformed. Overlapping systems characterized by emergence, chaos and flux. Unknowable risk. Actors must learn to manage unexpected feedback and live with ambiguity.	Now that actors in war anticipate and shape media coverage of their actions, how do they design war for media, and how is media designed for war? Now that audiences know these symbolic/representational games are being played, how do they find credible and authoritative information and analysis about war?

2

IMAGES

1. Introduction: Do Images of War Show or Hide?

The second phase of mediatization is characterized by some as being satiated and overwhelmed by a 'torrent' of media data (Gitlin, 2001). One of the central aspects of the competing 'control' versus 'chaos/complexity' debates over the dynamics of the flux of digital content concerns the nature, value and impact of the realm of the visual. The image has a special status in the study of warfare (as it does in the study of media), as we show in our subsequent chapters on Compassion, Witnessing, Genocide and Memory. As a tool of persuasion and, indeed, revelation or exposure of truth (particularly of the 'real' and brutal bodily destructive consequences of military conflict and terrorism), the resonance of the visual is unparalleled in the propaganda and counter-propaganda of warfare. The visual is taken as instrumental to the maintenance or loss of public and political support for military interventions and campaigns, and in debates over the morality of the representation and sanitization of images of the suffering, the dying and the dead in various mediated forms and contexts (see, for example, Sontag 1979/1977, 2003, 2004; Hallin, 1986; Taylor, J., 1998; Hoskins 2004a; Butler 2009).

It is important to state at the outset that the difficulties and complexities of accessing, analysing and managing image research has undoubtedly skewed an understanding of the historical mediation of war. Some researchers are reduced to analysing only those elements most easily available, code-able and quantifiable, even simply counting images.[1] The 'content analysis' of political communications scholars rarely appears, for example, in the pages of the journal of *Visual Culture*. We are not claiming to offer a ready solution, but at least an articulation of the problem. To this end, this chapter sets out the shifts in the nature, supply and circulation of images, both still and moving, in our new media ecology. We examine the practices of the principal providers, editors and interpretative actors or communities in shaping mainstream news coverage of images of war and catastrophe.

In the first part of the chapter we survey the role and status of the still and moving image in the history of modern war. The shift to digital media appears to unsettle the relationship between an image and what it represents, since the moment of truthfulness may no longer lie at the moment a photograph is taken, when the image is physically marked on film or captured digitally, but with the consumer or user who sifts the multiple and often competing images emerging from contemporary war and conflict events. What might this mean for whether an image can become iconic, today, and does the responsibility for images switch from producer to consumer? Second, we argue for a change of emphasis in the study of visuality and war, from a concern with the 'representationality' to that of 'mediality'. Instead of an exclusive focus on the objectivity and accuracy of an image to the object being represented, we suggest that the significance or 'impact' of images may lie simply in our relationship to them: the way we consume them, forward them to friends or family, and edit and recontextualize them ourselves. War and social media are interpenetrative realms. Were the Abu Ghraib photos shocking because of the torture being represented, or for the apparent normality of the photographers who looked as if they were enjoying themselves taking holiday souvenir photos? Analysis of the visual in war must account for both these representational and the medial dimensions. Finally, we identify how the 'emergence' of digital images shapes the status and legitimacy of events, and illustrate this through an analysis of the mediatized delivery of the execution of Saddam Hussein. Two sets of footage emerged: first, the official Iraqi-government sanctioned edition, which was relatively sombre and dignified, and then unofficial mobile phone footage of the event, which included the jeering of those present and presented a far more chaotic situation. Audience research suggests that people objected not so much to the representation as to the medial aspect of the event: the lack of dignity of those involved and the symbolism of the timing of its filming and release.

Running throughout our account is the question of what images do. It is not simply that images exist, but that they can become something else: weapons, symbols of cooperation, markers of territory, and so on. This distinction builds on Judith Butler's (2005) assessment of the work of Susan Sontag on the interpretative power or otherwise of the photograph (which we return to develop below). Butler argues that 'the frame takes part in the interpretation of the war compelled by the state; it is not just a visual image awaiting its interpretation: it is itself interpreting, actively, even forcibly' (2005: 823). We explore this 'performative' dimension of images again in chapter 9. Identifying the function or effect of images is a critical challenge in the second phase of mediatization. A recurring question is whether images from war or conflict amplify fear or shock, or whether images can serve to nullify or contain such impact. The image(s) that shock and disturb news publics, delivered by a journalism that is unable or unwilling to be sufficiently reflexive about its weaponizing effects, are ultimately rendered *less* potent, precisely through the familiarizing recursivity of repetition and endless recontextualization.

One view is that there are too many images to make sense of, to filter out;

we are overwhelmed and cannot make any political evaluation of the war we are witnessing. For example, Nicholas Mirzoeff argues: '[T]he weapon-image overcame its opponents by sheer relentless persistence. So many images were being created that there was never time to pause and discuss any one in particular . . . a dramatic visual moment could be top of the news one hour, only to be discarded to the dustbin of the present moments later (2005: 74). He argues that there is a 'deliberate effort by those fighting the [Iraq] war to reduce its visual impact by saturating our senses with non-stop indistin-guishable and undistinguished images' (ibid.: 14); in other words, a *counter-weaponization* of distraction, a saturation of coverage intended to obfuscate the death and suffering hidden beneath and beyond the visual 'shock and awe'. Indeed, this may not be new: the idea of the mediated satiation of our senses as a means to hide the real and terrible consequences of warfare was a popular interpretation of the coverage of the 1991 Gulf War (if on a smaller scale) – in other words, applicable to the period of the *first* phase of mediatization (Virilio, 1989).

This sounds an attractive thesis. But for all the churn of the fast throughput of images in real-time (or near to real-time) news coverage of breaking and ongoing events, most expositions of the weaponization thesis are incomplete. In fact, the default mode of both continuous and extended and even the more punctual (bulletins) television news coverage is repetition. 'Recognition' and even 'familiarity' actually sit with novelty, immediacy and surprise as news values. As Silverstone argues on the news coverage of 9/11:

> [T]he shocking and the threatening has to be made into sense. Despite the sin-gularly catastrophic moments of September 11 the media have a stock of images, frames and narratives available in their conscious and unconscious archive which will hold as well as explain. This is the container of the familiar, the familiar which is claimed, sooner or later, to soften the blow. There is safety in the cliché. There is comfort in the tale. (2002: 2)

The second axis of diffused war refers to the manner in which the mediati-zation of warfare leads to uncertain relations of cause and effect. The flux of digital data unsettles the relative stability of the control of images. For example, the dominant visual culture of warfare, subject to such careful management, premediation and censorship, acquires a new fragility in the second phase of mediatization. The meaningless but seemingly newsworthy fragmented vision afforded by the embedding of journalists in the 2003 Iraq War, for instance, did not contain the story of the war for very long. The uncertainty principle is fed by the potential of images to emerge at any moment, which can shatter attempts to develop or sustain a version of warfare around which public and political opinion can cohere, exemplified by the emergence of the transcendental images from Abu Ghraib prison which first publicly circulated in April 2004. The phe-nomenon of 'emergence' is critical here and we interrogate this phenomenon in more detail shortly, and in chapter 5. But it is also that the public and political outcry, and the proliferating mass of academic analyses (e.g. Danner, 2004; Sontag, 2004; Mestrovic, 2005; Eisenman, 2007; Mitchell, 2008a, 2008b) on the Abu Ghraib scandal signify a crisis of the visual in the second phase of mediatization. The risk for all the agents/victims of the emergence of the visual (authors and their chain of command, subjects, mass-mediators, and audiences) is exemplified by the panic over the glut of interpretations and remediation of the Abu Ghraib images. Tangled in these debates is actually something that goes beyond the visual. What is distinctive in terms of the crisis of the visual is the second phase of mediatization. By specifying the visual image as the object of analysis and the primary measure of the saliency or impact of an event, we miss the fundamental relationship we have with mediation itself, or what we analyse below as mediality.

2. Photograph and Flux

The photograph has a privileged status in the study of mass media and this is also the case in the study of war and media. For instance, the resonance and longevity of photographs in the memory and history of warfare has been seen in relation to ideas around their physicality, artefactuality and permanence. Thus, as Douwe Draaisma writes: 'As analogies for visual representations photographs particularly stress the *immutability* of what is stored as a memory: they suggest a memory that forgets nothing, that contains a perfect, permanent record of our visual experience' (2000: 121). This status also affects their treatment as objects of study and the photograph has been used as a kind of transparent selection of a piece of reality across a number of disciplines. The historian Raphael Samuel, for example, argues that 'historians [are] content to take photographs on trust and to treat them as transparent reflections of fact . . . as though depository had the same authority as source' (1994: 329). In the first phase of mediatization, the photographic affordance of any given event was challenged with the advance of television and video. For example, Michael Ball and Gregory Smith make the case for comparative if not holistic investigation of the visual: 'Photographs constitute still or frozen images of an instant. In order to explore the processual and sequential character of visible social arrangements – what Garfinkel (1968) has termed the "now you see it, now you don't" character of social life – the comparison of photographs and video is necessary' (1992: 4).

Yet, it is the photograph that seems – precisely because it *is* a still image – to possess a resonance that the moving image does not. Photographs may be presumed to endure because they represent a single moment snatched and preserved, and are not merely part of a larger sequence of frames, as with video and film. Sontag, for example, argues that '[p]hotographs may be more memorable than moving images, because they are a neat slice of time, not a flow. Television is a stream of underselected images, each of which cancels its predecessor' (1979/1977: 17–18). One is moving and intrinsically ephemeral, while the other is constant and fixed. Television is relentless in its immediacy, in its delivery of the present and its selective redelivery of the past, but this real-time temporality and apparent flow may function to obscure its impact, unlike the indelible marking associated with the medium of the photograph. In his study of Vietnam War photography, Patrick Hagopian argues:

> [T]he power of the still image lies in its very stillness. Because it exists in space but not in time, it can endure for the viewer. We can fix on a particular configuration of forms and we can hold it in our gaze. We can possess it as we stare at it. In contrast, the moving image exists in both space *and* time. Its verisimilitude may be enhanced by movement, and its content multiplies with the micro-movements within each successive frame. . . . Compared with the time we can spend studying a photograph, the existence of a moving image is a fleeting thing. (2006: 213)

The iconicity of Vietnam images for many commentators (Sturken, 1997; Moeller 1999; Hoskins 2004a) is explained by their remediation as black-and-white photographs, displayed in books, galleries, exhibitions and museums, for example. Two of amongst the most iconic of Vietnam War images in the West were taken from photographs – 'Vietnam Napalm' by Nick Ut (Huynh Cong) (1972) and 'The Execution' by Eddie Adams (1968) – rather than from the existing film footage of these events. As Marita Sturken (1997: 90) argues, there are a number of possible explanations for the establishment of a primacy of the photographic over the film of the same events. These include the photographic capturing of the definitive moment in terms of the contorted expression of terror on the face of the Vietcong suspect milliseconds before being shot in the head at close range, as well as abruptly sanitizing out the horror of what follows; the relative confusion of the video of the naked girl (Phan Thi) Kim Phúc following a South Vietnamese Napalm strike; and, again, the detail of the facial expression of Phúc in the photograph over the film (ibid.). The impact of the photograph is evident from the awarding of a Pulitzer prize to the AP photographer Ut in 1972, whereas the NBC cameraman Dinh Phuc Le, who shot film of the same event, did not attain recognition to this extent.

However, there is also a set of moving images of the Vietnam War which have become engrained in the mediated memory through their remediation in television news and documentary programmes (as well as in cinematic depictions). These 'stock' images include US troops jumping down and running away from a helicopter hovering close to the ground, and chanting and placard-waving protestors representing opposition to the war at home. The resonance and status of these and other moving images of the Vietnam War are also attributable to their recording onto film, rather than onto videotape. As Sturken, for example, argues: 'They have the sharp-edged, gritty quality of film images: as they have aged, their grainy black-and-white and faded color have enhanced their historicity' (1997: 90). In this respect, the relationship between the original medium of record and the later veracity or otherwise of the images produced at the time, and the significance of the still versus the moving image, appears to be less clear-cut. Furthermore, the photograph can be lingered over by video or film to mirror the stillness of the medium being remediated in television or cinema. One can argue that the photograph that is afforded an extended present in film or video possesses even greater power than the photograph alone, as each medium of its remediation adds another cycle of fixing the gaze anew.

The power of photography, however, has long been acclaimed with reference to the work of Walter Benjamin, who saw the introduction of the technology of film as responding to the 'shocks' of the emergent conditions of modernity and the 'increasing rapidity and abruptness' and thus providing 'a representational equivalent to the disjointedness of life' (Henning, 1995: 229). One of the most cited passages of Benjamin's work emphasizes the twin temporalities of the rupture of the moment of capture and the potentiality of the extended duration afforded to the image:

> Of the countless movements of switching, inserting, pressing, and the like, the 'snapping' of the photographer has had the greatest consequences. A touch of the finger now sufficed to fix an event for an unlimited period of time. The camera gave the moment a posthumous shock, as it were. (Benjamin, 1969: 174–5)

How does the emergence of digital photography affect the status of the once 'snapped' still image or 'filmed' moving image?

Much has been written on the relationship between the mediums of photography, cinema, television and time (including Doane, 2003; Mulvey, 2005; Hassan and Purser, 2007) and an overview is beyond the scope of this book. However, we place the visual mode of representation centrally as part of the 'connective turn' (Hoskins, 2011), and we go on to explore how this bears upon war and media.

The connective turn of the digital transforms the photograph from a discrete object to a node (or many nodes) in a network. Fred Ritchin considers that the paradigmatic shift underway is that of 'hyperphotography'. He writes: 'The digital photograph, unlike the analog, is based not on an initial static recording of continuous tones to be viewed as a whole, or teased out in the darkroom, but on creating discrete and malleable records of the visible that can and will be linked, transmitted, recontextualized, and fabricated' (2009: 141). Furthermore, that which was once analogue is also, in the second phase of mediatization, subject to digitization, affording it the same if not similar properties as if it had been captured in the digital era. For example, despite the dominance of the 1968 photograph by Eddie Adams (referred to above) as an iconic representation of the Vietnam War precisely because it slices the fractional moment just before the act of execution, it is today newly connected and reconnected via the Internet to an unlimited set of contexts (including the images captured on film). Thus, as Ritchin puts it: 'If the reader clicked on the famous photograph of the execution of a member of the Vietcong, he or she could see the images that preceded and followed it. If the reader clicked on the man doing the shooting, he or she could find out that he later opened a pizzeria in Dale City, Virginia' (ibid.: 140).

This is an example of the temporal and spatial diffusion of the image in the digital flux of the new media ecology. As Lisa Gitelman argues, 'digital images recomplicate the notion of a photographic index altogether' (2006: 5). The ways in which a photograph is taken as indexical to the truth, since *that* was *there*, may no longer hold for digital images. Today, where, when and with whom does the truthfulness or veracity of an image lie? The connective turn affords the simultaneous existence of multiple and conflicting narratives on events past and present that are no longer restricted by the scarcity-led model of the broadcast era. This is not, however, to ignore the role of the stock images of warfare used in television and cinema, and which are also remediated across multiple other media platforms. Rather, in the condition of diffused war, we require analysis of the ongoing interpretations and reinterpretations of images, even (and perhaps especially) of those images presumed to be the most engrained in collective consciousness. For example, the critique that Butler (above) makes of the transitive interpreting force of the image needs contextualizing in terms of the ongoing and potentially counter-remediations and translations of the same image. This is not just a question of alternative and competing narratives of the meaning of media content. Instead, a more temporally sensitive approach is needed to take account of the impact of 'some form of temporal coincidence, of simultaneity, as the mark of the real' (Doane, 2006: 36).

Much has been written, for example, on the shaping of content and the interpretation of content by television news and what we have called the medium's 'economy of liveness' (Hoskins and O'Loughlin, 2007). The status of the image lies in an open process, not a moment of closure. So, as Doane argues, 'Benjamin's snapping of the photographer has moved from the realm of production to that of reception. The event becomes that of the user's engagement with the technology' (2006: 36). Here then the two phases of mediatization become more distinct in relation to the shift from the idea of the power of the analogue-era image as a comparably static mass-consumed object to the power of digital mediation through the connection and diffusion of the image into intrinsically unpredictable and ongoing interpretative realms, communities and individuals.

If the impact of each new instance of reception is a marker of the real (in Doane's terms), does this transform the extent of vicarious responsibility for what is clicked on by the user? Whereas the watching of video or film is associated with a more passive mode of consumption, 'viewers of still photography in a hypertext environment can choose to pursue their own curiosity in a variety of ways. They begin to bear some of the responsibility of collaborator and "coauthor"' (Ritchin, 2009: 110). We return to consider some of the implications of the connective turn on 'witnessing' in chapter 4.

What we might call the 'fabric' of our new media ecology – the multiple connectivities of the production, exchange and consumption of increasingly digital content – fundamentally concerns how we engage with that which is 'mediated'. Today, what appears to be missing from the endless analysis of the production, circulation, reception, interpretation and impact of media images and other content is attention to the continuity and familiarity of media representations and events represented by our own everyday media practices, their *mediality*, in shaping our understandings and responses. We now turn to address this.

3. Mediality

A principal focus of enquiries into broadcast-era mass media pivots around the idea of 'representationality'. This includes a concern with the accuracy, veracity and objectivity of representations. So, analysis of media content often involves looking at journalistic practices in the selection of materials for the construction of news, at the dominant language and visual or audiovisual 'frames' that are employed in constructing media texts, and at how audiences consume, interact with or ignore media content. 'Mediality', by contrast, refers to the way in which media texts are interwoven into our lives; that is, how the continuity and familiarity of these representations interact with our everyday media practices. This is not to say that mediality completely replaces representationality as a mode of enquiry into contemporary media or how we orientate ourselves towards media. Rather, the prior emphasis on representationality is complicated or even displaced because of our own affective (emotional, sensory) relations with, and uses of, the gamut of digital technologies, the very technologies that we recognize as also used in the production and distribution of diffused war.

Mediality is perhaps less established as a concept in US and UK media, communication and cultural studies than it is elsewhere in Europe (for instance, it may be linked in part to the work of Régis Debray on what he calls 'mediology'). Richard Grusin is the leading scholar employing the idea of mediality (and affect) and what he calls the 'media everyday' to enhance our understanding of the workings and impact of 'security' in our new media ecology. His argument is underpinned by the notion developed in a number of fields that, 'humans have historically evolved with technology, distributing their cognitive and other functions across an increasingly complex network of technical artifacts' (Grusin, 2010). So, Grusin articulates a position that includes, but goes beyond, an interest in cognitive and epistemological accounts of media interactivity that 'is also bodily and affective' (ibid.). He argues:

> In all of our media relations we establish affective networks or feedback systems or cybernetic loops that distribute our affect across various media forms, technologies, and practices. To understand these affective relations, we need to think in fairly concrete terms about specific interactions among humans, technology, and media. (Ibid.)

In the field of war and media a scholarly tradition perpetually concerned with the analysis of media content, institutions and ownership has resulted in mediality and mediatizion being underexamined or ignored completely. Stephen Crocker (2007), for example, argues: 'As long as we remain focused on questions of media ownership or the meaning of messages, we miss our deeply tortuous relation with the fact of mediation itself.' And it is mediality that becomes more significant in the second phase of mediatization.

Mediality is itself a diffused phenomenon. It is often in the background of our media practices. The 'everyday', be this our connection with and our uses of media everyday, or more wider ideas of the everyday, are overlooked, given that they are routine and unexceptional and we do not ordinarily reflect upon such activities in themselves. In this way, we draw upon an emerging scholarship that applies Nigel Thrift's notion of a 'technological unconscious' to describe 'the very basic sendings and receivings of sociotechnical life – and the modest but constant hum of connection and interconnection' (2004: 175). Grusin (2007) for example, employs this idea in his analysis of the responses to the public emergence in April 2004 of photographs depicting scenes of torture and abuse on Iraqi prisoners by members of the US Army at Abu Ghraib prison. Grusin questions whether concerns over the criminal abuse exposed in the photographs, and the horrible and disturbing events they depicted, are the only explanation for the ensuing public and political outcry. He asks:

> Rather than consider the Abu Ghraib photographs as transparent windows through which we could view unthinkable, horrible practices of torture and humiliation . . . what would it mean to consider them as sociotechnical artifacts, operating within a premediated network of media practices similar, if not identical, to those practices widespread among students, tourists, parents, pet-owners, photo-bloggers, and in the military itself? (2007: 47)

Grusin appears to give more weight to mediality than to content in his explanation for the global media attention afforded to the Abu Ghraib photographs. He concludes his essay on this study: '[T]he media publicity created by the photos from Abu Ghraib lies less in the significance of what they show us than in the sensation they produce, the feeling that in looking at the Abu Ghraib photos we are participating in our ordinary practices of mediality' (ibid.: 60). Indeed, Susan Sontag (2004) earlier hinted at the significance of the mediality of the images:

> There is more and more recording of what people do, by themselves. At least or especially in America, Andy Warhol's ideal of filming real events in real time – life isn't edited, why should its record be edited? – has become a norm for countless Webcasts, in which people record their day, each in his or her own reality show. Here I am – waking and yawning and stretching, brushing my teeth, making breakfast, getting the kids off to school. People record all aspects of their lives, store them in computer files and send the files around.

In line with Grusin, we do not treat 'content' and 'mediality' as necessarily exclusive categories. However, one of the characteristics of diffused war is the combination and even the intersection of these two phenomena as explanations for the differing resonance and impact of mediatized events. One example of what became much more prevalent with the advent of the Iraq War, and can be taken as evidence for the weaponization of media, is the 'hostage video'. The two principal and ubiquitous media – portable recording equipment and web upload facilities – were effectively combined to facilitate the rapid production and dissemination of video depicting the imprisonment, torture and killing of Western hostages by Iraqi insurgents. These videos were most often partially or heavily edited by broadcasters to enable their inclusion in Western television news programmes. However, as Brian McNair argues, the sanitization of such materials to conform to national broadcast regulations and conventions (as well as being in keeping with presumptions on the part of programme editors as to what their audiences would deem 'acceptable' viewing) did not necessarily diminish their intended impact, to terrorize: '[T]he knowledge that they [decapitation videos] were available to be seen on the web – that they existed, out there in cyberspace – had a profoundly disturbing emotional impact. They brought geographically distant atrocity into the living room, from where it entered the collective imagination as the stuff of nightmares' (2006: 8). This attention to the mere *knowledge of the availability* of the full shocking videos on the web (the real horror of which was only glimpsed via the censorious mainstream media) can also be considered in relation to the very mediality of searching the Internet, downloading and viewing videos, as well as the practice of producing amateur videos and posting them on the web, and the rapid growth in image and video sharing sites such as Flickr and YouTube. The previously more distinct personal and public domains of our everyday mediated experience both collapse and collide through our connection to and our uses of the Internet.

Although trophyism amongst soldiers in terms of taking, keeping and sharing images of their injured, mutilated and dead enemies is not a new phenomenon (US soldiers were even accused of attempting to send home enemy 'trophy skulls' from Vietnam in the 1970s – see Boorstein, 2007), the availability and portability of digital recording equipment transforms the potential for all parties in warfare to document atrocities and for these to be quickly disseminated. For example, the site nowthatsfuckedup.com (NTFU) was set up in 2004 initially for the trade of amateur pornographic images. Chris Wilson, the owner of the site, allowed US military personnel to exchange images of themselves in the field for access to the site, allegedly in response to their being unable or unwilling to use credit cards in their operational zones. Although the initial photographs sent were benign, soon American soldiers serving in Iraq and Afghanistan were submitting trophy images of mutilated and dead bodies. After the site became a global news story in the second half of 2005, it was finally shut down by the US authorities in 2006 and this URL now links to the local Sheriff's Office with the message: 'The investigation resulted in the prosecution of Christopher Wilson, the former web master of this website. The Polk County Sheriff's Office now maintains this URL to prevent further transmission of obscene material.'

The second phase of mediatization is thus characterized by attempts to contain the uncontainable (it is claimed that some of the graphic images from NTFU were later published on the more innocuously named documentingreality.com). More recently, in May 2009, the Pentagon was forced by legal action by the American Civil Liberties Union to release dozens of previously unpublished photographs of abuse of captives carried out by members of the American military in Iraq and Afghanistan, beyond those of Abu Ghraib. There is, it seems, an accumulating legacy to the phenomenon that, as Kelly Oliver writes, 'digital technology feeds, if not produces, the compulsion to record life as a sort of proof that it has been lived' (2007: 73). Perhaps it is the self-production of the Abu Ghraib photographs and their associated mediality that exemplify their greatest (although mostly unsaid in a news media obsessed with the images themselves) impact.

However, it is the very existence of a glut of recordings of images and video, amateur and professional, incedental and intended, and their *potential* to emerge and to transform all-that-is-established about an event, that fundamentally unsettle the second phase of mediatization. The future of the mediation of warfare, we maintain, is to some extent dependent upon 'emergence', which is the phenomenon we now turn to examine.

4. Emergence

A key condition of our new media ecology (NME) – and which Urry (2005: 5) argues is central to complexity – is 'emergence' (cf. René Dubos, 1987 [1959]; Johnson, 2002). Accounts of and uses of this term vary between disciplines and over time. Briefly, 'emergence' involves 'the processes whereby the global behavior of a system results from the actions and interactions of agents' (Sawyer, 2005: 2), or, more straightforwardly, the 'collective phenomena that are collaboratively created by individuals, yet are not reducible to individual action' (ibid.: 5). In terms of causality, phenomena cannot be reduced to the actions of major institutional actors such as governments, militaries, media or publics. This is precisely one of the ways that mediation is modulated. For example, to take a useful analogy from biology:

> The microbiologist René Dubos was the first to coin the term 'emergence' as a way of describing the temporality of biological evolution. By 'emergence', he understood not the gradual accumulation of local mutations, but the relentless, sometimes catastrophic upheaval of entire co-evolving ecologies; sudden field transitions that could never be predicted in linear terms from a single mutation. (Cooper 2006: 116)

However, we propose a more inclusive definition of emergence to incorporate the massively increased potential for media data literally to 'emerge' in unpredictable future times. The second phase of mediatization is characterized by a move beyond the relatively ordered and institutional mediation and documentation of events of the first phase to an expansive 'run-time' recording culture. The intended and the random recording of public and private events via professional and amateur mobile media (and the blurring of these distinctions) has been enabled through the global portability and availability of such devices. Consequently, there is a radical new potential for a mediatized record of events to emerge – to be 'discovered' and/or disseminated – instantaneously, at unprescribed and unpredictable times after the moment of recording, and so to transcend and transform that which is known, or thought to be known, about an event. Consequentially, legitimacy, trust and reliability are all increasingly difficult to attain by governments, politicians, militaries and NGOs, as they are increasingly subject to operating under conditions of the entirely unpredictable emergence of visual and audiovisual media fragments, especially of injury, death and torture, in the context of diffused war. The global spread of online video clips or images such as Abu Ghraib or the execution of Saddam Hussein exemplify this phenomenon.

Images recorded via mobile media and their transferability and circulation can be said to contribute to three dimensions of emergence. First, the visual reporting, culture and history of modern warfare has been absolutely transformed on account of the proximity to sites of conflict now afforded through the mobility of journalists and, indeed, anyone with a mobile phone that incorporates a camera. Second, the ubiquity of digital recording devices and the relative universality of access to the Internet, where such digital data is freely disseminated, feeds a new immeasurable potential for the retrospective transforming of a received understanding of events and the challenging of the declared or perceived legitimacy of acts. The first dimension is exemplified by the news coverage of the 9/11 attacks on the US and the 2005 London bombings. The second dimension will become increasingly fundamental in the political and military management of the news media in reporting war. The sudden and speedy dissemination of the unofficially recorded mobile phone footage of the moments preceding and those of the actual hanging of Saddam Hussein, examined below, exemplifies the second dimension of emergence.

The third and final dimension of emergence that is significant in shaping the mediatization of warfare is the manner in which images become drivers and, indeed, determinants of events being treated and reported as 'news'. The emergence of an image or set of images around even an old story can inject sufficient newsworthiness in itself to warrant the revisiting and replaying of the story. Thus, the emergence of images contributes to an increasing recursivity in news agendas, a kind of self-fulfilling news cycle.

The trials of those charged with terrorist offences, for example, often acquire significant additional or primary news value with the release of previously 'unseen' stills and increasingly, it would appear, video footage of those accused. This links to and feeds an obsessive media focus on accounting for the actions of terrorists and especially those deemed to have become 'radicalized' into committing or plotting to commit terrorist activities. For example, in the wake of the 9/11 and the London and Madrid bombings, the visual biographical mapping of those found or thought to be responsible was a key mechanism through which (British) media narratives constructed the acts and the perpetrators of those acts, via a taxonomy of normality (see Hoskins and O'Loughlin, 2009a). What is specifically new in this third dimension of emergence is that a significant proportion of the media data (images, sounds, words) upon which these biographical narratives are constructed, and thus the reported rationale for such acts, are in fact *auto*biographical. Such clips and images are self-recorded by the to-be-accused in their everyday lives. Notably, one of the interesting and underexplored dynamics of emergence in accounting for terrorist acts is in the self-produced recordings that afford a new (later) visibility to what is reported as 'terrorism' or 'radicalization', for example. We might ask also, from a critical perspective, whether the recording by US/UK media of US/UK-led 'shock and awe' bombings in the 2003 Iraq War also constitute self-incrimination.

We live in an age of unprecedented accessibility of a 'long tail' (cf. Anderson, 2007) of the past, so that that which is selected for representation and circulation in so-called mainstream media – that which is routinely and often repetitively 'seen' as 'news', for instance – becomes increasingly juxtaposed with content that is judged unshowable by those same mainstream 'gatekeepers'. Consequently, there is a greater reflexivity about that which exists just beyond 'what we are permitted to show'; the news content we are routinely presented with is increasingly embedded in a self-conscious discourse as to its partiality. A double discomfort is afforded at both the horror of the event or act being reported and also its active censoring through its representation (as with the related significance of 'representationality' and 'mediality', above).

In this way, the traditional media editorial practices and controls and the institutional norms around 'taste and decency'[2] (managed by journalists, editors and programme managers) are shrunk into a 'mainstream' that reveals rather than hides its increasingly anachronistic status in the new media ecology. The connective turn has accelerated news' decline into the bland and the banal, with war reporting epitomizing the 'comfort zone' of the mainstream, and the acceleration of what Martin Bell (2008) identifies as 'the death of news'. The shifting timidity of mainstream news reporting and the tension with the wider new media ecology in which it is embedded is exemplified in the case we now turn to consider, the reporting of the execution of Saddam Hussein.

5. Saddam Hussein's Execution

Saddam Hussein's death was one of the most public executions of the modern period, public in a number of ways. Yet despite the mediatized publicness of his hanging, which was relayed around the globe on 30 December 2006 (or at least in mainstream news media the before and after of the act itself), and the control, order and dignity conveyed by the 'official' Iraqi government video, the whole management of this execution (and any legitimacy this may have conveyed) was shattered only a few days later by the emergence of the unofficially recorded mobile phone footage of the last moments of the former Iraqi president. The footage was uploaded to an array of websites, copied onto videotapes and sold on the streets of Baghdad, and remediated globally on television and as stills in print media.

The symbolism of Saddam's execution and death beyond the Middle East was not lost on the West, especially given the US and UK's persistent demonization of the Iraqi leader, particularly since Iraq's invasion of Kuwait in 1989. The initial Western television coverage of this story (e.g. on BBC, Sky News and CNN) showed clips taken from Iraqi TV, heavily embedded in the televisuality of graphics and commentary with the overlaying of the Western news stylistics on top of the replaying of the Iraqi TV tape. This presentation is framed in the othering of its source at one step removed – a visual and immediate justification for its broadcast was that this is Iraqi TV showing the footage.

As the hours and days passed by, however, and once the video footage had been extensively remediated, its presentations become less tentative. Once 'out there', and perceived to be 'out there', the repetition of even very graphic images accrue a certain credibility and authority as part of the public record; no longer just news, but public document. Warnings were issued by many of the UK broadcasters over this period about what viewers were about to be confronted with. The Channel 5 News anchor said: 'This shows the moment that the noose is actually put around Saddam's neck.' Over time, however, as the story lost its recency, the broadcast of such cautionary statements diminished. It was as though the story moved from news to historical document, or rather that there was a presumption by broadcasters that viewers had become accustomed to seeing it and were thus desensitized, and no longer needed to be warned over images with which they were already familiar.

However, within three days of the broadcast of the original news story containing extracts from the official Iraqi government video record of the hanging, a second piece of video emerged, recorded illicitly by mobile phone. This second clip, showed again in news programmes around the world, provided an entirely different audiovisual account of the hanging of Saddam Hussein. One form of violent propaganda was replaced by another. The calm and relatively contained silent official video was transformed into a PR disaster by the counter-modalities of the shaky and grainy footage and the mob-like jeering of the co-present witnesses to the hanging. English translations to the taunting of Saddam Hussein (in Arabic) were added to a number of Western news reports. The initial news reports of the relatively successful (orderly) execution of the former president in accordance with Iraqi law was swiftly transformed into a story about the disorder of Iraqi justice, given that even some of the official witnesses to the execution were jeering at the apparently chaotic spectacle, as well as at the illicit recording of the hanging. The emergence of this footage fundamentally undermined the Iraqi government's presentation of the management of the execution of Saddam Hussein as dignified and non-sectarian (and thus any legitimacy these impressions may have conveyed). This is one example of the emergent power of mobile media to quickly challenge and to subvert narratives facilitated through the astonishing connectivity of the web and other electronic and digital media. Thus, legitimacy, trust and credibility are all increasingly difficult to attain by governments, politicians and militaries, as they are increasingly subject to operating under the conditions of the entirely unpredictable emergence of visual and audiovisual media fragments – especially of injury, death and torture.

An audience ethnography conducted in the UK demonstrated that people responded both to the representationality *and* to the mediality, and that a transitivity of the images was achieved as they became perceived as weapons. Footage of the execution of Saddam Hussein was played in 10 interviews and focus groups in different cities in the UK. Interviewees were asked to respond to the footage, to recount how they originally learnt of the story and who they watched such news with, to reflect on news media's decision to show the footage, and for their interpretations about the role and responsibilities of mainstream news media when such events occur. Most had seen it with families, with children around. Many had the news forwarded to them on the Internet. This indicates the variegated processes through which news 'travels' when a critical news event breaks, both as *transmission* from the execution site to the physical and virtual locations and addresses at which audiences 'receive' or 'pick up' the story, and as a *ritual* process – the family, gathering round, consumed socially, spoken about and interpreted in ways that confirm identities – of Saddam, of 'the Americans', and of the audience members themselves (Carey, 1989).

Many respondents identified a weaponization at play – that is, media being used as weapons within a larger political-military context. 'Big D', an Algerian asylum-seeker and IT engineer living in Cardiff, had originally seen the footage on his mobile phone. He said the video was made 'to prove a point to the current regime in Iraq, to the Baathists, that Saddam has been truly hanged'. He added that the trophy status of such footage might counter some conspiracy theories: 'When someone who used to decide on other's life, it is always difficult to believe his death. I have . . . heard of some Iraqis here in the UK wondering if Saddam's sons really have been killed.'[3]

One researcher, Sadaf Rizvi, asked participants in a focus group of Muslim women in Oxford why the execution had been shown when usually an image of the dead body is taken to be sufficiently convincing. Nazima, a graduate student on a teacher-training course, replied: 'They wanted to show that even if he is dead, they have still got hold of him, just to show that "we are still controlling him" and also to show to the Muslim world that [is] how they can be treated.'[4] Several respondents suggested that the execution was an act by the US to send a message to Muslims, and that showing the video was an act intended to demonstrate power over Muslims. For Saddam Hussein's execution date to fall on Eid was viewed as an act of provocation intended to create humiliation: humiliation of Saddam Hussein, who had already been humiliated by earlier photos released of him being discovered underground and inspected by medical staff; and humiliation of Muslims in Iraq and worldwide. The following quote is indicative. Here is Munira, a 50-year-old Muslim woman also in Oxford:

> It almost puts things in perspective, doesn't it? In my mind it immediately puts things in perspective, that it is almost like when you read a poem and the teacher asks you to identify what's symbolic about it. It is almost like that. This hanging is symbolic. As you say, 'gardan tor di', to break somebody's neck. It is exactly that. This is what is symbolizes to me, that they say we have broken your neck. *It symbolizes the entire situation.* (Emphasis added)[5]

The chaotic aspect of the emergence of the footage was noticed by most participants. The question arose, does technology create a media *beyond* responsibility? Enrico, a 44-year-old Italian living in East London, noted that the tape was not broadcast for a few days, but that the existence of the footage on the Internet forced editors to broadcast it: 'I know there's no dignity in that, but . . . if we could get that news on the Internet then why not put in on television, on the front page, all the world had seen that stuff and all the world wanted to see that stuff.'[6] Another interviewee, Shafiq, a 35-year-old teacher in the London suburbs, also said 'because of the Internet we had to see it', and described the incident as a 'minefield' for broadcast news editors.[7] On the question of whether such footage is necessary to document history, Enrico was sceptical, saying that its broadcast was 'more for the benefit of show than for history. . . . The way he was shown at the moment of hanging gave nothing to history, other than revenge for those Iraqi people.' Some also asked who was responsible for the consequences of the showing of the execution, including, for instance, a possible increase in tensions between Sunni and Shia groups in Iraq. More viscerally, a group of Muslim women in Oxford spoke of copycat executions in Pakistan and the US:

HM: . . . I heard that GEO showed and even in Pakistan a child tried to do it himself. He tried to do an experiment with himself.

SR: Oh really?

HM: Oh yes and he died.

MA: Yes, exactly. And it is not only one case, several children have died
      like this. In Multan [Pakistan] a boy hung his sister like that.
HM: Yes, in America also a child did that.[8]

They wondered why Western news media had ignored these consequences, even as they still reported and analysed the Saddam Hussein execution story. Or, how could Western broadcasters retain sufficient control to filter out or block the emergence of these copycat incidents for Western audiences? But would this be temporary, since the long tail of digital images in the new media ecology could mean the sudden appearance of such stories. Big D applied this principle to the likely emergence of footage of the execution of Saddam's half-brother: 'but I do think they have filmed it and [are] keeping it waiting for an occasion to broadcast it. Well, I'm not sure. As I said before, technologies of communication and information are too developed as no one can hide such important things.'[9]

These audience observations support our thesis that representationality and mediality are two intersecting ways through which audiences (and policymakers) engage with media coverage of war. This indicates the dimensions of analysis necessary to understand the role of images in situations of war and conflict.

6. Conclusion

The shaky mobile phone footage of the execution of Saddam Hussein served to amplify his unscripted, undignified and chaotic end and undermined the cause of those desiring an orderly execution to demonstrate the competency of the then fledgling Iraqi Administration. Furthermore, the verbal taunts by the small gathering of witnesses to the execution (and Saddam Hussein's responses), even before translation to a non-Arabic speaking audience, afford visceral impact to the recording. These multiple modalities of this footage became even more significant with its remediation on file-sharing sites (for example YouTube, Revver) – and its reintegration back into news coverage – as well as on thousands of other websites covering a whole spectrum of mainstream and niche, legal and illegal. And it is on these sites that different modalities of the video have been edited, added, enhanced and cut, including textual and verbal translations and music, not to mention its embedding in and linking to an array of institutions and causes online. That this entire event involved (i) the existence and emergence of the mobile phone footage, (ii) its remediation and multiple editings and translations (amateur and professional) and (iii) its reintegration into mainstream news discourses could not have occurred before the mid-1990s. This is indicative of the shift that we have identified as a second phase of mediatization.

A focus on the image itself and/or what is depicted in the image, as evidence of the weaponization of the media, does not sufficiently address the temporal and medial dynamics of our new media ecology. It is not just a question of the difficulty of researching the visual, but that a focus on representationality leads to a failure to interrogate the multiple modalities (visual and non-visual, representational and medial) and how these are embedded and connected. Diffused warfare is fought amidst more unpredictable dimensions of reflexivity, as Mitchell argues: '[T]hanks to the invention of digital media, these spectacles, the violent dismemberments of the biopicture, can be cloned indefinitely and circulated globally. They are the poisonous "gift that keeps on giving", taking on a perverse life of their own in the world's nervous system' (2008b). The function, impact or transitivity of media in shaping warfare is not limited to a single modality, then, but rather comes from its connectivity. Diffused war is fought at all these levels of mediated consciousness and is not somehow isolatable and separable to any one of them. It is with this call to step beyond the traditional focus that we now turn to address the nature of and the prospects for 'compassion'.

3

COMPASSION

1. Introduction: What is Compassion Fatigue?

When we tire of media coverage of suffering, pain and death in wars, conflicts and catastrophes close to or, more typically, far from home, we experience compassion fatigue. When audiences or journalists themselves lose interest in a story, this feeds back into news organizations' decisions about what to show (Moeller, 1999). If editors believe that audiences have lost interest in a war or famine, they will stop covering the story. They will assume the story is not in the public's interest, and so perhaps not part of the national interest. Or if news editors still feel compelled to cover such a story, they will make their coverage simplistic. As Moeller writes: 'If images of starving babies worked in the past to capture attention for a complex crisis of war . . . the starving babies will headline the next difficult crisis' (ibid.: 2). Simplification will be accompanied by sensationalism: If audiences tire of a certain level of atrocity, then journalists must find greater horror and suffering to capture their attention next time, or at least present the next event as more severe and tragic even if it is not. Finally, if editors suspect that audiences are tiring of a war or famine, they will move onto another event even if the war or famine is ongoing and worsening. As such, compassion fatigue appears to be a process that skews news editors' and journalists' priorities and inhibits public knowledge. Moeller suggests that a vicious circle occurs: '[T]he droning "same-as-it-ever-was" coverage in the media causes the public to lose interest, and the media's perception that their audience has lost interest causes them to downscale their coverage, which causes the public to believe that the crisis is either over or is a lesser emergency' (ibid.: 11). Compassion fatigue would seem to lead to audiences being misinformed and ultimately ignorant of war, conflict and humanitarian crises.

However, 'compassion fatigue' is a hypothesis, not a fact – just like the 'CNN effect' (Tester, 2001). The proposition runs thus: continual coverage of distant suffering eventually causes audiences and even journalists themselves to lose interest, even if the suffering continues. The role of visual images and various mediums are usually embedded in this proposition, as we set out in chapter 2. For example, Susan Sontag writes: 'An image is drained of its force by the way it is used, where and how often it is seen. Images shown on television are by definition images of which, sooner or later, one tires' (2003: 105–6). Television is central to this hypothesis and dominates the literature we explore below, though as more news is consumed via the more interactive Internet, we might ask whether our engagement with images of suffering will change.

So is there any evidence to support this hypothesis, or is it simply a myth, much like the notion that US media 'lost' the war in Vietnam in the 1970s by showing US audiences the bloody 'reality' (Hallin, 1986)? Until we are sure there is evidence to support the proposition, then compassion fatigue is not a fact. Rather, as Stanley Cohen states:

> Compassion fatigue [embraces] all the connotations of overload, normalization and numbing. It is also over-used – vague as a description, and even vaguer as an explanation. At times it means getting used to bad news, at other times a reluctance or inability to respond to demands for help. All the while, the facts are not denied; they are only too well known and their meaning acknowledged. The 'fatigue' refers to burn-out – which may be emotional (a diminished incapacity to feel anything), or moral (a diminished moral sensitivity). (2001: 191–2)

Accordingly, this chapter examines three aspects of the problem, which can be the basis for testing whether compassion fatigue exists in any situation:

1 News values create a 'hierarchy of pity' whereby the suffering of some places and people receive greater coverage than others (Chouliaraki, 2006: 189). Which journalistic practices explain how and why this happens?
2 How can spectators/audiences relate to sufferers?
3 How is the relationship between spectators and sufferers constructed by media? How are our feelings as audience members shaped and structured by the news report or text?

Each section offers a set of factors or a framework for analysis of these questions, which can be applied to past, present and future news events. The first section draws on interviews with journalists and news producers, undertaken in our 2004–7 *Shifting Securities* project,[1] and on the work of Susan Moeller, to identify the reasons that lead journalists to cover some stories more than others. The second section draws on the work of Adam Smith and Luc Boltanski, who offer a framework for mapping and analysing relations between spectators, sufferers and the persecutors or benefactors involved in a crisis. The third section presents Lilie Chouliaraki's framework for analysing news texts, including the visual and verbal techniques used to appeal to audiences' sensibilities. Each of these sections, then, offers a 'way in' to analysing aspects of the compassion fatigue hypothesis.

The notion of compassion fatigue is not new, but how it plays out in the new media ecology deserves close attention. The hypothesis, if true, suggests a way in which media have a direct effect on audiences: news media stop us caring about distant suffering. But can this hold in the chaotic, nonlinear and emergent conditions of diffuse war?

Yet the topic also demands we think about certain unchanging questions:

- *Truth.* Can we trust news about distant suffering? Should media prioritize sensation[2] and urgency over objectivity and factuality in order to make audiences care?
- *Ethics.* How does it make us feel? How are we supposed to feel? Many foreign correspondents justify their vocation by declaring they are motivated by compassion and sensitivity for those they report on (see Tumber and Webster, 2006: 72–4). Should spectators necessarily feel compassion – are they 'bad people' for not caring (Tester, 2001: 16–17)? Do we always feel compassion to those we physically meet in normal life, unmediated?
- *Representation.* How much suffering should media show? What are the appropriate ways to represent pain and misery?
- *Power.* Who benefits if distant suffering is low or absent from the news hierarchy or agenda? Will newer global news networks such as Al Jazeera and China's CCTV change who has the power to shape what counts as a crisis to global public opinion?

We begin our discussion with a 'classic' case of compassion fatigue: the apparent failure of Western media to offer adequate coverage of the crisis in Darfur from 2003 onwards.

2. Why News Values Keep Some Stories Off the Radar

In February 2003 a war began in the Darfur region of Sudan. On one side were the Sudanese government and the Janjaweed militias; on the other were a set of rebel groups from different ethnic tribes. The number killed by violence, disease and starvation resulting from the war is disputed, but allegations of genocide were public in 2005 and by September 2006 the United Nations suggested a figure of 400,000 deaths, with 2,000,000 people displaced.[3] Controversy persists as to how and whether the international community could have intervened earlier to prevent these deaths. Yet it also persists as a war that has received sporadic media coverage in the West and elsewhere. Researchers showed two clips about the Darfur crisis to five university students in London in November 2006, one clip from CNN and another from Channel 4 News in the UK. The discussion was part of a much larger study with UK audiences of all ages, but it encapsulates many of the ways we found audiences think about the reporting of war and disasters. The students were asked how they would like TV news to cover such disasters:

Fatima: It should be informative.
Jessica: To treat these things equally in sort of their importance to the world, on the global scale. Whereas, some things are taken out of proportion . . .[4]

But what does 'equal' or 'proportionate' mean? How are these measured and ranked? What 'information' is relevant? Discussing Darfur, Fatima said, 'it made me think about, you know, the tsunami and how that occurred and really the people after Boxing Day, everybody that was around sorted of started, like, collective community . . . where everyone wanted to hand in charity just the day after . . . people were affected and . . . felt really touched and planned to do something about it.' The tsunami stood at the top of a *news hierarchy* because Westerners were directly 'touched'. It stood above Darfur, which seemed distant, tribal and of no consequence beyond the region. Between the two was the Israel–Hezbollah war of 2006, because, according to one of the students, Khalid, 'the Middle East has an economic value . . . the players in the Middle East are on an international scale'. Hence, although Westerners might not see 'people like them' in pictures of the war, the war affected stability in the region and, therefore, oil prices in the West – an indirect way of being touched. It is also important that the students interviewed reflected on Darfur by comparing it with other events not in the broadcasts shown to them. No event exists in isolation, and importance or news 'value' is always relative, and therefore contestable.

Given the numbers killed, injured and displaced, and the brutality of the violence, why did Darfur remain a low-level story on news agendas? This case is important for unpacking a series of questions around compassion fatigue and media coverage of distant suffering. Theo Murphy, East Africa Researcher for Amnesty International, offers a practitioner's view of the conflict. Interviewed in September 2006, he speaks about the difficulty of getting media to cover Darfur:

> First, the war has gone on for too long. It is not news anymore, it does not captivate the audience. Second, the conflict is not framed as nicely as the North–South one was, there is the lack of that Christian versus Muslim framing, although you do have the Arab versus Black African framing. Third, Africa is less interesting than, say, the Middle East, and especially Iraq. And finally, there is no Western involvement. So you need to find something new, something big to get the media attention. In general, though the lack of reporting is a major problem for us, as there is a grave situation, which we are unable to publicize enough.[5]

For an NGO worker, it is a struggle to make the crisis 'news'. Darfur must be made not just interesting but 'captivating'. It must also be made intelligible to those not familiar with the conflict, by imposing clear ethnic or religious frames that viewers will understand and possibly relate to, or by showing there is Western involvement and hence that the West has 'a stake' in events.

Murphy: You need big changes to get Darfur on the map again, you need a big event. I guess that the celebrity effect, with George Clooney and others taking interest does not hurt. But to get it back on the agenda, you need to push the envelope.

Interviewer: How would you do that?

Murphy: You need to push the statements and be more and more sensationalist. You can also criticize things that others do

> not criticize, for example the Abuja peace process which has been a failure. From our point of view, we can't criticize political decisions, such as the peace process, without an human rights angle. So, we always need to find such an angle in order to push statements.[6]

Yet even if Darfur could be made more sensationalist and framed in these terms, Murphy recognizes that if journalists can't even access the region, there can be no news to frame. The mediatization of war – the first axis of diffused war – is not a universal, completed process, but varies by locale. Moreover, how can such a massive catastrophe be caught in an image?

> The lack of access is a major problem as it reduces the number of stories you get. At the same time, the lack of images is also important. This is another problem with Darfur. There are not enough images of suffering coming out, and in any case, the images that do come out do not show the scale of the crisis. In the end, how do you show 200,000 displaced people? Not to mention the total number of 3 million. At the same time, the media go for a personal story, and with limited access there are very few of those. This also goes back to the problem of having something new to say, and this usually comes from outside, such as UN resolutions or celebrity involvement. If the International Criminal Court (ICC) had a milestone, then it would get reported. But it is so slow and so obscure, that it could only be a story on slowness.[7]

Was the crisis in Darfur, then, too monumentally big and slow for audiences-cum-publics to grasp or for journalists to make interesting? Was it a failure of the capacity of representation and mediation itself? Darfur is an example of the way in which the news values of media determine whether distant suffering – from violence and conflict to natural disasters and humanitarian crises – is shown to audiences. While Darfur did become more prominent on Western news agendas in the spring of 2006 due to the 'looming end' of the African Union peace operation and a 'publicity drive' by celebrities such as George Clooney,[8] the war in Lebanon between Israel and Hezbollah in August displaced it (Michalski and Gow, 2007: 169). The latter offered graphic images from journalists and from the PR campaigns of each party; Darfur offered what 'appeared to be no more than standard images of Africa, perhaps with famine present, but with no evidence of ethnic cleansing' (ibid.: 169).

Interviews with journalists and media practitioners shed further light on why some stories receive greater coverage than others. In the next quote, Lindsey Hilsum, International Editor of *Channel 4 News* in the UK, compares wide-spread coverage of the Israeli–Palestinian conflict with the lesser coverage of war in the Democratic Republic of the Congo. She argues that this is due to the strategic importance of the former in geopolitics, and also the cost and difficulty to news organizations of making the report. But this leads to a self-fulfilling prophecy where 'expensive' or tricky stories get ignored, which makes them seem less important, which makes it even less likely they get reported:

> [I]f you talk about violence in the Middle East between Israelis and Palestinians, it gets a lot more television coverage than violence in the Democratic Republic of

Congo. Now, there are a number of reasons for that, obviously one reason has to do with how geo-strategically, the importance of where those places are in relative terms, but Israel and Palestine have the largest number of cameras around, I mean nobody farts in Israel without somebody filming it. And say you have a tremendous number of images at all times, whatever happens you will have an image of it and that inevitably means that they will get on the television, while in the Democratic Republic of Congo, if you want to report a story it involves a tremendous investment of time, energy and danger for your correspondent and camera person to go and find that story. Inevitably that is not going to get on the television as often as the other. And so if you take these things together (because obviously Israel-Palestine can be regarded as more geo-strategically important), that's why it gets much coverage, than it becomes a self-fulfilling prophecy because all the resources go into that story.[9]

For Jennifer Glasse, a journalist with the US broadcaster PBS, the Congo war only became a Western interest when it emerged it had minerals needed for Sony Playstations:

[I]t goes back to ratings, it's ratings driven. You know if you could find some way to make it interesting to your audience, be it a British audience or an American audience. It's kind of like, you know the war in Congo, in eastern Zaire, the conflict there only became super-interesting to the West – or, kind of, it's been a long-running war, it's been running almost 10 years . . . It only re-emerged in about 2000. The conflict became very important again to the West. Why? Because one of the minerals mined there, and can only be found there, was a central component in the Play Station! . . . It's all about making those kinds of connections, it's like, 'What, my kid can't have a Play Station because there's war in the Congo? I'm interested'. And those are the kinds of connections you [as a reporter] have to make.[10]

On such trivial connections do audiences take notice and feel affected. Alongside the problems documented so far – lack of journalist access and resources to reach distant insecure areas – Fiona Lloyd Davies, a former BBC *Newsnight* producer, speaks of 'three Ts' of news values:

The key problem is that people think it is 'worthy' and 'worthiness' is thought of as particularly not compelling television. We are living in a climate now where foreign current affairs is almost becoming a thing of the past. The most important thing for current affairs is to have a gimmick, or the three Ts – tone, talent and treatment.[11]

Hence a current affairs show may feature a celebrity presenter ('talent'), such as George Clooney presenting a report on Darfur as mentioned above, or approach a topic from a shocking angle ('treatment'). Davies argues that *Newsnight* allowed Salam Pax, the 'Baghdad Blogger' who reached a global public audience in 2003, to film reports for the programme because he had the three Ts. His tone was laced with irony and humour, which would appeal to the up-market news audience *Newsnight* attracts. He had talent, insofar as he was part of Iraqi society yet also educated in Austria and fluent in English. And he offered appealing treatment of the ongoing Iraq story. For instance, in one report, he offered 'a kind of alternative guide to how not to get killed in

Baghdad, whether it was hair gel, slightly too tight jeans, anything that's red, and a number of other things. And a Western journalist couldn't do that.'[12] *Newsnight* also allowed Pax to present an obituary of Saddam Hussein: 'It was the blogger's style with an ironic view of the life of Saddam.'[13]

In *Compassion Fatigue* (1999), Susan Moeller looks at many of the reasons explored so far in the context of the US media, looking at problems of money and access, sensationalism and simplification. In addition, she argues that American audiences in particular seem prone to ethnocentrism, the tendency only to identify with those like oneself. So Americans will only watch overseas reporting if the story involves Americans; coverage of different nationalities, ethnicities or religions is less interesting to home audiences. Whether this is true, and whether other national populations are less prone to ethnocentrism, is a matter for research. But Moeller adds a final reason which should not be overlooked: accident/luck. She cites Carroll Bogert, foreign correspondent at *Newsweek* magazine, who said that decisions about which stories the magazine covers is often slightly random:

> There was one editor who just for a long time had a thing about Yugoslavia. You know, it's a lot of messy ethnic things, and the editor felt Americans didn't know or care about Bosnia. Some editors find China tedious. Other times I think it's just quirks of fate. Media watchers and others often see conspiracy, but it's not something that's deliciously complex. We just want to get the story out. There's a lot that's just accidental blundering and happenstance. (1999: 23–4)

To summarize, student interviewees identified a 'news hierarchy' whereby some stories seemed to receive disproportionate coverage at the expense of others. Proportionality is not the primary value in news, however. Coverage depends on journalists' and editors' assumptions about what interests their audiences, and what audiences feel affects their own interests. Journalists' and editors' decisions are shaped by news values such as novelty and drama, and whether the tone, talent and treatment in a report is 'catchy'; editors may assume too that news is also more intelligible to audiences if it has a clear framing, such as 'us versus them', 'good versus bad', 'perpetrators and victims', as well as clear religious or ethnic differences. The amount of coverage a story receives also depends on practical matters, such as whether it is safe for journalists to access a war zone, and whether a news editor happens to be fascinated or bored by a region that week. Importantly, each of these many factors can interact. As Lindsey Hilsum noted, if journalists can't access a region, we remain ignorant of what is happening there, so we cannot assess whether it affects our interests, and resources remain diverted to stories we are sure do affect our interests. Practical restrictions can interact with news values to create vicious cycles whereby certain stories remain unfamiliar and therefore less intelligible to audiences, and so are less likely to be covered. Hence, to understand why a story is 'off the radar', we must not only identify distinct reasons, but examine how these reasons reinforced each other over time.

The alert reader may by now have asked whether news editors and journalists are correct in their assumptions about what audiences are interested in. Next, we ask why audiences or spectators connect to some stories more than others.

3. Exploring Spectator–Sufferer Relations

Why do viewers feel more connected to some stories than others? What shapes who we feel close to, and who we feel a distance from? And from where do we look? We saw earlier in this chapter how five students in London discussed the Darfur crisis. Later in their conversation they turned to broader relations between Britain and the developing world, beginning with US/UK relations with Iraq before moving to their relations with Africa. We can discern where, politically and geographically, they are speaking *from*, with what identity they are speaking *as*:

> Khalid: And it's awful because in 1998, [US President] Clinton attacked
>   a major resource of medicine . . . a factory in Al-Shifa, which
>   used to aid millions of people and he said there was chemicals
>   there. It was medicine and it was attacked and you don't even
>   hear about it, nobody knows about it, and now [in Darfur] it's
>   completely different [i.e. the West wants to help] . . . so some-
>   times you hear for example, they talk about aid for Africa . . .
>
> Amina: And, like, why aid? Why not tools? Why not help the people to be
>   independent?
>
> Fatima: It's because they want to fire money to the problem, they want us
>   to be dependent.
>
> Amina: That's their colonial mentality, their thing.[14]

All three here speak of Britain as 'they'. While Khalid was born in Palestine, Fatima speaks of Africa as 'us'. Hence, despite living in London and being addressed by British media such as the BBC and Channel 4 News, they view distant events through different identities. By not identifying themselves with an imagined, typical British viewer, they are positioned to criticize '*their* colonial mentality'. The presence of diasporic or migrant audiences is central to the new media ecology; in any country there will be people who bring different geographical, ethnic and religious perspectives to local or national news. In the case of Amina and Fatima, their identity contributes to their critical (perhaps cynical) opinions about the US and UK.

How we relate to the story may also depend on our ability to empathize or put ourselves 'in their shoes'. Somebody who has been assaulted will feel differently towards a story about an assault from somebody who has not. The person who hasn't been assaulted will feel less empathy, if any. They might try to imagine how the assault victim in the news story feels, to overcome the distance through an act of imagination. But do they imagine themselves in that situation, or do they imagine how the assault victim must feel? It will matter to whether we feel we might be an assault victim one day, or whether the suffering depicted is simply not something experienced in their society. A Western viewer may not expect to be made a refugee after a land war.

We may also feel we have a 'stake' in the story. Sontag writes: 'To those who are sure that right is on one side, oppression and injustice on the other, and that the fighting must go on, what matters is precisely who is killed and by whom' (2003: 10). Political loyalties and attachments can colour our interpretation of reports of suffering. The pain of others can signify your safety and success.[15] If 'our boys' are winning a battle, does this take primacy over any relation we might have to those on the receiving end? This is both a matter of social groupings and loyalties, and a historical question.

Alongside the identity and perspective of the viewer, it matters whether audiences trust what they are seeing. To be committed to acting in response to a story about distant suffering, we must trust that the report is accurate in the first place. Boltanski (1999: 32) identifies three aspects of trust. First, the report must be falsifiable. It must be possible to show that the information is not simply rumour or an invention of the reporter. So it must be possible to triangulate, to get a second opinion from another trusted source or, for instance, a reliable witness. Second, news about one disaster must be justifiably more important than news of another disaster. When our attention is limited, we need to trust that news will be ranked by the same criteria of importance to which we hold. News values must align with audiences' expectations about what is important. Third, the framing of the news must be justifiable. We expect a degree of objectivity and impartiality (we can't have a public sphere where we can debate matters if there isn't at least some commonly agreed-upon information we can argue about), yet to grab and move the audience the newsmakers may omit some detail and prioritize that which pulls our heartstrings. We must have confidence that this selection process is not skewing the report in a particular direction that leads to a basic inaccuracy in our understanding of the event as a whole.

Nor does everyone consider morality in the same terms. We each have different criteria of 'worth' or common good (Boltanski and Thévenot, 1991/2006). Studies by Carol Gilligan are instructive here. She found that men tend to think in terms of justice, and evaluate situation in terms of abstract ideals; the morality of women, in contrast, was centred to a greater degree upon care and evaluated in terms of meeting people's needs (In most cases people mix these two forms of morality together – see Gilligan and Attanuci, 1988). She also found that people feel outrage differently. A person whose morality centres upon justice will feel shame that the injustice exists, and guilt about not acting and thereby failing to live up to one's ideals. A person whose morality centres upon care will feel outrage at the failure of people to relate to and respond to each others' needs (Gilligan and Wiggins, 1988). Based on Gilligan's studies, Tester (2001) hypothesizes that a 'justice' person will be provoked by a report that emphasizes the unfairness of a situation and that nobody has acted (a lack of charitable donations, say). A 'care' person will be provoked by a report that constructs an emotional connection or attachment in the viewer.

The student of compassion fatigue requires an analytical framework for mapping the relations between spectators, sufferers and others involved in the distant story reported. Adam Smith addressed this issue in *The Theory of Moral Sentiments*, written in 1759 – these are not new questions! He identifies a set of actors – as shown in figure 3.1. The ordinary spectator is straightforward: the person watching, whose reaction we can record. But alongside the ordinary spectator is the figure of the ideal spectator: the person whom we imagine to be observing our conduct, and whose presence guides our moral actions – the imaginary person we should be able to account for our response to, and whose

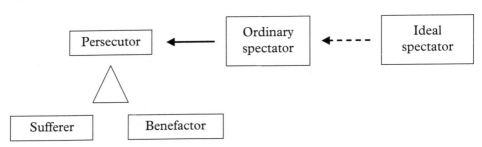

Figure 3.1 Adam Smith's Model of Sympathy

values and perspective we would fear offending (Smith, 1976: 113–14). In other words, the ideal spectator stands for general opinion in our society, which the ordinary spectator will take into account. We are aware, for instance, that it is inappropriate to talk about others' suffering in very factual, detached terms (unless one is a doctor). We tend to mention how witnessing that suffering made us feel, thus fulfilling expectations about a genuinely 'human' response. Or think of watching breaking news coverage of a terrorist attack on a large screen at an airport or train station: we are part of the crowd and in reacting we take into account those around us. It would seem inappropriate, for instance, to start laughing.

Both persecutor and benefactor are considered by Smith to be 'agents', people with the capacity to act: the persecutor acts to cause harm, and the benefactor acts to relieve the harm caused. The victim feels grievance to one, gratitude to the other (Smith, 1976: Part II). The spectator or audience member will feel connected to all three: to the persecutor the spectator will feel resentment; to the benefactor, sympathy (for the spectator would like to do the same); and to the victim, the spectator will feel an indirect sympathy.

We are able to analyse these relations – how media represent the triangle of sufferer, persecutor and benefactor – and then find audience responses to these media representations, for instance through online forums, opinion polls or other data on public perceptions of events. This is a relational approach which allows for the mapping of relations between actors, where distance is in effect eliminated in the analysis (see chapter 7). Incorporating the ideal spectator into analysis is difficult. Each ordinary spectator may imagine the ideal spectator (public opinion) differently, and the repertoire of culture they share.[16] Heroism, suffering, 'just' intervention – can we identify our society's shared understanding of these moments? Identifying these social expectations is central to media regulation of what standards of 'taste and decency' media must adhere to when representing scenes from war. Regulators are assuming or second-guessing, in effect, an ideal spectator. That ideal spectator indicates the norms of acceptability. When a news story infringes these norms, public complaints will notify the regulator of the breach. In this way, the regulator can be said to identify the ideal spectator. But in the new media ecology, audiences are not necessarily unitary wholes existing within a nation-state container. We must ask whether and how norms and repertoires become diffuse.

Let us take three ways or 'modes' by which people relate to those suffering in media reports, as set out in Boltanski's *Distant Suffering* (he calls the modes 'topics'), and use Adam Smith's mapping of relations to illustrate them. Each mode comes into play and may be valid at certain times, but none applies universally and all have their limits. The three modes are *denunciation, sentiment*, or an *aesthetic* connection to the event. In other words, we can react with indignation or tender-heartedness, or view the scene purely as a spectacle. (Note that these are ideal-type constructions and demand empirical substantiation.)

Denunciation occurs when the spectator is powerless to intervene in the distant suffering. Their pity turns to indignation: an anger that cannot be turned into action. Only speech is possible, and the only form of speech is accusation. Attention is not to the sufferer but to the persecutor. However, it is not always easy to identify a persecutor – it is not always clear who is to blame for a conflict, a famine or other disasters. Additionally, the spectator may identify with the victim or sufferer (they might be of the same nationality or religion, say), and be over-quick to identify a persecutor based on their own existing prejudices. One group or collectivity may attribute collective blame to another group in an unreflective, 'contagious' way (Boltanski, 1999: 59). Following George W. Bush's description in 2002 of the war on terror as a 'crusade', Muslim audiences aware of certain historical connotations of the term – the Crusades began in medieval Christian Europe in an attempt to claim Jerusalem from Muslim possession – may have thought, 'It's those Christians on another crusade'. But that may have been to misread Bush's intended meaning entirely.

So let us ask: under what conditions can indignation (for Boltanski) be valid and appropriate? Instead of knee-jerk, blanket condemnation of another group, for denunciation of a persecutor to be valid, the spectator must first be sure that the victim is in fact a victim. It must be established that that person is suffering an avoidable misfortune because of a third party, the persecutor. A degree of causality must be evident. News stories may construct a notion of causality through comparison. To show the 'cause' of poverty, a television story may show shots of a slum interspersed with shots of a skyscraper or other symbol of financial wealth (or 'greed'). Such a story would appeal to implicit conventions about economic justice and fairness, and suggest that the poverty of the slum inhabitants is due to the actions of the 'rich' in the skyscrapers. Indeed, attempts to construct a causal story will rest upon a theory of power (ibid.: 62–3). Marxists and socialists will see some suffering as caused by forces in political economy – power relations between classes. The oppressed class will be indignant and seek to turn their indignation into political action. But is their indignation towards an individual ('the boss', a police chief) or towards 'the system'? Similarly, news reports on war and conflict may convey implicit or explicit theories of power to explain what is causing things to happen in a war zone. However, these theories may be questionable. For example, from the 1990s when the Kosovo Liberation Army (KLA) fought for independence for Kosovo from Yugoslavia and then Serbia, there was doubt about whether it represented victims or persecutors, and hence whether or not Western agencies should be offering support. There was uncertainty therefore regarding the cause of suffering for Kosovar Albanians and towards whom indignation should be directed. Conflict in Rwanda and the Democratic Republic of the Congo since the 1990s has involved killing by both

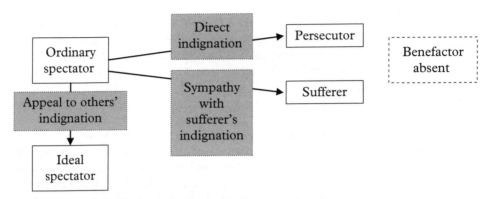

Figure 3.2   Relations in the Mode of Denunciation

sides, but is it fair to depict Hutus at all stages of the conflict as more often the aggressors and worthy of indignation and Tutsis as worthy of pity?

Denunciation demands a degree of investigation, then, to establish blame and responsibility. Do journalists always provide this, and how can audiences be sure that journalists have done a thorough job? The accusation towards the persecutor must rest on proof – ideally, sufficient proof to convince both a general audience and the persecutor. The subjective emotion of the accusation must be seen to have an objective basis. Emotion must be controlled: the case must be agonistic (seeing the opposition as there to be persuaded) not antagonistic (seeing the opposition as an enemy to be eliminated). Most compelling, for Boltanski, would be if an investigation had also asked whether the apparent persecutor is in fact a victim himself. Here, the spectator would exhibit 'enlightened indignation' (ibid.: 59). For example, critics of the US-led invasion of Iraq in 2003 might pause to examine the extent to which US policymakers and publics after 11 September 2001 identify themselves as victims, and investigate and take into account how justifiable that claim is.

Denunciation is open to criticism, then (see figure 3.2). Since it relies on speech rather than action, critics may complain that 'it is only words'. Nothing is risked by the accuser. So perhaps the sense of indignation is false; and if it is false, the accuser is a hypocrite. Indeed, the lazy accuser could himself be accused of irresponsibility, for raising the level of debate which may cause further harm to the sufferer, or inciting a mob mentality. The charge of falseness and hypocrisy could also be levelled if the spectator has never shared the sufferer's position or experience (for example, civilian travellers who appear to gain some thrill from visiting conflict zones are often labelled 'war tourists'). Yet if you are part of that suffering group, then your denunciation may appear self-interested. Finally, denouncing a group or collective appears contradictory. If you simply denounce everyone in a group, it is difficult to prove that all members of the group share responsibility for actions done in the group's name. If, then, you allow that some of the group may not be responsible for the suffering caused by the group, then that group must be divided into two groups: those responsible and those not. At that point it is no longer possible to blame the group. Note that this is a difficulty within Al-Qaeda's discourse: can all US or UK citizens

Table 3.1 Boltanski's Three Modes of Spectatorship

Mode	Form the relation takes	Problems
Denunciation	• The spectator is powerless. The only possible action is speech, in the form of accusation. • Attention is on the persecutor not the victim. • Judgements may be based on group loyalties.	• Investigation and proof are needed to be sure the victim is a victim and the persecutor alone caused the harm. • Accusation is mere words. • Either you have not experienced and so cannot feel the pain of the victim, or, if you have experience as part of the victim group, then your accusations are self-interested. • If you denounce a whole group, are all members equally complicit?
Sentiment	• The spectator's priority is to see the victim's suffering end. • The spectator sympathizes with the victim's gratitude to the benefactor. • No attention on blaming a persecutor. • Judgement is based on emotion: whoever spontaneously feels touched grasps the truth of the situation.	• The spectator's self-indulgent emoting obscures the suffering of the actual victim. • The spectator's discovery of their emotional sensitivity means they gain pleasure from others' pain. • The spectator ignores the cause of the suffering.
Aestheticized	• No relation. The victim is simply an object to gaze at. • What counts is how the spectator experiences spectating – e.g., a sublime moment of moving from confusion to comprehension. • Stands as a critique of the hypocrisy, resentment and selfishness of the other modes.	• What spectators choose to look at is a matter of individual taste, not public interest or the urgency of the victim's plight. • Power inequality: the victim is merely an object put on view. • Standing outside society's norms offers little scope for action.

be responsible for the actions of their governments? What if they voted against their governments? Are they responsible for not overthrowing the democratic system? Ellis writes about spectatorship of suffering more generally: '[B]y the very act of looking, individuals in the witnessing audience become accomplices in the events they see. Events on a screen make a mute appeal: "You cannot say you did not know"' (2002: 11).[17]

The second mode of spectator–sufferer relations is sentiment. The *denunciat-ing* spectator felt indignant at the persecutor, and sympathy with the sufferer's

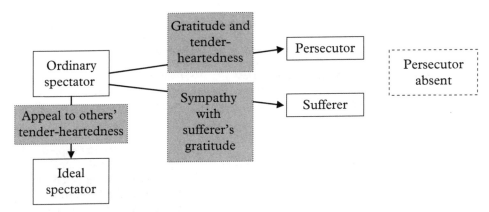

Figure 3.3 Relations in the Mode of Sentiment

resentment to that persecutor. The *sentimental* spectator sympathizes with the sufferer's gratitude to the benefactor. Instead of feeling indignation, the spectator feels tender-heartedness. There is no direct relation to a persecutor. In the topic of sentiment, questions of responsibility and blame are set aside. The primary concern is an urgent demand to relieve the suffering (see figure 3.3).

If responsibility and blame are set to one side, there is less need to investigate the cause of the suffering, to assemble proof of causal links or to appeal to principles of justice. Rather, the appeal to others (to the ideal spectator and to potential benefactors) is based on *interiority*: the spectator reveals their interior – their emotions. They appeal to the heart, to others' interior states (heart-to-heart). We ask who else has been touched as we have been. Emotion is the signal of truth, or, if truth is interior, then the displaying one's interior state – showing how we feel – is the manifestation of truth. As Boltanski writes (1999: 82), the moment when the spectator witnesses the suffering is the 'moment of truth' because it is then that the spectator feels touched. Additionally, the truth-value of emotion is bolstered by the fact that spectators don't intend to feel touched. They just do, and that is a signal the feeling is genuine. In contrast, if in a news story the reporter appears to fake his or her emotional response to the suffering, this becomes a significant offence. Such 'artifice' or sensationalism will fail to convince or move audiences because it is a false revealing of emotions – within a framework in which emotions are the mark of truth – and because it makes presumptions about the audiences' interiority or emotions. The foreign correspondent has tried to second-guess and play upon the audience's feelings.

We might add that it matters who the depicted sufferer is. The gender, ethnicity and class of the sufferer matter, and the spectator's perspective will be shaped by cultural norms about the 'worthy victim' (Hoijer, 2004). Take the images of a wailing man in Iraq standing over coffins of his dead family, published by Reuters on 2 April 2003 soon after the start of the invasion. For many Western spectators, the man's grief could stand for (metonymy) the horrors or injustices of war, and invoke a universal morality whereby 'we' sympathize with anybody who has just lost their family. Yet he is in full Arabic dress and headscarf; in one shot he is standing barefoot, and has his arms thrown up in a tragic gesture. These aspects may problematize any natural bond of sympathy for the spectator: is it 'right' for a man to grieve so dramatically? Isn't it more typical to offer sympathy to grieving women? Why has the father failed to protect his family? And the man's dress appears stereotypically 'Arab', and therefore, for Westerners, 'other' – not 'us' (Konstantinidou, 2007). Standing barefoot, the man is also somehow not part of 'our' modernity.

Spectators whose response falls within the topic of sentiment are open to criticism too. They can be accused of self-indulgence, for where is the limit of how much one should and could describe one's emotions? The spectator's own self-descriptions could end up 'swamping' the position of the sufferer (Boltanski, 1999: 98). Indeed, the spectacle of suffering can bring pleasure: the pleasure of discovering one's own humanity, and affirming it by feeling moved. Hence, the sentimental spectator could be accused of self-interest, or of voyeurism (war tourists, again). Equally, why should it take *this* story of suffering to move the spectator, when there is general or systemic suffering aplenty in the world? Finally, is it really valid for spectators to ignore the question of what is causing the suffering? As soon as the spectator begins to consider why this suffering is occurring, the limit of sentiment is reached and the topic of denunciation is present. Hence, NGOs and humanitarian organizations may wish to avoid denunciation and the 'blame game' and concentrate on presenting suffering in ways that simply allow for an empathy between victims and potential donors.

There is a third way to experience the spectacle of suffering, Boltanski argues. So far, we have seen that pity can turn into indignation or sentimental tender-heartedness, and that both of these reactions can in some cases be criticized, for instance as self-interested or hypocritical. The third mode or way of relating is when the spectator views suffering in aesthetic terms. This may include boredom, or pleasure at a panoramic spectacle. Instead of surrendering to feeling and looking to blame or display emotions, the spectator could simply accept the suffering and look it 'in the face' (ibid.: 116). This form of spectatorship is divorced from questions of political structures, responsibilities and inequalities. The horror could be anywhere, happening to anyone, at any time – it does not matter too much. What matters is the spectator's own experience. They may experience *the sublime*. This entails passing through two stages. Initially, the spectator feels horror and confusion as they struggle to comprehend the suffering on view. But then, the spectator enjoys a moment of comprehension and appreciates what it is they see. They undergo 'a delicious horror and painful enjoyment' (ibid.: 121).

The aesthetic mode can appear problematic politically. First, is it that some people experience boredom, pleasure, distress, the sublime when regarding suffering, and others do not? Is spectatorship of suffering a question of taste? That would make a 'politics of pity' difficult, as it would be impossible to arouse a fully public response or appeal to universal values. Taste is individual. As Boltanski notes, in this mode we appear to meet the separation of aesthetics from politics. Taste is a subjective, private matter, for the discerning few, while politics is often conceived as outward-looking, a matter for the demos or public or a 'common good'. Second, the spectator does not feel symmetry with

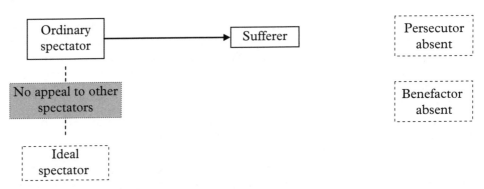

Figure 3.4   Relations in the Aesthetic Mode

the sufferer. The spectator does not think, 'That could be me'. The sufferer is irrelevant; the sublime experience depends on the spectator's subjectivity and gaze ('beauty is in the eye of the beholder'). Both the spectator and the person delivering the representation – the news reporter or photographer – are mobile. They can look at different things, at different times. But the sufferer is *stuck*, a mere object '*put on view*', to be looked upon (ibid.: 128).

Let us return to the 'wailing father' in Iraq, in Konstantinidou's study of photographs of the 2003 Iraq War in the Greek press. The father does not look at the camera. He is alone in his state of grief and despair. As such, 'the photographs "offer" the wailing father's misfortune to the viewer as an item of information or as an object of contemplation' (Konstantinidou, 2007: 155). A caption underneath the photograph reads: 'The pain is unbearable for the Iraqi who lost his six children in an air bombing. *Absolutely nothing could be done to console him*' (ibid.: 157). Nothing is being asked of the reader. No political action would make a difference. Moreover, because of the non-Western setting, the chaos, it is unlikely that many readers of the newspaper would think 'That could be me'. It would seem that the asymmetric character of the aesthetic topic makes it apolitical. With no persecutor or benefactor, we are free to take or leave the spectacle.

So what can spectators do? Given that most news consumers are unlikely to get up and go to the disaster zone, Boltanski suggests that our options are to pay, speak or demonstrate (see table 3.2).

In summary, this section has suggested several reasons why viewers feel more or less connected to those depicted as suffering in news reports from war zones and humanitarian disasters. These include the national, religious and ethnic identity of the viewer, their capacity to empathize with the sufferer's situation, whether the viewer has a stake in the conflict or disaster, whether they trust the report about the conflict or disaster and whether their moral compass is centred more upon justice or upon care. This was followed by the setting out of a framework for mapping and analysing the relation between spectator and sufferer (and persecutor and benefactor), based on Boltanski's theorization of three 'modes' of relation – denunciation, sentiment and the aesthetic. This led to a brief consideration of the political action each mode leaves available to the spectator to act to relieve suffering from a distance.

Table 3.2 Boltanski's Forms of Response to Suffering

Form of action	Advantages	Disadvantages
Paying (e.g. a charitable donation)	• A clear action, quantifiable.	• Requires an intermediary, an institution to collate donations and organize their distribution. • Loses all specificity: your donation is absorbed into a larger sum. There is no connection between donor and receiver. • Anonymous: we don't know who else cares and has donated, so we cannot mobilize together.
Speaking (e.g. writing to a newspaper or just telling your friend)	• Speech can help form groups, allowing a politics of pity to emerge. • Politicians take account of opinion polls. Opinion polls are instances of citizens speaking.	• Often requires an intermediary to turn single voices into 'public opinion', e.g. polling agencies, NGOs. • May not require much sacrifice: 'talk is cheap'.
Demonstrating	• Public, collective, may have a written manifesto.	• None.

Source: Boltanski, 1999: 17–19, 171–92

What we have yet to introduce to the analysis of compassion fatigue and distance suffering is the precise role of media texts in these processes. How can a news report be constructed and framed by journalists and editors to entice a particular connection? What characteristic of a news report or text makes compassion more likely?

4. How Do Media Enable or Restrict Compassion?

Returning to our five students interviewed in London in 2006, we see that they objected to the quantification of victims in one report about the Darfur crisis:

Maria: I just remember when it was 9/11, when they said the amount of people who died, there really was an emphasis on 3,000 or however many, but here he quite simply said 400,000 – do you know what I mean?

Amina: I agree, it's such a dispassionate way of speaking – the way of saying 400,000. My feeling is not, 'People died?' *You might have been, like, rocks!*

Maria: Yeah, it's not really like they're talking about people, with, like, the whole region of Africa, sometimes you feel like they're *talking about cattle* or something like that. There's no individuals and . . .

> they don't care who they're filming, it's a person, they're skinny,
> they've got really big tummies, and it's really really generalist.

Large numbers of dead and injured can play a role in a narrative. For example, increasing numbers of casualties in Iraq after 2003 were interpreted in various ways: rising figures as signifying 'unnecessary loss', as a Vietnam-like 'quagmire' in which the Coalition military was stuck; falling figures as 'success', 'progress', 'proof the situation is increasingly under control' and 'the return of security' (see Hoskins and O'Loughlin, 2007: ch. 6). On the other hand, however, numbers can appear too large to tell the story, dehumanizing the victims by representing each individual as part of a mass sum – like 'cattle', as Maria says.

The use of statistics in news is just one way media can create an interest or, conversely, prevent audiences from feeling connected to a story. Another is scripting. Hammock and Charny (1996) argue that media coverage of distance crises follows the convention of a morality play, to the point where coverage is seen as naturally that way and couldn't be any other. They identify five conventions:

1 The crisis comes from nowhere. It is suddenly here.
2 Roles quickly emerge: heroes such as Western aid agencies, and villains such as UN bureaucrats or local military authorities who obstruct aid.
3 Suffering, not the causes of suffering, receives attention. The story is about an aid operation, and the suffering party is only ever a recipient of aid, never an agent of their own destiny.
4 The credibility of heroes is never questioned. Whether these aid agencies are best placed to act, whether their track record is good, and what their motives are: all go unquestioned.
5 The efforts of local agencies are overlooked.

Certainly we are familiar with such reporting. The cyclone that hit Burma in 2008 became an international news story of military generals obstructing well-intentioned international aid (though political crisis in Burma is not a new story). But if this routine 'script' was the case, why do people still feel sufficiently connected and concerned to make donations? Tester writes, there is 'no necessary link between the report or representation and the perceptions and feelings of the audience' (2001: 102). So what are the sufficient conditions which alone or together can trigger such feelings?

To understand compassion fatigue fully, we must get to grips with the complete range of techniques of representation through which media portray suffering. An important study on this theme is Lilie Chouliaraki's *The Spectatorship of Suffering* (2006). She argues that Western media coverage of distant disasters constructs a hierarchy of pity (ibid.: 189), which chimes with the 'news hierarchy' identified by our students earlier. The hierarchy of pity is constructed by imposing one of three scripts on events: *adventure, emergency* and *ecstatic* coverage. Reporting of a disaster that follows the adventure script is akin to a Greek romance, in which our hero wanders through a strange landscape where random, distinct events occur. News offers a description of the victims (number, nationality, occupation) and the circumstance (location, manner of disaster, cause), but in terms of multimodality – the verbal and visual aspects of the coverage – there is no verbal narrative constructed. Take the news headline, 'separatist rebels attacked in Indonesia yesterday': there is no explanation of why. Like an adventure, things just happen. Visually there may be a map given but the space-time is 'cut off': a map with dots and coloured regions does not allow us to visualize what happened. We may get static shots of a disaster zone, such as a flooded area, but this does not help us envisage a possible future for the zone. And such a report will present the victims as entirely lacking in agency, or the capacity to alter their circumstances. Static shots of floods appear as a biblical catastrophe, part of an eternal repetition; the story omits the role of humans in causing flooding through lack of agricultural planning or preventative technologies. Labelling the victims in terms of numbers ('40 dead') or nationalities ('two Americans and three Germans died') also dehumanizes those involved. It is, as we saw above, difficult to think of numbers as people.

In short, news-as-adventure strives for objectivity, with camera shots 'from a position of nowhere' or 'universal' perspective (ibid.: 107). However, not only can this create distance for viewers, but it constructs hierarchies of worth. In a story that has no on-location interviews, the lack of voice and agency of those involved or attention to the cause of the disaster both suggest a hierarchy of human life. This can be reinforced if the story is low down on the news running order. There is also an implicit hierarchy of place: if no Westerners are killed, then the incident is simply represented as dots on a map. With an event such as the Bali bombings of 2004, in which Western tourists died, journalists reported from the location, providing interviews with those involved, allowing viewers to engage; interviews offer a voice to those involved and so, we might imagine, it is easier to feel pity for the survivors, their families and hospital workers, and denunciation towards the perpetrators. Furthermore, Bali became a place connected to other places – one of many possible holiday resorts that terrorists might still target – and thereby connected to the past and future. Bali became relevant to viewers because it was represented as part of a chain of terror attacks within which the viewer may one day be entangled. But without such multimodal narrative-construction (and speculation), adventure news creates distance and possibly compassion fatigue. Disasters 'just happen', leaving audiences in a position to do nothing about it nor connect to those involved.

News as emergency *can* produce pity. In box 3.1 we summarize three examples of emergency news, from longer case studies by Chouliaraki. In the final example in particular, we see how news may offer spectators options for action; the disaster is distant but bridgeable. Unlike the static shots and minimal voices of adventure news, emergency news offers a more complex array of ways to engage the viewer; unlike a single space-time, emergency news tells a story that connects here and there, past-present-and-future; and emergency news offers the possibility of agency. Chouliaraki finds that emergency news offers the strongest connection between spectator and sufferer. The difference between the situation depicted and our own experience is what pulls the spectator in, and the final story offers the possibility that the spectator can get involved and help.

Table 3.3 Chouliaraki's Three Types of News of Suffering

	Adventure	**Emergency**	**Ecstatic**
Multimodality	Simple narratives. Verbal: simple reporting of facts. Visual: minimal, abstracted representations.	Complicated.	Live flow, mixed.
Space-time	Singular. An isolated place, a one-off event.	Concrete, specific, multiple, mobile.	Now *and* historical, local *and* global, connects all humanity.
Agency	None.	Conditional.	The viewer is sovereign.
Moral mechanism	Othering without pity.	Suffering without pity.	Reflexive identification.
Spectator's role	Sufferer.	Actor.	Unstable: both protected *and* engaged.
Compassion fatigue then?	Little possibility.	More context and explanation, but still offering only token engagement.	Less, due to distancing and reflection.

Box 3.1

Rescuing African refugees: high-adrenaline spectacle
A Maltese coastguard boat attempts to save North African and Somalia illegal refugees 44 miles off the Malta coast. News shows a video clip and voiceover describing the action. Shots are erratic and water is on the lens. The montage of shots constructs a narrative; it appears as 'real-time story-telling', with the present tense used and 'live' pictures. There is little explanation or context, just drama, and no follow up afterwards. Spectators witness an urgent need but it is not placed within any historical context. Perhaps this happens often, but the viewer is not told. The rescuers carry guns and have medical face-masks and uniforms, which distances us from them, but the story is heroic, even cinematic. The spectator is therefore in an ambivalent position.

Famine in Argentina: icons of starvation
The report combines archive and satellite pictures that take us between multiple places: homes, streets, hospitals – overall suggesting a widespread problem. The visuals focus on particular children and situations, but the voice-over is general, about the broader starvation. The particular children are powerful icons of the general suffering. One village is named, making it familiar to us. Some children gaze at the camera (us), but we only see the torsos or arms of others. The only agent is a US aid donor, but their aid

has stopped. Hence the only agents with the power to change the situation are failing. The spectator is moved, but can do nothing.

Death by stoning in Nigeria: symbols of inhumanity
News of the stoning to death of a mother in Nigeria, Amina Lawal, in 2002, offers greater potential for connection to audiences than other stories. First and most superficially, the story is personalized: it is immediately about one woman, not a group, community or city. Amina Lawal is shown in a courtroom with her baby, followed by a protest by Amnesty International representatives and then a violent mob in Nigerian streets. The sufferer is named, she is given agency – unlike rescued Somalis or starving Argentineans, Lawal at least 'had her baby' – and even though she does not speak, her passivity invokes a resource in a shared cultural repertoire: 'woman as silent sufferer'. Her dignity is contrasted with the mob and Sharia justices, positioned as barbaric persecutors. Second, audiences are encouraged to connect to the story as a situation that can be changed. A speaker for Amnesty encourages 'everyone' to sign a petition. This may be a minimal act asked of viewers, but it is presented as part of a process that could make a difference. Unlike the stories of floods, starvation and terrorism, this story asks 'why?'. This is a story with a historical and political trajectory, not an isolated instance. Finally, by inviting 'everyone' to sign the petition, the story appeals to an undefined public. Often, Western publics are addressed by national broadcasters as national publics; an address by Amnesty International is an address across many countries (as would be an address by, say, Nelson Mandela or the UN). As such, it invokes ostensibly universal values and appeals to individual viewers as part of a universal consciousness. Overall, then, in the Amina Lawal story, viewers are asked to step beyond their ordinary concerns to share in empathy to an individual, share awareness of a political process whose outcome can be altered, and join an undefined community of the concerned.

Ecstatic reporting is the final way disaster news is conveyed to Western viewers, argues Chouliaraki. Live coverage of 9/11 was the exemplary ecstatic event. Chouliaraki suggests that there was such uncertainty about what was happening – the event seemed out of time and place, out of our understanding – that spectators felt ecstasy, meaning 'when a minute seems to last a lifetime' (ibid.: 158). In US news coverage the event should have offered maximum engagement between spectator and sufferer: both shared the same identity as Americans, and the suffering was shown from multiple camera positions, including from cameras moving through the streets of Manhattan. Yet mediation involves 'noise' and hence distance. Dust on the lens reminded spectators they were not physically there, that the event was mediated. The breakdown of routine journalism increased awareness of the chaotic mediations being delivered, and hence our *medial* relation to the event. As reports moved to the Manhattan skyline and lingered on the burning iconic towers, the long shot fostered aesthetic contemplation, inducing horror and awe. From that position, we do not see the sufferers. The horror leads to realization of our own safety. This is comparable to Boltanski's aestheticized viewing (above), in which the spectator derives enjoyment or boredom from gazing upon a spectacular scene of suffering. But this moment of reflection quickly opened up thoughts of other, future attacks; this event becomes linked to other times and places, to a new story we came to know as the 'war on terror'. Hence an ecstatic event such as 9/11 moves the spectator – hypothetically – between different registers: concerned and empathetic, denunciating, and also reflection.

Of Chouliaraki's studies of adventure, emergency and ecstatic news, only the Nigerian stoning story offered Western viewers a connection to non-Western suffering, because it explored *why* the mother was to be killed. Yet many journalists *do* want Western audiences to care (see chapter 4 on the 'journalism of attachment'). It simply seems that the news values and conventions of professional journalism inhibit the creation of such human connection. Alongside journalists, however, how do news organizations position themselves? For in the relation between spectator and sufferer, media also construct their own position, as an actor who has a relationship to the sufferer and others involved. We as spectators might wonder 'how are we supposed to feel?' and imagine a social consensus about the 'right' response. Is it the same for media workers? News organizations are like spectators insofar as they are social actors who present themselves to others (to audiences, to other news channels, to shareholders and regulators) with an eye to their reputation and credibility. In the terms of Boltanski's framework (above), the ordinary spectator feels a pressure to appear concerned or upset in response to a particular news story. The relation between news organization and audience maps onto the relation between ordinary spectator and ideal spectator.

At the beginning of this chapter we presented part of an interview in which students had watched a clip of CNN's coverage of the Darfur crisis in 2006. CNN, the ordinary spectator, cannot know exactly how its audience will feel towards the story, but through audience research and feedback it will have a general idea. Hence CNN modifies its presentation of news in line with its expectation of audiences' expectations. However, in the new media ecology in which media content may be viewed in any country, at any time, it is not clear who the 'ideal spectator' is. When this clip was shown to audiences in the UK, many individuals felt CNN's coverage was deceitful or emphasized racial and religious aspects of the story in ways UK audiences are not accustomed to. The UK audience may not have been the intended audience, the anticipated ideal spectator. The news values examined in section 2 of this chapter vary from country to country, and the repertoires of evaluating situations that audiences bring to news – as explored in section 3 – will also vary. Consequently, we now see that the ways in which news frames distant suffering can resonate or jar with audiences, because both news content and news audiences are diffuse: content produced for a US home audience is viewed in other countries, and those in other countries bring unexpected identities, cultural repertoires and comparisons to bear upon the news. Not only is this 'cultural chaos' a primary marker of the new media ecology (McNair, 2006). It indicates that the compassion fatigue hypothesis is more complex than news editors and journalists acknowledge (Tester, 2001: 11–12).

5. Conclusion

This chapter has set out three areas and sets of questions for testing the hypothesis that audiences feel compassion fatigue. First, do news values lead to a hierarchy of pity? Which journalistic practices explain how and why this happens? Second, how do spectators relate to sufferers? And third, how is that relationship constructed by media? How are our feelings structured by the text? For each area, we provided the basis of an analytical framework for further exploration of these questions. For each, we drew respectively on the work of Susan Moeller, Adam Smith and Luc Boltanski, and Lilie Chouliaraki. It is imperative that students, scholars and news organizations themselves carry out research in these areas, because compassion fatigue is not only a hypothesis. If enough news editors and journalists believe compassion fatigue to be a fact, and act as if it is, then they will deliver stories on the assumption that audiences have little toleration for news of distant, difficult situations. In the long run this will make news from distant places seem more unfamiliar and difficult to comprehend, generating compassion fatigue that was not there in the first place.

How, then, can we test these theories of compassion and spectatorship in the second phase of mediatization? Conceptually, it is possible to identify a modulation between *amplifying* stories of emergency and adventure from those vectors triggered by catastrophes and *containment* of alarm and urgency in the reporting of long, slow crises such as post-conflict situations or refugee movements. We can identify instances in which images of past or forgotten crises re-emerge into the public eye due to the diffusion of that image and story. We can analyse the ways in which premediation shapes our relation to distant others; for instance, do media prepare us for thinking about how we should and could act, ahead of a disaster or conflict actually happening? We can also explore the twin axes of representationality and mediality. For the former, we can conduct multimodal textual analysis of the combinations of images, captions, maps and verbal text in different media reporting of crises, conduct audience studies of their interpretation of these representations, and interview those producing and disseminating such representations in an attempt to elicit compassion, such as NGO workers or journalists. Questions of mediality are key too. How do audiences feel about being targeted or confronted with images of suffering? Can we map a distribution of emotion or affect across borders in response to breaking news events, and correlate emotion with action – donations, protests and so forth – to explore the relation between mediality and politics? Do those filmed – the suffering, the injured, the bereaved – have rights over how images of themselves are used?

In the following chapter we extend this discussion of compassion by addressing the process of witnessing. The question is: how do we come to a shared perception of *a* or *the* 'truth' of war? The chapter examines how soldiers, journalists, humanitarian workers and audiences act as witnesses in varying ways.

This follows directly from the three areas of this chapter: which news gets reported and which doesn't, who feels for and identifies with whom, and how media can make the situations of others appealing or, perhaps, repellent. The phenomenon of witnessing forces us to think about who takes responsibility for recording and interpreting war and conflict as it happens, both to form an accurate memory and to guide present and future policy and action.

4

WITNESS

1. Introduction

'Some people are closer to the truth than others', said a colleague. We were discussing the difficulty of knowing what's happening in Iraq. He meant that some people are literally closer, physically, to incidents – to marketplace bombings, attacks at checkpoints, and militia executions of local civilians. The authority of somebody who witnesses a suicide bombing down the street lies in their proximity and presence at the event. But it is likely that all they know is what they saw. To know the 'truth' of the suicide bombing might also mean knowing who the bomber was, what their motive was, and the experience of those unfortunate enough to be caught up in the explosion. Yet the appeal of proximity is instinctive. Moreover, Deirdre Boden and Harvey Molotch (1994) argue that there is a 'compulsion of proximity', as co-presence affords trust, commitment and detailed understanding. And news media attempt to achieve the status of co-presence, even and especially through the act of media-tion. Why else did BBC Radio 4's *Today* programme send its lead presenter John Humphrys to broadcast a live edition from Baghdad in October 2006 (Luckhurst, 2006)?

Media make us all witnesses, a fact that leaders of Al-Qaeda have invoked in trying to justify attacks on Muslim and non-Muslim civilians alike (Devji, 2005: 99–101). Unless oblivious to news, we will have noticed that US forces are present in Middle Eastern locations and, for bin Laden, are acting against the interests of Muslims. The media historian John Ellis writes: '[B]y the very act of looking, individuals in the witnessing audience become accomplices in the events they see. Events on a screen make a mute appeal: "You cannot say you did not know". The double negative captures the nature of the experience of witness. At once distanced and involving, it implies a necessary relationship with what is seen' (2002: 11). As we become witnesses, through our experience of mediality, we are drawn into ethical and political relationships; yet any such relationship depends on a certain faith in the veracity or truth of the coverage media offered us.

This chapter begins by surveying different modalities of the truth of war. Is it a journalist's duty to deliver truth, accuracy, fairness, balance, authenticity – some of these modalities, or all – or rather, are these merely ritualistic features of news discourses that are rarely if ever comprehensively achieved or achievable? Having established these as common modes of the discourse of representing or delivering the 'truth' of events, we present a picture of the different witnessing roles possible around war and media: journalists, soldiers, humanitarian workers and audiences all become implicated as witnesses in different ways.

We ask how these roles are shifting or more complicated in the connectivity of diffused war. For instance, the blogs of citizen journalists can be used to raise funds to send the blogger to a war zone and report back to those who read the blog and 'donate'. Here is the Back to Iraq 2.0 blogger Christopher Allbritton:

> Hi there! . . . This summer I went stumbling around Iraqi Kurdistan, the northern part of Iraq outside Saddam's direct control, looking for stories. (Some might call it 'looking for trouble.') Well, now I want to go back in time for the war. So I'm asking your help supporting independent journalism! Send me back to Iraq to report on what's happening . . . Click on the PayPal icon below to donate. (Cited in Wall, 2005: 163)

His wish was granted: 320 donations followed. Not only money was received: readers posted story leads and links to further information, and did their best to fact-check Allbritton's reporting. This demonstrates one way in which new technologies facilitate new ways of organizing witnessing – collaborative, participatory, somewhere between the subjectivity of one and the overview of many.

The rest of this chapter is in two parts. In the first, we examine the difficulties of establishing the truth of war, the manner in which media are systems with enduring practices of news gathering and presentation within which only certain things can count as 'news', 'facts' or 'truth', and we set out the intricacies of terms commonly used in these matters: what counts as objective, realistic, accurate, authentic, balanced or certain? In the second, we see how frontline journalists, documentary-makers, soldiers, NGO workers and even audiences become witnesses to war and suffering, and the terms in which they present the truthfulness of their accounts. Issues of technological change, ethics and the legitimation of war cut across our cases. The role of the witness is a lynchpin analytical category for understanding war and media. To what extent, we ask, do new practices of witnessing enabled by the mediatization of war result in a flux of media content making control of 'the message' of war more difficult, or does this mediatization simply enable new forms of control of information and opinion about war?

2. Representation and the Truth of War

Mediation brings what is beyond our human sense experience. It brings us representations of that which is beyond our immediate surroundings. You might have been present at an event. I was not, but media re-presented it to me live on TV. That which is present to us if we are *there* is re-presented to us by the media from where we watch, *here*, wherever we consume media. This is increasingly a real-time phenomenon as the concatenation of 'NowHere' (Friedland and Boden, 1994) suggests. As Roger Silverstone argues, our world is made up of these mediations *and* of the everyday life we experience (2007: 108–11). But mediations or re-presentations have a presence in our lives, and it can be difficult to disentangle mediations from non-mediated experience. Hence, Silverstone writes, mediation is 'the fundamentally, but unevenly, dialectical process in which institutionalized media of communication are involved in the general circulation of symbols *in social life*.' (ibid.: 109; emphasis added). Dialectical process refers to an exchange, for instance an argument is met by a counter-argument which may lead to a new position. Thus mediation (thesis) interacts with our everyday lives (antithesis) to produce our understandings of the world (synthesis). And as discussed in chapter 1, some events are not simply mediated but mediatized: the event in question becomes considered by those participating in it as a media phenomenon; its publicity is constitutive of the event; the event happens the way it does because media are built in to it. The original, to be mediated and re-presented to us, was designed with that mediation in mind.

To know of war, we must depend more on media than on our own experience in everyday life, unless we participate directly in a war. Silverstone argues that as far as news of war goes, 'the media are becoming a second-order paramount reality, fully equivalent to what would otherwise be understood as the world of the tangible face-to-face' (ibid.: 110). Media coverage of war does not replace sense experience altogether (cf. Merrin, 2005), but if we have no sense experience of war, then we depend on media for the 'truth' of war. Media 'pick up' events and re-present them to us, often neatly packaged, and, in receiving the package, we become witnesses of a sort.

But we cannot take at face value the coverage that the mass media bring us. Once we ask how these representations or 'mediations' are generated, we see how difficult it is to speak of media re-presenting an original and essential truth of war. According to Niklas Luhmann, mass media offer two realities which blur together. The 'reality of the mass media' refers first to the operations of mass media themselves, such as reporting and broadcasting. But there is a second reality: that which appears to them – the observations made by mass media and our observing (as audiences) of what media observe. This second reality – the 'out there' that mass media observe and bring to us – gets blurred with mass media's delivery of it. Take climate change, for example. Climate change is a media topic and a real process 'out there'. When media report on climate change – the *phenomenon* out there – they report it as part of that *topic*, 'climate change', which they have reported on previously. New events connected to climate change are organized into that prior media memory. This 'recursivity' operates across the various elements of news discourses, institutions, blogs and other forms. Michael Schudson writes: 'There is, we might say, a rhetorical structure to social institutions, a patterned way in which language comes to be used; once used, referred to; and when referred to, remembered and drawn upon as part of what 'everyone knows' (1990: 118).

Or think of the 2003 Iraq War. News media blurred together the actual war, on the ground, with their delivery of it. 'What happened' in the war could only meaningfully be what media had brought us. To make the war intelligible to audiences, journalists had to build upon what they assumed audiences would already know, or even what they might remember from the 1991 Gulf War ('remember when we brought you' Operation Desert Storm).[1] Truth is *recursive*, Luhmann argues: '[T]he prerequisite that [the topic] is already known about and that there is a need for further information' (2000: 12). Topics are presented on the basis that audiences already know about them, that these are 'accepted' topics, and mass media will bring a new report when journalists reckon that something novel or significant has happened within that topic.

The Bush Administration was well aware that the reality of the Iraq War could be established *for* US media, not discovered *by* US media. Prior to the war, when intervention required justification, news media were supplied with a steady, voluminous 'flood' of 'war stories, replete with mushroom-cloud imagery', which, for Bennett et al., 'acquired the illusion of credibility largely because they so dominated the media stage' (2007: 7). Rather than seek independent evidence of the situation in Iraq and existence of weapons of mass destruction, US media focused on how effectively US politicians created images for those same journalists. The choreographed 'media events' provided by President Bush, such as his arrival on an aircraft carrier in a 'Top Gun flight suit' to stand before a banner stating 'Mission Accomplished', became the story (ibid.: 6). Bennett et al. write:

> The fascinating aspect of such [reporting] is that the news itself is the completing link in the image creation process. Reporting stories according to a calculus of government power and dramatic production values often makes the news reality emanating from Washington an insular, circular, and self-fulfilling operation. News and politics loop quickly back on each other because of the press's preoccupation with how well powerful officials manage their desired images in the news. Thus, in early Iraq coverage, potentially important contextual details such as the dubious reasons and evidence given in support of the war became incidental to the fascination with whether the Bush administration had the image-shaping capacity and political clout to pull it off. (Ibid.: 7)

While journalists should report political leaders' propaganda efforts as such,[2] we might not think that such propaganda efforts are 'the news' in-themselves. The tendency of journalists to report the decisions, statements and gestures of powerful actors – 'calibration' to power, in Entman's terms (2004) – allows political and military leaders to create events which fulfil news values but tell audiences little about what is happening in Iraq. We might ask, why are journalists content to play such a role?

In Luhmann's analysis, mass media are a system within which meanings are self-referential: the meaning of any news rests on the existence of a prior set of meanings which this 'news' adds to. 'Truth' is a product of an *enclosed* system. Journalists are trained to regard certain types of events as 'news', and this system reproduces itself as senior journalists pass on their values to their juniors (Deuze, 2008: 18–21). Luhmann labels this process autopoiesis: 'Autopoiesis signifies the closure of a system's organization, i.e. the self reference of the complex of components and component-producing processes that mutually produce themselves and unify the system' (1989: xii). It is not that media manipulate audiences by denying them 'the truth', but that mass media have routine professional practices within which only certain things count as 'true' or 'factual'.

Both media and military can be viewed as systems with their own practices of determining whether something has happened. The generation of the truth of war depends, for instance, on the testimony of eye witnesses, the verification of the identity of bodies by families and medical staff and reports on damage to infrastructure or technology by official authorities. By piecing these different levels of evidence (or opinion), a version of truth is constructed. What we trust, as audiences, is not that media deliver a definitive truth, but that their piecing-together operations are trustworthy, so that what media deliver is *credible*, not absolutely and comprehensively true necessarily. '"Credibility" in the moment has replaced "truth" as the test and guiding principle of news', Merrin writes (2005: 71). Our awareness that some news that media bring us is 'false' can only be based on counter-claims that media bring us. Merrin points to an argument of Baudrillard (1994: 54): a report is only discredited by being 'refuted virtually', whether on air, in print or on the Internet. Since we cannot often experience the original event by being there, co-present, we cannot assess the truth of a news report (if we depend on news for our information of the event, we cannot know better), only whether it seems credible. What counts as true or false is produced entirely within the mass media system, and so it is a matter of trusting, or at least the taking for granted of, the operations of mass media.

We might ask whether news offers a realistic representation of an event, but what does *realism* mean? The convention of realism refers in this context to photographs or other media that are 'widely accepted as standing in for the real thing' (Taylor, 1991: 1). Realism suggests a closeness between a sign (e.g. a media image) and the thing signified.[3] This can never be wholly realistic in terms of conveying the 'lifeness' of the situation (Wood, 2008). But do realist photos take us *closer* to the truth?

> [W]hat they [readers] see through the 'window' of photography is nothing more than the pictorial analogue of the texts. In other words, the photographs are not 'windows' at all. There is no possibility of moving through them, only of sliding from them to the text (or vice versa): a planar movement of the eye, and a movement that remains actually and metaphorically bonded to the appearance at the *surface*. (Taylor, 1991: 4)

Photos in a newspaper or online news article offer a given world put on display for us. We cannot move into that photo/world and through it (though sites such as Google Earth and various news sites do make the user active, able to click on images and zoom in or search for other images of the thing in question).

Furthermore, our understanding of the photo is generated by moving between it and the words of the report. Hence realism is not actually given, but constructed by the form of the text and how the viewer engages with it (Jerslev, 2002). In a study of Greek newspapers, Konstantinidou found that realism in war photographs was constructed through the composition of the newspaper page. He describes a Greek newspaper running a double-page spread story on an Iraqi father who has lost his family during the 2003 Iraq War: '[T]he photographs are arranged in such a manner that the man standing up in open and uncontrollable grief seems practically "surrounded" by the corpses of his wife and children in their coffins' (2007: 156). The arrangement of text and images works to reinforce the veracity of what is being shown:

> The accompanying articles – appearing on the left-hand page under the heading 'Blind strikes cause baby victims', and on the right-hand page under the heading 'They kill anything that moves. Americans are terrified of kamikazes' attacks' – provide some contextualising information (precise time, location, circumstances, official declarations, NGO statements, general progress of war enterprises, etc.) and, through this, try to 'lock' the photographs into their 'indexical', 'eye-witnessing role'. (Ibid.)

The text is not objective, of course, but rather steers interpretation towards particular readings of the story (as we know, for every fact selected, another is not, and much news text is less 'straight reporting' and more editorialising).

To summarize so far: to demonstrate some of the difficulties in establishing the truth content of news media, which is necessary if one is to act as a witness to war and conflict, we have described news media as a system that generates facts ('news') about distant events and delivers them to audiences. We have suggested that facts are something pieced together and audiences must place their trust in journalists' ability to carry out this piecing-together role. We may also ask whether the result of this piecing-together seems to depict a realistic picture of events. But the truth of war is not just a matter of facts and a simple visual correspondence to the real, original thing. What about *experiences* of war? To know what happened, do we not need to know how the war was experienced by those in it?

By definition, images cannot offer '*accurate*' representation of *experiences* of war. For, as Guerin and Hallas ask (2007), how can trauma be adequately represented? What images would stand as evidence for, or verification of, a traumatic experience? Photos taken of survivors of Nazi concentration camps when they were liberated in 1945 depicted masses of emaciated people. Such photos may offer a representation of Nazi atrocity by presenting the effects, but the photos neither captured the actual atrocities themselves nor allowed the prisoners to speak of them. Such photos could not capture 'either the existential or metaphysical reality of the prisoners' debasement'; indeed, the images could be interpreted as dehumanizing the prisoners as a sheer mass of bodies (ibid.: 2–3). Photographs from Abu Ghraib prison of the abuse of Iraqis by US troops do not 'show' wider or systematic abuse, only the acts present in those photos (Bennett et al., 2007). Yet, the multiple levels of interpretation exemplified by the mediation and discourses on Abu Ghraib may make this a mute point.

What then, for example, is the value of verbal representations? The truth of an experience is the person's subjectivity – their point of view, as the person they are. This explains the value placed on autobiography, 'considered most authentic because it spoke or wrote from an individual and deeply personal experience that did not claim to represent the experience of all those who suffered' – just the individual (Guerin and Hallas, 2007: 7). The subjectivity of individuals suffering in a twentieth-century war zone or genocide could not be captured on film because victims of genocide or invasion hardly had access to cameras; they could not take photos as they were being killed. At best, handwritten notes or diaries could be smuggled out.

If verbal representation is not present, a *proliferation* of images of a phenomenon could lend credibility and realism to a story. The new media ecology permits realism through the aggregation of multiple perspectives due to the diffusion of mobile phones and other devices for recording and distributing media content. The founder of Wikipedia, Jimmy Wales, argues that such aggregation means 'You can get a really good *consensus picture* of what's going on that any one news organization could offer' (cited in Allan, 2006: 8; emphasis added). For an event such as the Asian Tsunami of 2004, when major news organizations were slow to access the disaster zone, the aggregation of images provided by 'citizen journalists' constituted a composite realism, but, as Luhmann would contend, ultimately there is a convergence of the audiovisual record through the recursive operation of the mass media. We shall return to citizen journalism below.

If suffering cannot be verbally *or* visually represented, it cannot proceed to be politically represented, notes Elaine Scarry (1985). It cannot become a public issue. Torture poses problems of representation: it is likely to be unseen, and the victim may no longer be able to talk. Those who campaign against torture try to find ways to make pain visible or audible. An organization such as Amnesty International may represent the pain caused by torture through images of weapons – that inflict the pain – or images of the effects: damaged bodies. The same goes for war more generally: anti-war groups may publicize images of weapons or images of those harmed in war (particularly children). Here lies a significant consequence of the images from Abu Ghraib: what was supposed to be hidden, and what is normally unexpressable such as the pain and humiliation of torture and the emotions of the perpetrators, became visible and public. Here, images were held as revelatory of a hidden truth.

Films or novels could offer a representation *about* an event – the experience of those involved, the context and background – whereas news reports aim to offer a representation *of* it, through realism and accuracy (cf. Zimmerman, 2007: 72). Hence movies or novels may portray the reality of a war situation better than a news report. In a *New York Review of Books* essay Sue Halpern (2008) addressed a clutch of books, films and TV series that had emerged by late 2008 about the ongoing wars in Afghanistan and Iraq . Each tries to represent 'how it is'. Listing them illustrates the possibilities they afford, collectively, for audiences to piece together an impression of these wars. There is the brutal materialism of a book of medical case studies (including graphic photographs of injury) in *War Surgery in Afghanistan and Iraq: A Series of Cases, 2003–2007*. There is the HBO miniseries *Generation Kill* and HBO film *Baghdad ER*, each showing the over-lapping relationships of war; the former follows a troop of US marines, who kill and injure Iraqis, while the latter depicts the consequent attending to Iraqi and American casualties in a city hospital. Another HBO film, *Section 60: Arlington National Cemetery*, focuses on the mourning of US families. Finally, Halpern reviews a traditional war correspondent's account of the two wars, Dexter Filkins's *The Forever War*. Each of these works may spotlight different actual or fictional individuals, but all offer a view of the central categories: protagonist, victim, physical consequences and emotional aftermath – and how they have actually connected. This ensemble provides a richer impression of the character of these terrible situations.

But is relying on fictional accounts for the reality of war problematic? We may desire to find a reality that conforms to what we expect of reality, or how we expect reality to be. We might then be less inclined to face up to actuality; it will be less interesting. Umberto Eco, on a trip to Disneyland, wrote:

> Disneyland not only produces illusion, but – in confessing it – stimulates the desire for it: A real crocodile can be found in the zoo, and as a rule it is dozing or hiding, but Disneyland tells us that faked nature corresponds much more to our daydream demands. When, in the space of twenty-four hours, you go (as I did deliberately) from the fake New Orleans of Disneyland to the real one, and from the wild river of Adventureland to a trip on the Mississippi, where the captains of the paddle-wheel steamer says it is possible to see alligators on the bank of the river, and then you don't see any, you risk feeling homesick for Disneyland, where the wild animals don't have to be coaxed. Disneyland tells us that technology can give us more reality than nature can. (Eco, 1987: 44)

Some modalities offer more excitement: by surrendering any aspiration for veri-fiable correspondence to the actual event, a recalled experience can be embel-lished and altered to fit expectations of what will excite an audience. Personal accounts are subjective, lacking *objectivity*: the person providing the account is not viewing the event from an external position, but is part of the event being accounted for. In theory, an objective report would be able to take into account more information and perspectives, as well as assume an unbiased, impartial point of view.

Personal accounts may offer questionable veracity and an absence of objec-tivity, but they do provide *authenticity*; what only that person could offer of the situation. The *Oxford English Dictionary* defines 'authentic' in several ways:

- original, first-hand, prototypical;
- real, actual, 'genuine';
- really proceeding from its reputed source or author; of undisputed origin, genuine;
- acting of itself, self-originated, automatic.

Authenticity could become a matter of performance, then: of acting in a manner that projects genuineness, through modes of speech and gesture, not what is said (a bit like authority and 'to be authoritative'– see Sennett, 1974). And any media culture may have its own norms and conventions of what performing authenticity looks like. Hence, unlike realism or accuracy, authenticity appears more malleable and perhaps, as a consequence, a less reliable record of events.

Balance is another criterion of the truth of war. Fox News and Al Jazeera both justify their perspective in terms of restoring a balance that was allegedly missing from media menus – balance in terms of political ideology. Fox News's tagline is 'fair and balanced', offering a conservative counterpart to an alleged liberal media. Balance is also a matter of who gets to speak. Al Jazeera claims to offer a 'voice to the voiceless' (Burman, cited in Al Jazeera, 2008), allowing Arab voices to speak into the global media air (to paraphrase John Durham Peters, 1999) which had been dominated by Western news organizations; this was the channel's 'emancipatory' potential for many Muslim and Arabic audiences in Europe and the Middle East, for instance (Hafez, 2008).

Overall, then, we have varying expectations of what kind of truth media bring to us – accuracy, authenticity, realism, objectivity, balance and, no doubt, others. What none of these modes of representation offers is *certainty*, yet perhaps certainty is what audiences seek above all. Media offer some order and coherence to life (Silverstone, 2007: 111–12). When a security crisis breaks, news will deliver it, but also contain it within a narrative and framework: it is *this* type of event, a type you are familiar with (Luhman's recursivity). A certain type of comfort may be found in following a story in which the plot is not too unsettling. For instance, a breaking news event on a 24-hour television news channel acquires a rhythm. News *contains* anxiety (Hoskins and O'Loughlin, 2007; Richards, 2007). We can be certain we are getting 'news', it's true, but whether we can be certain about anything the news bring us, as true, is another thing.

This survey of forms of truthfulness indicates the different modalities available to people involved in war or conflict to represent what is happening to others. We shall see next how different witnesses use these various modalities. Frontline journalists, documentary-makers, soldiers, NGO workers and even audiences themselves can all relate to war as witnesses, possessing *some* truth of war that they can relay to others.

3. Witnessing

'For a witness to perform an act of bearing witness, she must address an other, a listener who consequently functions as a witness to the original witness', write Guerin and Hallas (2007: 10). For you to be a witness, reader, you must offer your testimony of what you experienced to another audience – a jury, a television audience or just the people you are with. To be a witness is to tell somebody. It is in the telling that the 'truth' emerges. It is for the audience to decide whether your truth is valid. A witness is a person who re-presents to a listener an experience of being *there* and seeing *that*. Both witness and listener must share a faith in their relationship, that each is who they claim to be, and they must have faith that experiences can be re-presented at all. This is different from believing that CCTV footage or a photograph is true, in the sense of an accurate correspondence to an original entity. The image produced by a witness's words – a shared or intersubjective mental 'seeing' between witness and listener – does not depend on an image as a material, technologically produced artefact (unless one counts the brain as a material technology). CCTV footage counts as proof, provided you trust it. But it is not a witness.

In psychoanalysis, for instance, the trauma victim's mind blocks out the horror the moment it occurs. What happened, the horror, is repressed, and only emerges later (Felman and Laub, 1992). In effect, the truth of the situation for the victims occurs for the first time only when telling or narrating to the listener. In addition, the listener is now given the role of sharing the burden of this knowledge, of enabling it to become part of collective memory or 'our' history.

In his seminal essay on 'Witnessing', John Durham Peters (2001) sets out a detailed framework on the topic. In terms of its use as a verb, Peters argues:

> to witness . . . has two faces: the passive one of *seeing* and the active one of *saying*. In passive witnessing an accidental audience observes the events of the world; in active witnessing one is a privileged possessor and producer of knowledge in an extraordinary, often forensic setting in which speech and truth are policed in multiple ways. What one has seen authorizes what one says: an active witness first must have been a passive one. Herein lies the fragility of witnessing: the difficult juncture between experience and discourse. (2001: 709–10)

In war, this fragility is evident (and, as we argue, is diffused) on a number of levels in the mediation of warfare where experience and discourse conflict and conflate to legitimize or undermine military, diplomatic or humanitarian actions and inactions. Furthermore, the multiple roles of witnesses clearly can conflict; for example, military forces do not necessarily want journalists or NGO workers to witness the effects of military action, or for them only to witness particular desired effects and remain unaware of civilian casualties. Let us explore these different witness roles.

Journalists as witnesses[4]

Journalists reporting from zones of war and disaster witness history being made and have the opportunity to testify and explain events to their audiences, often near-instantaneously, 'live and as it happens'. Delivering such testimony allows the journalist to claim a mission to alleviate audiences' ignorance of the situation being reported, a calling to deliver 'the truth' about world-historic events, to be 'humanity's eyes and ears' at the 'front row of history'. Through a long set of interviews with such reporters, Tumber and Webster note 'there was a *passion* for their vocation' (2006: 72).

This passion leads to a dilemma for reporters of war and conflict. Is their role simply to report events objectively, as professional journalists, or to make audiences care about the suffering they report on? 'Are we reporters or are we social workers – or are we human beings?' asks Janine di Giovanni, a reporter who has covered conflict in the Ivory Coast, Rwanda, Sierra Leone, the Balkans and Chechnya (cited in Schmeizer, 2007). The *New York Times* reporter Nicholas Kristof, for instance, bought two girls out of captivity and returned them to their families when reporting on Cambodian sex slavery (Kristof, 2005). The BBC's

John Simpson claimed to have 'liberated Kabul' (see box 4.1) (Simpson, 2001). This is more than bearing witness: it is intervening in the events being reported on.

Box 4.1 John Simpson liberates Kabul

Extract from 'The journey into Kabul', by John Simpson, BBC world affairs editor
Tuesday, 13 November 2001, 17:39 GMT
Kabul lay temptingly close below us now.
The small BBC team decided to head on into the city, on our own, and on foot – so no one would think we were soldiers.
We ploughed on – radio side-by-side with television.
As we walked into Kabul city we found no problems around us, only people that were friendly and, I am afraid, chanting 'kill the Taleban' – although as we understand it there are not going to be that many Taleban around.
It felt extraordinarily exhilarating – to be liberating a city which had suffered so much under a cruel and stifling regime.

The act of witnessing war at first hand appears to generate a heroic self-identity on the part of many war correspondents. An 'ethic of resistance to manipulation' (Tumber and Webster, 2006: 18) is part of the heroic self-image that frontline reporters have. World-weary, cynical, sceptical reporters do not see themselves as a potential dupe of less-experienced PR staff. War correspondents may feel part of a collective heroic force, with newspaper journalists in particular prone to living in a 'press pack' in a particular hotel, sharing information, living the war in parallel to the militaries they are reporting on and, like many soldiers, rarely meeting up when they return to the home country and family life (Morrison and Tumber, 1988). Heroism may also be a consequence of such a dangerous job, which requires a 'calling'.

However, as with the 'journalism of attachment' (Bell, 1998) they feel profoundly involved in and affected by what they witness, to the extent that they may compromise their goal of objectivity in order to depict the experience of suffering they witness (Tumber and Webster, 2006: 72–4). Additionally, as we saw in chapter 3, to grab and move the audience, the newsmakers may omit some detail and prioritize that which pulls our heartstrings. The journalism of attachment offers a journalism that 'cares as well as knows' and that does not 'stand neutrally between good and evil, right and wrong, the victim and the oppressor' (Bell, 1998: 51).

What makes journalists special as witnesses is their training, experience and self-discipline, argues Kieran (1997). Their claims for objectivity do not imply that ideally they would achieve it, but that by following professional standards they will at least avoid inaccuracy (Tuchman, 1972). Their professionalism does not guarantee objectivity, but they can claim to be moving towards it.

Nevertheless, there are numerous obstacles. The ability of frontline journalists to witness war is dependent upon the access provided by military authorities. Following US defeat in Vietnam and the perception that the US media lost the war for their military by showing images that turned the public against it – the myth of the 'Vietnam War Syndrome' later exposed by Daniel Hallin (1986) – Western militaries became more stringent in their control of journalists. The British government operated a 'pool system' during the 1982 Falklands/Malvinas War, in which only certain reporters were allowed access to the Islands and their reports had to be 'cleared' by a military censor (Knightley, 2003; Cottle, 2006). A pool system also operated in the US-led 1991 Gulf War and 2001 Afghanistan War. In the 2003 Iraq War, a new system was introduced by the US military – called 'embedding' – in which journalists from selected news organizations were assigned to live and travel with military units. The military units would guarantee their safety, enabling them to witness some of what was happening in Iraq at first hand. We explore the tensions this creates below, for, as interviews with frontline reporters indicate, journalists are particularly attuned to attempts to manipulate them (Tumber and Webster, 2006).

The centrality of embedding to the US military media strategy in the 2003 Iraq War made sense. Frontline journalists have become 'major players' insofar as military press operations have attempted to conduct perception management campaigns *through* reporters (ibid.: 5). These reporters are the face of war, trying to explain what is happening to audiences. When any report can be uploaded to YouTube and disseminated globally, reporters can testify to the progress (or lack of it) towards security goals and the protection of human rights. As such, frontline journalists have a central role in the legitimation of war.

Frontline journalists can become a familiar, reassuring presence to audiences, acting as a 'buffer' between the potentially horrifying event and the audiences at home, even speaking as if for the audience, referring to 'what *we* have heard' or 'as far as *we* can see', as if the audience is part of a shared perspective (Hoskins and O'Loughlin, 2007: 91). In the 2003 Iraq War the BBC journalist Rageh Omaar became the 'face' of the war. The channel's coverage of the Asian Tsunami of 2004 was notable for the lack of such a star reporter presence. Consequently, the BBC received complaints via one of its television viewer feedback shows: referring to another BBC foreign correspondent, one viewer demanded, 'Where is *John Simpson*'? (Hoskins and O'Loughlin, 2007: 48).

Even if journalists are able to access war zones and compile reports, their capacity to report what they have witnessed is conditional upon the degree of censorship and regulation of the media organization they report for. British journalists, for instance, are subject to the Official Secret Act, libel laws and 'Defence Advisory Notices', which are sent by military authorities to news editors instructing them to keep certain stories secret. A further question concerns the failure of journalists to become embedded with 'the enemy' and thereby provide an understanding to audiences of the people against whom 'we' are at war (Lynch, 2003). In the US/UK-led interventions in Afghanistan and Iraq in the early twenty-first century, could journalists have embedded with local civilian populations? What legal, professional, commercial and political pressures have prevented journalists from fulfilling these functions?

Tumber and Webster outline several ways in which frontline reporting has changed in the new media ecology:

1 *Increased danger.* The job of frontline reporter has become more dangerous, though the majority of journalists killed in Iraq are local – figures are available on the websites of Reporters Without Borders (www.rsf.org), Committee for the Protection of Journalists (cpj.org) and the International News Safety Institute (www.newssafety.com). Violence towards journalists has increased from both governments and militia; all have come to identify journalists as tools of conflict, not objective, impartial professionals 'above' politics. The Al Jazeera headquarters in Kabul and Baghdad have been attacked by US forces, and the TV station headquarters of Al Manar was attacked by Israeli forces during the Israel–Hezbollah war of 2006, as they deemed Al Manar to be Hezbollah's propaganda outlet. The kidnapping of Western journalists has become routine. Western journalists have become more likely to undertake training in security and safety, take out more expensive insurance and use bodyguards. The use of bodyguards in particular reduces their mobility and restricts their ability to mingle with local people.

2 *Greater use of fixers.* If Western journalists have become targets in war, it makes sense for Western news agencies to employ local journalists or local people who can translate or facilitate access to situations that overseas journalists would not have ('fixers'). Fixers will have greater access and knowledge of the area, including how safe it is to enter and how local media are covering matters, and will arrange interviews and protection. However, this simply shifts the risk onto local journalists. Palmer and Fontan note that in the first year after the March 2003 invasion of Iraq, roughly half of media workers killed in Iraq were Iraqi nationals, but that in each year since, Iraqi nationals have been the vast majority of those killed (2007: 6). In addition, it is not clear that fixers or local journalists can generate the same information as Western journalists would for Western audiences. Lindsay Hilsum of Channel 4 News complains that Iraqi journalists do 'their journalism . . . [and] ask different questions' from those she would ask.[5]

3 *Parachute journalists.* In the second phase of mediatization, reporters may spend less time in the zone of conflict or disaster than once was the case. Instead of living there for weeks, months or even years and acquiring expertise and fluency in local languages, reporters today can be flown to a 'hot spot' from where, using mobile technologies, they can film, edit and disseminate their report within hours before flying back ('parachute journalists' – see Hess, 1994; Hamilton and Jenner, 2004; Palmer and Fontan, 2007; Volkmer, 2008). With 'liveness' a premium news value, technology increasingly enables this, even if the reporter does not witness anything live and simply stands in the war-afflicted hot spot and reads a report written back in his or her home country. We might ask whether the increased speed and mobility of journalists implies a trade-off at the expense of reflection and analysis, though of course analysis can be added in the newsroom or studio.

4 *Younger journalists.* Greater mobility and danger have made frontline reporting a job for younger, fitter journalists. Additionally, financial restraints for

major news organizations that lead to reduced budgets for foreign correspondents creates a situation in which only young, aspiring journalists in their
twenties will have the freedom to travel to foreign countries and learn to be
frontline reporters; there are fewer permanent posts for those, perhaps with
families, who demand a steady income.

5 *More women.* As in the military, since the late twentieth century far more
   women have become war correspondents, and sexism towards female war
   correspondents has decreased, if not disappeared altogether, according to
   recent interviews with frontline correspondents (Tumber 2006: 443–5).

6 *Technological tethering.* Just as media connectivity makes all users increasingly
   'tethered' to each other and their technologies in various ways (Turkle, 2008),
   so the connectivity between a media organization's home newsroom or studio
   and 'the field' in which the journalist reports from renders the journalist 'on
   call' and accountable. The editor at home can double-check the journalist's
   report with other reports online from the area and even think they know
   better what is happening than the journalist in the field. That editor may be
   correct, since journalists can only report what they witness, and one person's
   perspective is limited. This enables the editor at home to guide the journalist to where 'better' action is, but it may also result in conflicted relations
   between the editor and journalist, both of whom think they are correct about
   what is happening. Additionally, some journalists are happy 'early adopters'
   of new technologies and more likely to adapt their working practices to fit
   new requirements that technology makes possible (Deuze, 2008).

7 *Embedding.* Foreign correspondents have always depended on the authorities
   in areas they report from for access and security. In 1944 Paul Winterton,
   Soviet correspondent for the *News Chronicle* in the UK, complained about
   the treatment of foreign journalists: 'We were simply marched off by Soviet
   officials like a crocodile of schoolgirls, and were required to follow a fixed
   and usually rigid schedule which we had no hand in drawing up' (cited in
   Cockett, 1988: 519). This resulted in a paradoxical situation in which the
   British reporters' editors in London began to believe the reports sent, which
   were in effect Soviet propaganda, to the extent that when the reporters
   returned to London and told them about actual conditions in Moscow, their
   editors did not believe them. Is this analogous to contemporary warfare?
   Evidence suggests that, counterintuitively perhaps, embedded journalists
   today are more likely to deliver balanced and proportionate reporting about
   war than journalists in the safety of the news studio. Without embedded
   reporters, media may have to rely on military briefings for information
   (Lewis and Brookes, 2004). While a single journalist has only a very partial
   view of the broad picture in any situation (a 'soda straw' view), their perspective is at least their own. On the other hand, Lewis and Brookes ask, if news
   broadcasters prioritized the live, first-hand reports of action by embedded
   journalists, did this reduce consideration of the causes and consequences of
   such actions?

   Embedding also raises ethical questions: what if an embedded reporter is
   shot in a live broadcast? How much delay can be inserted by news organizations for a report still to count as 'live'? If significant delays are inserted (e.g.

more than 60 seconds), does this allow military authorities to monitor and possibly censor footage?

Military forces do use media not only to convey news of battlefield progress or victory, but to air grievances and complaints. While writing an article for the *New York Review of Books* as an embedded reporter with US forces in Iraq, Michael Massing realized that a US Captain, Brett Walker, was taking him to scenes that did not indicate US progress:

> [H]e had decided it was important for me to see it so as to understand that it was not 'patty cake.' He had also wanted me to speak with captains and sergeants who were leaving the Army so that I could grasp the heavy toll the war was taking on the troops. In fact, he told me, he himself was planning to get out as soon as he could. (Massing, 2008)

Hence the embedded reporter was shown 'the war through the eyes of the US military' but was being used as a conduit so that a disgruntled Army could convey its grievances to a home audience.

Practices of embedding may be nothing new, but we must understand it as part of a broader mediatization of life, not just war. Since the rise to prominence of reality TV in the 1990s, journalists are 'embedded' with families, hospitals, driving instructor schools and all manner of everyday institutions. This is part of the mediatization of all aspects of life; why should war be any different?

It remains an open question whether these new trends and conditions for frontline journalism better enable reporters to communicate a 'truth' of war, and we can consider how each modality of truth (objectivity, authenticity and so on) is altered by this changing context. Does the reporting coming from Iraq, Afghanistan or any other war or disaster zone enable journalists to 'connect' to audiences, or enable audiences to 'connect' to the events taking place?

Documentary journalists as witnesses

Leslie Woodhead has been making documentaries for nearly 50 years, starting at Granada TV in the UK in 1961, producing and directing the prime time series *World in Action*, later producing documentaries for HBO in the US. In an interview in 2006 he described his career as spanning a shift from an era in which documentary-makers had autonomy to define their own agenda, to a more ratings-driven, constrained situation. This matters for conceptualizing the documentary-maker-as-witness, since it indicates that the role of the audience – to which the witness testifies – has become more prominent. What remained constant, Woodhead said, was: 'I've always thought that the audience is far smarter and more able to deal with difficult material than the broadcasting gurus ever allow for.'[6] Yet he admits: 'There's very little sense of what the audience is thinking and feeling out there apart from very crude measures of ratings.'[7]

As with many frontline journalists, and, as we shall see later, for NGO workers too, it is possible for documentary-makers to feel emotionally attached to the phenomenon they witness. Here, Woodhead talks about his relationship to the former Soviet area and how it shaped his experience of making a documentary about the Srebrenica massacre of 1995, *A Cry from the Grave* (1999):

> I did become, and still am, hypnotised by the Communist and now the post-Communist experience and what that means and formed a lot of contacts, a lot of relationships, spent a lot of time in Russia and in Poland and in Slovakia and all of that. So, I'd not been to the Balkans ever before the Srebrenica film but it was that accumulated interest in that part of the world that got me seriously interested. And the thing [about] meeting the people who'd been at the centre of those events, I mean, I can't recall anything really reaching me personally as all that did, really really [smacked] me, and I couldn't get rid of it. It was like I was at the bottom of a swimming pool with all the stuff going around, and [it] became a real personal engagement . . . Beslan had that quality, the Srebrenica film certainly had that quality.[8]

Yet incredibly such an experience was simultaneously banal. He continued:

> And I find it simultaneously hypnotic, addictive, and so boring in Eastern Europe, and I felt the same in China: how can somewhere this interesting be this boring? The lack of sensory input, the sheer drabness of everything, the wretchedness of inter-personal relationships, the awfulness of the architecture, the ghastliness of what people do to one another. You think, why would anybody want to spend more than five minutes in the thick of all of [this.] Yet for some reason it grabs my [attention].

Behind this paradoxical relationship of excitement and boredom lies a similar motive to other witnesses of war – 'making a difference'. Woodhead explains why he returned to make a second film about Srebrenica, *Srebrenica: Never Again* (2005):

> The issues about telling the world how it is, bringing this to as large an attention as you can possibly do. In some cases when you get really lucky and . . . hoping you can make a tiny bit of difference . . . Why I made the [second Srebrenica] film was because I'd never really stopped thinking about the people I'd met in the first film and I genuinely wondered what the hell had happened and how there might be a way to see through them whether any improvement, healing, change had taken place in that story.[9]

This documentary-maker shares certain priorities and objectives with frontline journalists in general, such as the duty to report. Yet Woodhead expresses little sense of his audience. He added: '[I]f we get three letters for something like Srebrenica it's as much as you ever get [from audiences].'[10] However, with much longer to reflect on things, and no mandate and pressure from an editorial desk, the pressure of presumed audience expectations and numbers are removed.

Soldiers as witnesses

Since the 2003 Iraq war, the issue of soldiers speaking publicly about military life and policy has become prominent. New technologies allow military personnel to share their experiences of combat, their frustrations or boredom, and their hopes. Producing and posting representations of their experience and actions may help soldiers reaffirm their identities, and overcome uncertainty about what they are doing (Bhattacharyya, 2008: 67–8). However, the emergence of the blog, mobile phone and email mean the private communication of military personnel can easily become public, since content can be instantly disseminated and archived. For instance, we explored the scandal of the website nowthatsfuckedup.com (NTFU) in chapter 2. It is feared that national security could be compromised as well as the operational security of military personnel involved. As Tatum Lytle documents (2007), since 11 September 2001 US army personnel have been punished for revealing information deemed classified about the location or movement of troops, casualty rates, or general strategy. He cites a memo from Chief-of-Staff General Peter Schoomaker, written in September 2005, stating: 'The enemy aggressively "reads" our open source and continues to exploit such information for use against our forces' (Lytle, 2007: 607). This has led to soldiers wondering whether they reveal more sensitive information than journalists in the field do; as such, these 'milbloggers' begin to think like journalists. They must consider the impact on their presumed audience, and what happens if their writing is picked up by mainstream media and they acquire a degree of fame.

The existence of many soldiers' blogs alters the relationship between media and military because a journalist can potentially find a story directly from a soldier rather than indirectly through an authorized military press officer. By removing this layer of mediation, journalists may be able to report stories more quickly, and, in theory, this would force that military organization to respond to the story itself. In a UK context, soldiers have used new media technologies to make public their grievances about pay or a lack of equipment in Iraq or Afghanistan. Such stories are difficult for journalists to verify, but the voicing of discontent is, in itself, a story.

The capacity of now-mediatized soldiers to instantly and publicly testify to what they are witnessing and relay information to journalists became subject to censorship. In October 2006 the Ministry of Defence banned access to ITV News because it had broadcast an interview with a serving soldier who testified that British troops were being treated in NHS hospitals rather than military medical facilities. (Hewlett, 2006: 4). The head of news at the Ministry of Defence, James Clark, accused ITV News of invading the soldier's privacy by recording him returning to Birmingham Airport without his permission, but the footage was too blurry to identify him. In August 2007 the Ministry of Defence introduced new regulations concerning soldiers' use of information, blogs and other media technologies. In a US context this dilemma is different because of First Amendment freedoms, though the free speech of military personnel is more tightly regulated than that of the general US public (Lytle, 2007). Indeed, military authorities are encouraged to 'foster instinctive obedience, unity, commitment and esprit de corps' such that personnel do not think to dissent (Goldman v. Weinberger, 1986; cited in Lytle, 2007: 599).

It is not just blogging or speaking to reporters. Soldiers can also use their mobile phones to record life in the war they are in, recordings that can make their way onto the Internet. The post-2003 conflict in Iraq is 'the first YouTube war', writes Cox (2006). Soldiers' videos are characterized by music soundtracks and gallows humour, but little comprehension of the war or their purpose. Cox argues that this may be a product of the US media culture in which the soldiers are literate: Nintendo, Arnold Schwarzenegger movies and MTV. She cites an anonymous *Wall Street Journal* commentator who describes the films as 'kind of like the ESPN highlight reels – music is pumping and everyone was running round'. Indeed, on 21 July 2006, MTV broadcast a special section of these films, 'Iraq Uploaded'.

The Abu Ghraib images perhaps exemplify the limit case of this relationship between media literacy from a particular culture and soldiers' attempts to document their experiences. Judith Butler (2008) argues that the torture of Iraqis by US soldiers can be understood as part of a US mission to bring modern (Christian) civilization to an irrational, childish and unmodern Islamic world (see also chapter 9). She cites the document 'The Arab Mind' distributed within the US Department of Defense in the 1970s, which argued that Muslims were characterized by certain social and psychological features, notably sexual vulnerabilities which could be targeted in torture situations. Paradoxically, then, torture was a way for US soldiers to prove both their own comfort with certain sexual practices (they smiled in some photographs) and that the victims of the torture – because they found these practices distressing – were in need of civilizing. 'The army considers itself more sexually "advanced" because they read pornography or impose it upon their prisoners', Butler writes (ibid.: 16). Butler's argument, supported by Mirzoeff (2006), is that the soldiers' behaviour was a manifestation of broader cultural and institutional processes. Whether or not one accepts this, it is indisputable that media technologies enabled those soldiers to document their wartime activities and thereby incriminate themselves.

NGOs as witnesses

Non-governmental organizations, such as humanitarian aid agencies, are another set of actors who witness war and conflict. Often they seek to use their testimony of suffering to raise funds or awareness of the conflict. Witnessing is central to this role. Theo Murphy of Amnesty International argues that his authority comes from relaying the testimony of sufferers and from AI workers sharing their experiences:

> A key requisite for the authority by which Amnesty claims to speak is the fact that the researcher (usually the media spokesperson) has moral authority. I think this comes from more than the organization's reputation. For me it's integral to the research methodology based upon the testimony. The act of hearing people's stories and recording in detail what has happened to them establishes a special link with the researcher. Where others report on what's happening, the people's story is only one part of the overall story (a journalist piece on Darfur could include more on local politics, UN, etc). But for Amnesty, the authenticity comes from the process of establishing empathy through direct contact with, in this case, the refugees. It may be a bit farfetched but I even think there is something of the researcher taking on the suffering he/she witnesses and when they speak about what is happening in Darfur they are able to transmit that; or perhaps better yet feel legitimate in

speaking so emotively about what is happening as it has in a minor way happened to them or at least they have in some way shared in the experience.[11]

Murphy makes several assumptions here about communication and compassion fatigue. For an Amnesty worker to 'take on the suffering' and then 'transmit it', and to speak of the suffering with emotion, suggests notions about the capacity of a witness to have an effect on an audience: to generate compassion through a particular mode of delivery (emotional). Media become weaponized, not as a weapon of terror but as a weapon of care. Murphy also justifies the NGO worker's place in the war zone – 'speaking . . . about what is happening as it has in a minor way happened to them'. We might argue that NGO workers have chosen to put themselves in that area, in harm's way, just as frontline journalists volunteer to put their lives at risk. Murphy's statement raises many ethical questions about the role of NGO workers.

Another NGO attempting to document suffering in order to raise awareness is Iraq Body Count. The organization has compiled an online database of civilian casualties in the 2003 Iraq War and its aftermath, based on a daily review of news reports emerging from the country which are used to assess who has died in each section of each village, town or city (for details, see www.iraqbodycount.org). By making public the name, age, gender and whereabouts of each civilian death, as well as the perpetrator and method of the death (US military, local militia, Iraqi military and so on), the organization makes visible more of the war and its effects. Such a project illuminates the chain of witnessing necessary to make a person's death public: a hospital worker who treats a person injured in a roadside bomb reports to an Iraqi journalist that the person has died; the Iraqi journalist passes this on to a Western news agency such as Reuters or Associated Press; a mainstream news organization such as CNN or BBC then receives the agency bulletin, and chooses whether this death has sufficient 'news value' to warrant being included in the running order or news agenda of that hour or day. To an NGO worker with, say, Amnesty International or Iraq Body Count, there may be some frustration at the many hurdles needed to be overcome for information about a death to become 'news'. Yet the construction of an online database demonstrates the possibilities in the new media ecology for an ongoing archive whereby the information is stored and retrievable. Even if news organizations do not pick up the information on that single death that day, the opportunity is there to return to it later if it seems to be part of a more systematic campaign of killing. Members of the public too can access the information.

Hence, NGOs have new opportunities to use the 'networked eyes' (Mitchell, 2006: 174). Indeed, Sam Gregory, Program Director for a human rights organization called Witness, hopes to see a 'participatory panopticon' such that the diffusion of media production technologies in citizens' hands allows them to 'document abuses by authorities' (Jenkins, 2008).

Audiences as witnesses

For Abercrombie and Longhurst (1998) there are three types of audience: simple, mass and diffused. A simple audience refers to a situation in which there are two fixed roles: performer and audience, and the audience is physically co-present at the performance (for example, a theatre or a ceremony), though kept separate – i.e. not on the stage. Since this co-presence is rare for audiences of war and conflict, we will focus in this section on mass and diffused audiences and how each can act as witnesses to war. We also consider here the role of audiences-become-journalists themselves – the phenomenon of 'citizen journalism' to emerge in the 2000s.

A mass audience is an imagined community of individual spectators who are aware of themselves as a collective. Audiences differ from spectators insofar as spectators are not aware of themselves as members of a single audience (Dayan, 2005: 45–7); spectators simply find themselves witnessing something. A broadcast audience is addressed as a set of strangers, and media content is designed to be intelligible to that audience. What is remarkable, Paddy Scannell has noted, is that media speak as if to a larger number of people – to millions, potentially – and yet often individuals find the broadcast speaks to them directly and individually. Scannell labels broadcast media 'a *for-anyone-as-someone* structure' (2000: 5). Broadcasts are designed as intelligible and useful *for-anyone*, as with any mass-produced goods (a toaster, say). Yet notions of mass media – messages sent to 'the masses' – are not supported by empirical evidence: individual members of audiences do not consider themselves merely part of a mass. Much media (novels, songs) speak to individuals as if it is to their selves, Scannell argues, and broadcast media achieve this too through particular modes of address: conversational, spoken by someone likeable, as if to an audience of one. Hence media is *for-someone* too. Scannell writes, 'The news is . . . appropriated by me as an aspect of my experience and yet at the same time this experience is shared by countless others' (ibid.: 11). We witness as individuals, yet our experience of witnessing is shared. Hence we have most-talked-about TV, water cooler moments and the generation of shared memory (see chapter 6). We testify to others about what we have witnessed. News producers are aware of this and try to make it happen. Paul Jenkins, a producer and director at the BBC, speaks of the need to create moments of intense witnessing and testimony:

> [Y]ou are looking for Hollywood or as a director friend of mine calls it: the 'fuck me Doris factor.' You imagine two housewives in Liverpool sitting down on a sofa the morning after a show, after a TV documentary, and one goes fuck me Doris I saw an amazing programme. That's the 'fuck me Doris factor'. You're looking for the jawdropping revelation.[12]

By addressing people in this way, creating this shared yet individual experience, media may enable a *public* to form out of audiences' experience. Around a particular issue, identity, programme or event a public will assemble. Daniel Dayan writes, 'publics are always the publics-of-something' (2005: 54), and global media events trigger the formation of publics. Many academics retain a distinction between audience and public. Political scientists assume publics to be sets of active, critically engaged and rational individuals who exercise power through voting or other forms of civic engagement, while audiences are the direct opposite: passive, private, emotional, their attention captured by trivial concerns (ibid.). Media audiences undermine democracy – if only we could return to face-to-face communication, the ideal of a town hall meeting, to get things done! In fact, the distinction is less clear and less useful.

That a public is formed matters because it is the moment at which audiences as witnesses can *act* in the light of what they have seen. As we wrote in chapter 3, audiences confronting mediated scenes of suffering may donate money to humanitarian agencies which may relieve the distress of those affected, or put pressure on political leaders who may have leverage over the actors causing the suffering.

Yet how do we know a public has been formed? Publics are mediated. We only know 'what the public thinks' via media. Public opinion is constructed through opinion polls, vox pop interviews, interactive participation ('email us your opinion') and focus groups. It is then relayed into the public arena as (usually numerical) facts; individual members of that society then know, apparently, what they and their fellow citizens think. Media make us aware of public support or opposition to war or particular aspects of war. Media are 'midwives' to publics if they allow people to express their opinion, become aware there are others who share their concern, and thus allow the collective to project their opinion out into the public realm. Equally, media can be 'abortionists' by preventing such movements from speaking out (ibid.: 63–4)

Of course, audiences do not always become publics. There are several stances that audience members can take in relation to news media – different modes of viewing. Table 4.1 suggests a number of ways (not exhaustive) in which audiences relate to news, and that media are not simply 'texts' that audiences 'read' and infer meaning from, but that media also constitute resources that audiences use to piece together their own interpretation of the world. Different audience members will have different competencies or media literacy based on their life experiences, the role of media in their family routines, and so on (Calavita, 2005). For example, Greg Philo and Mike Berry (2004) undertook a comprehensive study of the relationship between television news coverage of the Israeli-Palestinian conflict and the understandings, beliefs and attitudes of Western audiences. They found that for a large proportion of audiences they surveyed (their corpus included mostly students in Germany, the UK and the US), there was a very strong link between the extent of viewer interest and the degree of understanding of that being watched.

For mass audiences, news and media generally fit into daily routines, consumed at certain times (radio while having breakfast, iPod/newspaper on the bus to work, TV after dinner). But the relationship between *diffused* audiences and media is different. For Abercrombie and Longhurst (1998) diffused audiences have four characteristics. First, audience members are potentially always switched on; in a media ecology saturated by screens and sounds, a person can live in near-continual media immersion. Second, the media cycles that structured the news consumption of mass audiences come to acquire a comforting role: we find assurance through the presence of certain media at certain times of day or night. Third, members of a diffused audience are always performing or ready to perform if called upon – the West is now made up of 'performative societies'. No event, personal or public, goes unrecorded. Hence those taking part in events come to consider potential audiences, creating an imperative to

Table 4.1 Modes of Audience in Relation to News[13]

Mode	Purpose of news consumption	Relation to medium	Relation to sufferer
Dogmatic	Confirmation of worldview.	Unreflexive trust in favoured media, unreflexive mistrust of other media.	Depends on loyalty: the suffering is either justice done or a perfidious and predictable injustice.
Sceptical zapper	Compiling information and opinions by comparing a range of sources in order to construct their own news narratives.	More flexible, liable to be critical of all sources to a degree.	The suffering must 'cut through' the zapper's scepticism, perhaps through an arresting image.
Playful	News as entertainment, a source of pleasure (including enjoyable pain in the case of news as farce, too sad to be true).	Irresponsible – we do not feel that the situation in the news or those within that situation have any connection to us. Or, an event is deemed too farcical to treat seriously.	Possibly sympathetic but ultimately detached and not set on action.
Competent cosmopolitan	To make comparisons and contrasts of culturally diverse news sources as a matter of course in their everyday (transnational) lives.	The medium is a resource to gain material for building connections across cultures. Likely to access media in several languages.	Always open to the sufferer's plight and to finding ways to articulate it and make it intelligible to others.

perform. Fourth, the result of this perpetual acting-for-imagined-others that constitutes daily life is a 'virtual *invisibility*' of performance: it is so ubiquitous we stop noticing (ibid.: 72). While we have always been aware of ourselves as acting out certain social roles (mother, soldier, friend, student), the proliferation of media make an unprecedented degree of performance specific to our contemporary new media ecology. Performance is no longer tied to discrete events but has '*leaked out* into the conduct of everyday life' (ibid.: 75). At any moment, and routinely, we may be both producers and consumers of media. This results in an erosion of the distinction of public and private: personal, private occurrences can be recorded, disseminate and witnessed publicly in unforeseeable ways. Another consequence is a blurring together of forms of media. For example, mainstream/ professional journalism and citizen journalism appear increasingly to draw upon and shape one another, as the role of 'journalist' becomes rewritten thanks to new technologies of media production and consumption. We turn to this now.

Table 4.2   Mainstream/Professional Journalism vs. Citizen Journalism

Authorized	Unauthorized
Polished	Raw
Objective	Subjective
Second-hand	First-hand
Dependent	Independent
Packaged	Behind-the-scenes
Distanced	Connective
Top-down	Interactive
Lecture	Conversation

Not only are audiences potential publics, but they are also potential journalists. Audiences-as-witnesses can testify to others by broadcasting themselves and what they have perceived and experienced. As citizen journalists, they can also record and disseminate material themselves – user-generated content (UGC). This might appear to challenge the sovereignty of professional journalists: if ordinary citizens can produce media material themselves, including 'news' material, does this undermine the hierarchy that gives journalists their status as newsmakers? Audiences suddenly become co-authors in the news they watch (Bruns, 2005). News is not automatically a valued commodity, 'out there' to be bought and consumed, but something we can all contribute to.

This would appear to undermine Luhmann's conception of mass media as a closed, self-perpetuating system. Thanks to citizen journalism 'the system is porous', Mark Deuze writes (2008: 21). The values of ordinary citizens could infiltrate and alter the balance of traditional, systemic news values. Matheson and Allan (cited in Allan, 2006: 109) present the values of mainstream/professional journalism and citizen journalism as apparent in professional and amateur warblogs (see table 4.2).

In her investigation of non-professional blogs focusing on the 2003 Iraq War, Melissa Wall (2005) demonstrates that the blogs constituted a genre defined by personalization, audience participation (treating readers as co-creators), and story forms that are fragmented and interdependent with other websites. Are these characteristics coming to define 'traditional' journalism?

The relation between 'mainstream' and 'alternative' media is not zero-sum, with more of one meaning less of the other, or the values of one simply imposing itself on the other. A key challenge in the new media ecology is analysing how different forms or genres of journalism reinvent themselves by borrowing from each other to create new approaches. Big Media organizations such as CNN and the BBC encourage viewers/users to contribute their stories, photos and opinions, harnessing content generated by 'the masses' to make Big Media coverage more comprehensive and responsive. BBC News Online created a 'space for survivors' of the Asian Tsunami in 2004, writes Stuart Allan, in which they could 'post first-person accounts, photographs, and video items, as well as message boards for those hoping to post appeals for information about relatives, friends and colleagues' (2006: 9). In a less organized way, on the morning of the 7/7 London bombings in 2005, BBC News became a hub for user-generated content posted by what Allan calls 'accidental journalists' (ibid.: 9), those members of the public who happened to be proximate to the explosions and the aftermath. Such a role poses a problem even for a news organization of the BBC's size: all emails and images have to be checked, requiring many staff suddenly to be on hand (indeed, websites such as Wikipedia may offer more reliable and responsive coverage of breaking news events since their collaborative editing may be better suited). In light of such events, CNN launched I-Report in August 2006 to generate 'public journalism' in the hope that this would allow greater coverage of breaking news from anywhere that a person had a cameraphone or access to email (its greatest scoop at the time of writing is footage sent in of shootings at Virginia Tech University in the US in 2007).

Between the stereotype terms 'new' and 'old' media, we find *renewed* media: mainstream news organizations harnessing citizen or participatory journalism to enhance their news provision. Hence, during the 2003 Iraq War, the BBC's *Newsnight* programme hired Salman Pax, the 'Baghdad blogger', to report on life in Iraq for ordinary civilians during the invasion and occupation. A citizen journalist like Pax (a pseudonym) could provide access to areas too dangerous for Western journalists to visit. The BBC could 'see' more of Iraq, and offer an extra perspective – that of a local Iraqi – thanks to citizen journalism.

Mainstream news organizations reported on bloggers' coverage of the war. In the process, they lent credibility to bloggers as a legitimate set of participants in the new media ecology. Weeks after the opening of the war, the *Guardian* provided a guide to warblogs: 'the sites you need to see' (Perrone, 2003). After the invasion stage, Howard Kurtz at the *Washington Post* offered an evaluation of different bloggers wherever they might have been writing from (Kurtz, 2003). Of interest to professional journalists was not just whether blogs were pro- or anti-war, but the manner in which bloggers acquired and disseminated information.

It is important to note how rapidly the emergence of citizen journalism and renewed media has occurred. On 11 September 2001, the Internet as a technological infrastructure was simply not able to host the volume of emails and other communications about the event. Google was forced to post an advisory message: 'If you are looking for news, you will find the most current information on TV or radio' (cited in Allan, 2006: 58). As Allan documents (ibid.: 57–71), major news sites such as MSNBC were forced to run their pages without graphics. Their reliance on news agency wires meant the news offered by major sites was no quicker than what was on TV or radio – the promise of speed offered by the Internet was not then capitalized on. Many individuals close to the attacks, for instance those in New York City, were able to document what they witnessed that day on their personal webpages (and these were later followed up by professional journalists). However, this was before the emergence of mobile phones with video cameras; moving footage of the attacks and their aftermath was only available on television. The Asian tsunami and London bombings marked the arrival of citizen journalism as intrinsic to breaking news events, making those events mediatized. This was taken to another degree during the Mumbai attacks of November 2008, in which citizens – and the attackers themselves, it was rumoured – used Twitter to communicate about the ongoing situation.

We have identified, then, several modes by which audiences can relate to news of war and conflict. Since audiences are often aware that images can be manipulated and that stories may be biased, relations to mediated images may be ambivalent (Guerin and Hallas, 2007). We know that a report may not do justice to an event, let alone a single image. Hence, audiences as witnesses are in a difficult position, their media literacy tested in a new media ecology in which digital footage can easily be photoshopped. Ethical questions also emerge. We began the chapter noting that some claim that witnessing atrocities make audiences accomplices in the harm caused, but are we really *active* accomplices? Aside from doubts about the truth of a report about the atrocity, audiences do not know who else has seen and not acted, or how ready others might be to act, or the obstacles to action other audiences face (Boltanski, 1999: 16–17).

What is specific to the second phase of mediatization is the opportunity for audiences to transcend their category and become journalists too. This is creating new challenges and opportunities for both mainstream media organizations and citizens eager to harness new technology to report their experience to others, adding to the contingency of information emergence and distribution in diffused war.

4. Conclusion

How we respond to news of war and conflict depends on our evaluations of the truthfulness of what media deliver to us. The category 'witness' allows us to think through and analyse the many ways that those able to perceive war can then represent it to others, and the medial relations through which we feel close to or affected by war and its mediation. By relaying their perceptions, testifying to those not present, soldiers, journalists, NGO workers, documentary-makers and, indeed, audiences all help to piece together the truth of war. However, there are many modalities of truth – credibility, objectivity, authenticity, accuracy, balance and so on. Perhaps it is only taken together that these constitute the possibility for perceiving the reality, facts and experience of war.

The mediatization of war transforms many of the practices by which witnessing is accomplished, breaking down previously distinct roles as technologies allow anyone to both consume and produce media themselves. Soldiers, citizens and NGOs can report on war, challenging the sovereignty of the professional frontline journalist. This threatens to disrupt the linear cause-and-effect models of the first phase of mediatization in which it was believed that the 'flow' of communication could be managed by states and Big Media organizations. Yet an examination of how these roles are performed indicates instead a mixing and meshing of news practices and values. The military authorities and major news organizations that successfully adapt to these trends are becoming not old or new, but *renewed* institutions. It remains to be seen whether the (selective, strategic) harnessing of the 'collective intelligence' of bloggers and 'accidental' journalists can enable the control of communication by traditionally powerful institutions, or whether this more flux-like dispersal of information can enable the various modalities of truth to be better achieved.

5

GENOCIDE

1. Introduction

As we set out in our opening chapter, shifting technologies have transformed both the process and the perception of warfare. The character of mass killing is one of the key dimensions of these developments. For instance, Martin Shaw, one of the leading sociologists of modern warfare, identifies two principal elements therein: first, the increasing ease, scale, speed and remote means of mass killing and, second, the increasing military strategy of extending its scope of 'enemy' from the opposing armed forces to include society itself (2003: 24). In this respect, Shaw identifies a 'degeneration' of modern warfare which he sees as best understood as a 'dialectic between discriminating aims and indiscriminate results' (ibid.: 25). And it is this dialectic, the discourses over the legitimacy and illegitimacy of mass killing, that is becoming increasingly mediatized.

'Genocide', as a form of warfare, has come to frame and to define debates, actions and inactions, and even the modern history of conflict along that which Shaw sets out as a continuum of: 'war – degenerate war – genocide' (ibid.: 45). And it is precisely because the process of defining genocide is potentially so consequential and problematic that its use by political actors, militaries and journalists has particular resonance in debates about conflict today and conflicts that may occur in the future. Before we set out the parameters of this chapter in more detail, it is first important to note that the definition of genocide is enshrined in the United Nations Conventions on the Prevention and Punishment of the Crime of Genocide, adopted on 3 December 1948. Article II states:

In the present Convention, genocide means any of the following acts committed with intent to destroy, in whole or in part, a national, ethnical, racial or religious group, as such: (a) Killing members of the group; (b) Causing serious bodily or mental harm to members of the group; (c) Deliberately inflicting on the group conditions of life calculated to bring about its physical destruction in whole or in part; (d) Imposing measures intended to prevent births within the group; (e) Forcibly transferring children of the group to another group.

The UN's framing leaves a legacy, however. Shaw argues that a great deal of ambiguity over the definition of genocide derives from act (c) in Article II, in terms of the meaning of the destruction of a group (2003: 36). For Shaw, an emphasis on the uniqueness of the Holocaust in comparison to other mass killing, 'has helped to enshrine a maximum concept of genocide as the complete extermination of a group, involving killing of almost all of its members, in legal, popular, and even academic understanding. But this is clearly mistaken' (ibid.: 37). So, what looms large in any such claim concerning the occurrence of genocide is firstly about the past: the ubiquitous template, the prism of the Holocaust through which the meaning of genocide is forged and reforged. Second, claims about genocide invoke the moral, political and legal obligation to halt or prevent those acts defined as genocidal. We argue in this chapter that the linkage made between these two has become stronger because of what Andreas Huyssen has suggested is an increasing 'globalization of Holocaust discourse' (2003: 13). The link is also made possible through the use of 'media templates' – one of the principal ways the news media recycle the past in the framing of current and possible future events. In response, Shaw advocates greater clarity around the idea of destruction in genocide and identifies three elements to this end:

1 The identification of a social group as an *enemy* in an essentially military (rather than merely political, economic or cultural) sense – that is, as a group against which it is justified to use physical violence in a systematic way.
2 The intention to destroy the real or imputed *power* of the enemy group, including its economic, political, cultural and ideological power, together with its ability to resist this destruction.
3 The actual deployment of violence to destroy the power of the enemy group through *killing* and physically harming a significant number of its members, as well as other measures. (Ibid.; original emphasis)

The problem for Shaw arises from a misunderstanding that genocide requires the completion of the destruction of life, rather than genocide being seen as a destructive *process* (ibid.: 38).

In this chapter we consider the profound difficulties in actually defining, intervening in and preventing genocide, given the legacy of implicit or explicit comparative representations of the 'totality' of the Holocaust. Thus we ask, if a situation can only be described as genocidal once a group has been destroyed, rather than when a process that appears genocidal is under way, how can those charged with reporting atrocities hope to transform the responses of political and military leaders and, indeed, publics? In fact, our analysis suggests it is before or after genocide occurs that it is named as such. To this end, we distinguish conceptually between the media logics of 'pre-' and 'postmediation' as arbiters of genocide, rather than its live mediation. In other words, despite the ravages of mediatization that we have identified, and the immediate and penetrative force of mobile digital technologies, 'genocide' appears to continue to elude the real-time apparatus of contemporary news media. For all the apparent immediacy and relative accessibility of the tools of modern professional and amateur journalism, there nonetheless appears to be a disjuncture between mediation/culture of the news of genocide and the actuality of intervention.

Of course, twenty-first military operations are increasingly media-managed, be this through a tightly controlled inclusion of reporters (embedding in Iraq and in Afghanistan) or through exclusion (as with the 2008–9 Israeli assault on Gaza). As Martin Bell argues: 'Wars which are fought among the people are no longer reported from among the people' (2008: 221). The news reporting of genocide is of course fraught with additional complexities and difficulties, not least because its perpetrators most often wish their acts and their responsibilities for those acts to remain unmediated.

In this way, the likelihood of the mediation of genocide being vulnerable to the phenomenon we set out in chapters 1 and 2, namely, that of 'emergence', is differentiated or uneven. We define emergence as the massively increased potential for media data literally to 'emerge', to be 'discovered' and/or disseminated – instantaneously – at an unprescribed and unpredictable time after the moment of recording and so to transcend that which is known, or thought to be known, about an event. In relation to genocide, emergence is potentially transformative. Given the intrinsically *covert* nature of genocidal acts, and thus the diminished access, coverage and documentation available to mainstream journalism, what prospects do digital media technologies offer in facilitating identification of and intervention in genocide as well as the pursuit of its perpetrators? We pose this question particularly in relation to those moments, fleeting or extended, when there were 'windows of opportunity' to report, notably most often cast retrospectively in terms of the time and circumstance in which genocide may have been prevented or stopped.

In sum, the relationship between diffused war and genocide can be understood through principal components of its mediation. First, the media logics of pre- and postmediation shape a narrative on genocide that appears in (particularly Western) media and political discourses. These logics materialize chiefly through the routine application of a Holocaust 'media template' over news coverage and other media discourses on contemporary genocide and other atrocities. Genocides past or to come are only deemed intelligible, it appears, if they are compared to the Holocaust. Second, the dynamics of emergence may offer the prospects of rupturing such narratives. However, despite the much-heralded prospects of digital mobile media in preventing or limiting genocide through its promise of immediate and extensive visibility, this mobile footage is more often incorporated into the postmediation of a genocidal event. These components can be mapped onto Shaw's argument (above) over a misunderstanding of genocide as necessitating the completion of the destruction of life, rather than it being seen as a destructive *process* (2003: 38). In other words, the first (totalizing) definition presents a considerable threshold likely only to be met posthumously in the longer-term excavation, accumulation and analysis of evidence, whereas the second (processual) definition at least offers greater prospects for the emergence of evidence in time for a galvanizing of those with the political or military will and means to intervene. Of course, even news coverage of what is later established as ongoing genocide or the signs of its beginning does not necessarily equate to recognition or response, as with the Rwandan genocide, which we consider in conclusion to this chapter. Moreover, misunderstanding over the definition and thus identification of genocide *as* genocide may be related to the persisting trope of the Holocaust, the prism though which they are at least often initially mediated. In this way, this chapter maps the recent shifting mediations of genocide and the challenges and prospects for pre-emption and prevention therein. Furthermore, we contextualize these debates in relation to the specificities of 'the visual', and accounts of 'compassion fatigue' and 'witnessing', explored in the preceding three chapters.

2. Premediation and the Holocaust

One of the key issues in the relationship between media and genocide is that the prospects and, particularly, the failures of intervention to prevent or halt genocide are linked to the nature and extent of global and, particularly, Western news coverage. In other words, in the mass-mediated spheres of the governments (and their constituencies) most equipped with the (political, economic and military) resources to respond and to intervene, there is often an absence of information, including as 'news', concerning the actuality or likelihood of genocide. The 1994 Rwandan genocide is seen with hindsight as preventable, for example.

Yet, the very idea of the prevention of or intervention to stop genocide is bound up in the legacy of the Holocaust and it is to this relationship we now turn to address. One cannot ignore the Holocaust in either popular or professional history; in modern culture it is one of the most represented events of the twentieth century. It is there in literature, drama, film, television and countless other media. The scale of the documentation and mediation of the Holocaust is difficult to overestimate. In the pre-digital age, for example, 'a select bibliography lists close to ten thousand book entries in many languages and notes over ten thousand publications on Auschwitz alone' (Michael Marrus commenting on the field in 1987, cited in Weissman, 2004: 209). Today, thanks to advances in digital technologies and media, the ubiquitousness of the Holocaust is of a different order again. Yad Vashem, for example, Israel's official 'Holocaust Martyrs' and Heroes' Remembrance Authority', is committed to Holocaust commemoration, documentation, research and education. According to Dana Porath (2009), its content manager, in 2008 the Yad Vashem site received 8.1 million visits from 220 countries with an average number of 22,200 daily hits. Furthermore, in 2009, Yad Vashem launched four channels on YouTube in English, Hebrew, Spanish and Arabic, attracting more than 1.6 million video views by the middle of that year (ibid.).

However, it is precisely this ubiquity of mediations of the Holocaust that seems to have a paradoxical relationship to the reporting of, representing and responding to genocides that have occurred since then (and even retrospectively to those genocides that went before). Across the forms and scales of warfare, one can argue that genocide, through the prism of the Holocaust, is the most *premediated* of all. One of the driving rationales for the Holocaust as a universal trope is in relation to the idea that a media presence will help prevent such an event from happening again. Yet, despite the proliferating extent of Holocaust discourses and representations, genocides continue to occur in late modernity – in Rwanda, Bosnia and Darfur, for example. And it is this paradoxical relationship and the role and function of media as central to it, as well as the impact of this relationship upon the politics and the strategy of genocide, that is one emergent aspect of what we have called here diffused war.

So, as we set out above, it is useful to draw upon a new concept in media theory, that of 'premediation', to consider these relationships (Grusin, 2004, 2010; Erll, 2008). Erll for example, writes: 'The term "premediation" draws attention to the fact that existent media which circulate in a given society provide schemata for future experience and its representation. In this way, the representations of colonial wars premediated the First World War, and the First World War, in turn, was used as a model for the Second World War' (2008: 392–3). She continues: 'The American understanding and representation of 9/11 was clearly premediated by disaster movies, the crusader narrative, and biblical stories. Premediation therefore refers to the cultural practices of looking, naming, and narrating' (ibid.: 393). 'Schemata' we take as being a kind of framework and standard, which the unit of memory (mind, group, society) forms from past experiences and by which new experiences are expected, measured and also reflexively shaped (cf. Hoskins, 2011). The schemata of the Holocaust might be used for the representation and interpretation of genocide as genocide. However, part of the paradox explored here is that the use of this schemata may in fact impact upon potential prevention and intervention. Why? Imbued in premediation – the persistence of employment of 'the Holocaust' as a universal marker of genocide – is the idea that the Holocaust is nonetheless 'incomparable', a 'unique' event. Although the impact of 'the Holocaust' on interpretations of, responses to and the temporal trajectories of events deemed to be genocidal (as 'news' and later as 'history') is near inescapable, entwined with these debates is the claim that the Holocaust is 'unrepresentable'. Given its 'indescribable' and 'unimaginable' status, in terms of its industrial nature and scale and the horror of the suffering of the victims, any attempted representation is already and inevitably problematic – destined for failure. Forms of representation of the Holocaust, then, have difficulty in avoiding an underlying meta-discourse that they are 'not enough', being somehow insufficiently 'close' to the 'real' form of genocide that they seek to represent.

We now turn to consider the evolution of such representations and nonrepresentations in relation to shifts in media technologies, politics and culture, particularly as they connect with other elements of our account of diffused war as we have already explored, including theories of mediation and the politics of 'witnessing' in the previous chapter. The paradoxical premediation of genocide is an exemplar of diffused war. Given that news coverage of unfolding events is invariably framed in terms assumed to be familiar to audiences, a

Holocaust template is doubly problematic. This is because of the prevalent set of discourses, mentioned already, that define the Holocaust as a unique and incomparable event, which makes controversial its employment as a ready comparison. Second, running through this set of discourses is the related claim that the Holocaust is 'unrepresentable'. If the horror of the suffering of the victims is 'indescribable' and 'unimaginable', any attempted representation is already and inevitably problematic – destined for failure – as it cannot reproduce the 'reality' of such horror, no matter how vivid or well articulated the testimony, or however 'experiential' the museum encounter. This argument is central to the work of Gary Weissman, who goes further:

> Because writings on the Holocaust are replete with such phrases as 'imagining the unimaginable', 'speaking the unspeakable', and 'expressing the inexpressible', considering the subject in these terms has come to seem natural to both authors and readers. But these phrases point to the actual problem facing us, which is not that the Holocaust is unrepresentable, but that it is *only representable*. (2004: 209; original emphasis)

We can look at the issue of premediation from the opposite direction. Is it that the premediation of modern genocide or other forms of modern warfare, narrated and shaped as news events through the prism of the Holocaust, seem *un*real in that they exceed the bounds of expectation of representation of the Holocaust? Or, put another way, is it that such representations seem *more* real than the Holocaust and thus take on a semblance of hyperreality through their comparison? We will shortly develop this line of thought by considering one of the defining examples of the uses and effects of the Holocaust media template on modern warfare, namely in relation to the video footage and stills of an emaciated Bosnian Muslim, stripped to the waist, and apparently imprisoned behind a barbed wire fence in a Bosnian Serb camp at Trnopolje, filmed by Britain's Independent Television News (ITN) on the 5 August 1992 and quickly remediated around the world. However, first, we will develop our explanation of the significance of media templates.

3. Media Templates

Media templates are television's principal mechanism of instant comparison and contrast, as we identified in our 2007/9 study of news discourses and the mediation of terror and insecurity. Media templates not only involve the interpretation of current events; they also simultaneously reinforce or reshape the meaning of past events: an 'archival prism'. We examined how the extended aftermath of the 2003 Iraq War was readily and substantially interpreted through the 'quagmire' template of the Vietnam War. The continuing presence and casualties of predominantly US (but also UK) troops in Iraq was often narrated (in media and political discourses) directly through a retelling of the history of a war that was 'lost': Vietnam. This occurred despite – or perhaps because of – the considerable asymmetries of economic, military and political power in favour of the US. According to Jenny Kitzinger, analysing media templates is essential to enhancing understandings of how reality comes to be framed through the power of the media.[1] She argues: 'Media templates are a crucial site of media power, acting to provide context for new events, serving as a foci for demands for policy change and helping to shape the ways in which we make sense of the world' (2000: 81). In this way, the reiteration of the Vietnam template can be seen to provide leverage for those critical of US and UK foreign policy regarding the 2003 invasion of Iraq by offering a familiar narrative in terms of the ignored 'historical lessons' and a diminishment of optimism as to the likely consequences of prolonged occupation. Although the Vietnam template was used periodically, introduced at news-defined 'key' moments in the conflict such as anniversaries of action or the marking of a particular – again, news-defined – 'significant' number of US or UK casualties, it also mirrored more subtly the temporalities of the Vietnam War, in terms of a drip-drip of bad news modulating in and out of Western news publics' consciousness.

However, media templates of the Holocaust may impact upon the event being interpreted through the past in a different way. We suggested above that through the frequent evocation of the Holocaust, news coverage of contemporary atrocities has a problematic and paradoxical realism. On the one hand, it is difficult ever to meet the considerable expectations placed on representations of an event considered unimaginable (as in Weissman's position, above). On the other, the ubiquity of Holocaust representations across a spectrum of media instils and reinforces a globalized familiarity with its narrative, its defining acts, victims and locations. Indeed, there is an institutionalized presumption of this knowledge. For example, on a visit to Yad Vashem, the new Holocaust History Museum in Jerusalem, an international party of visitors, on running late for a talk to follow a tour, were hurried by their official guide: 'We'll go swiftly through Auschwitz as it is a history most of you know.'[2] But what is the function of this familiarity, real or assumed, in the mediation and response to emergent atrocities and genocide that are routinely embedded in and contrasted with the abundant iconicity of the Holocaust? Rather than mobilizing the action of policymakers and other political elites, templates of the Holocaust may function to diminish the prospects for response and intervention to emergent events because the very worst, the 'unimaginable', has already happened and has been already, if paradoxically, rendered familiar. Roger Silverstone argues: '[T]he endless repetition of image and the reiteration and reinforcement of narrative cements a version of the world which moves imperceptibly but entirely into the familiar and unexceptional' (2002: 10). Put another way, what is the capacity for mainstream news media to genuinely shock or to move its audiences in the new media ecology if the past, through which events are made sense of, is so abundantly and continuously mediated? Furthermore, even if representations of contemporary atrocity or genocide do evade or exceed accumulated understandings and tropes of 'what atrocity looks like', for example, such a shocking representation would not necessarily provoke action that will transform the event being represented. We return to consider these questions shortly in relation to debates over the media coverage of the Serbian prisoner camps near the beginning of the Bosnian war of the early 1990s. However, first we develop a more comprehensive outline of the characteristics and functions of media templates.

Jenny Kitzinger (2000) contrasts media templates with 'icons'. She makes the comparison through citing the work of Bennett and Lawrence (1995), who identified 'news icons' in their examination of the 1991 videotaped beating of Rodney King in Los Angeles by white police officers. Despite the similarities with icons, Kitzinger sees media templates working differently and 'defined by their lack of innovation, their status as received wisdom and by their *closure*' (2000: 75–6; original emphasis). She argues: 'Far from opening up historical reflection they reify a kind of historical determinism which can filter out dissenting accounts, camouflage conflicting facts and promote one type of narrative' (ibid.: 76). From this definition one see how 'the Holocaust' is readily available for 'keying in' as a media template given its ubiquity and dominance in the mediatized Western memory booms (which we consider in the following chapter). It is useful in this respect to outline in more detail the central distinguishing features of media templates as proposed by Kitzinger (ibid.: 76) as follows:

1 Media templates are key events which have continuity before and beyond the conclusion of any one news story they are used to interpret. Kitzinger also suggests that templates are defined more by their retrospective use in secondary, follow-up reporting of events, rather than in relation to current coverage.
2 They are employed through comparison to *explain* current events as proof of an ongoing problem.
3 They anchor a single primary meaning rather than being subject to multiple interpretations. Although the relevance of the application of the template may be debated, the event from which the template is drawn is rarely open to challenge.

In relation to these features, Kitzinger continues to set out 'implications' for their operation as follows:

1 *Simplification and distortion.* Media templates may blur details and frame out contradictory accounts and facts.
2 *Minimal opportunity for alternative readings.* Through repeated secondary reporting of the event, it becomes reduced to very basic details and thus less open to alternative interpretations from those who only have access to secondary accounts. Here, Kitzinger distinguishes between those who viewed the contemporary reporting – in 'event time' to use Todd Gitlin's (1980) term – and those who come to the news story later. However, she also acknowledges the likely influence of secondary reporting even on the recall of this group, in other words through repetition and reinforcement of the template.
3 *Osmosis.* Template events accrue meanings through *interaction* between them and subsequent cases to which they become linked. This is a useful formulation given its emphasis on the shifting temporal dynamics of templates. This is similar to our focus on the dynamic modulation, back-and-forth, of news

discourses between past and newly emergent events. In this way, there are parallels between Kitzinger's notion of 'osmosis', and the idea of diffusion that anchors our approach throughout this book.

In sum, Kitzinger tends to come down on the side of the significance of secondary reporting to media templates in the emphasis she places on their retrospective use. However, since the publication of her article in 2000, the balance between the significance of the use of templates before, during or after an event may have shifted. Advances in the recording, upgrading, digitizing, storage and accessing of media data have enabled the almost-immediate 'keying-in' of template material, and such media data can be shown/heard simultaneously with the broadcast of real-time or near real-time footage, in the same screen or frame. This has transformed the media template into a much more dynamic tool of modern news media, almost routinely feeding history into, and breaking, new events and creating newly converged histories. It is not just the ready collapsing (Hoskins, 2004b) of past/present/future into a single and immediate window of comparison that affords new power and complexity to media templates. The modulation and convergence of media data, events and their histories is dynamically shaped through media forms themselves. Media professionals – and increasingly amateurs – edit, remix and reconstitute news events iteratively on an ongoing basis. It is the remediation and retranslation of events through different media forms that is as significant in shaping templates as those iterations that occur intra-medium. We now return to consider the significance of these dynamics in perpetuating particular Holocaust discourses and in shaping news coverage of the early stages of the Bosnian War, and probe the paradoxes in responses (and their absence) to this news event. In other words, there is a 'lack of innovation' and 'closure' of media templates (as suggested by Kitzinger, above) which, rather than provoking action in response, may instead merely reinforce a sense of routine and helplessness and actually diminish rather than improve the likelihood of intervention.

The template event we now turn to examine is Western news reportage of the Bosnian Serb camp at Trnopolje, initially recorded and broadcast by ITN on 5 August 1992, although it is its translation by the British press the following day that provides the defining iteration of this story. Furthermore, this offers a rich case study of the shifting historical trajectories of templates across media and different discursive domains, not least owing to the controversy it generated and the extent of academic, historical and journalistic analysis that followed in response.

4. The Trnopolje Camp Images

The context for this controversy is the beginning of the 1992–5 Bosnian War. After Bosnian Muslims and Croats voted for independence early in 1992, Serbs, led by Radovan Karadzic, attempted to create a Serb Republic through persecutions and killings. Despite some of the complexities and turns of the Bosnian War, including the changing of allegiances by a number of groups, the siege of the capital Sarajevo, the Srebrenica massacre and the final intervention by NATO in 1995, the Serbian side was charged with the 'overwhelming burden of responsibility' (Gow et al., 1996: 1). In fact Gow et al. aptly capture the war's dynamics in disintegrating the country by naming it 'The Yugoslav War of Dissolution' in their important edited volume *Bosnia by Television*.

The set of images at the centre of the news story show Fikret Alic, a Bosnian Muslim man, who is topless, revealing his emaciated frame. He is caged with other prisoners, peering through a barbed-wire-topped fence. He can be seen stretching his hand out through the barbed wire towards the camera and shaking the hand of the ITN reporter Penny Marshall. These images were contained in ITN video reports led by Marshall and a colleague, Ian Williams, and broadcast on ITV and Channel 4 News programmes, respectively, on the evening of 6 August 1992. The most comprehensive analysis of these images and the ensuing controversy was undertaken by David Campbell and published in two articles in the *Journal of Human Rights* (Campbell, 2002a, 2002b). Campbell's work is anchored around debates about the Western media's use of these images in demonizing the whole Serbian people, thus legitimating the necessity and inevitability of US military intervention (2002b: 143). Campbell explores these claims in relation to a successful libel prosecution by ITN against *LM* (formerly *Living Marxism*) for an article published in February 1997 by a German journalist, Thomas Deichmann, entitled 'The Picture that Fooled the World'. This alleged that Marshall's and Williams's reports were fabricated through the use of 'camera angles and editing' with the intent of facilitating the use of a Holocaust template to frame the situation in Trnopolje. Deichmann's (1997) article provides a very different view of the Trnopolje camp:

> The other pictures, which were not broadcast, show clearly that the large area on which the refugees were standing was not fenced-in with barbed wire. You can see that the people are free to move on the road and on the open area, and have already erected a few protective tents. Within the compound next door that is surrounded with barbed wire, you can see about 15 people, including women and children, sitting under the shade of a tree. Penny Marshall's team were able to walk in and out of this compound to get their film, and the refugees could do the same as they searched for some shelter from the August sun.

However, a jury accepted that the camp was actually a prison and hence ITN's representation was justified. *LM* magazine was forced to close down following the costs of the successful libel case brought by ITN (BBC News, 2000).

Although ITN scooped the story with their video reports revealing the strategy of the Bosnian Serbs, it was the newspaper coverage the following day that most explicitly made the connection between the camps and the Nazi Holocaust. Notably, it was the still images grabbed from the ITN video that anchored coverage across much of the British national press on 7 August 1992. In the UK, the high-circulation tabloid, the *Daily Mirror*, used the front-page headline 'BELSEN 92' and the subtitle 'HORROR OF THE NEW HOLOCAUST', while the *Daily Star* opted for 'BELSEN 1992', all framing the image of Alic. The *Daily Mail*'s leader headline proclaimed 'THE PROOF' above a slightly wider shot of Alic and other prisoners behind the barbed-wire fence. The *Daily*

Mail not only employed the Holocaust template but, like other newspapers, extended the comparison to the mode of representation itself: 'They are the sort of scenes that flicker in black-and-white images from 50-year-old films of Nazi concentration camps.' The Holocaust template overran the news space.

In terms of the imperative of news values in impressing instant and familiar interpretations on recent and unfolding events, and also the comparative power of the visual image, the use of templates in such circumstances is unsurprising. As Susan Sontag, for example, argues: '[P]hotographs echo photographs: it was inevitable that the photographs of emaciated Bosnian prisoners at Omarska,[3] the Serb death camp created in northern Bosnia in 1992, would recall the photographs taken in the Nazi death camps in 1945' (2003: 84). And it is precisely this 'inevitability' in Sontag's terms that we take as arising through the media logic of premediation.

The lead story text in the *Mirror* on 7 August 1992 – by Mark Dowdney – was typical of the coverage: 'The haunting picture of these skeletal captives evokes the ghosts of the Nazis' Belsen concentration camp during the Second World War.' However, as Campbell's analysis shows, the image of Alic that dominated the press coverage only represents a fraction of the two television reports, twenty seconds of Marshall's six-minute report and only five seconds of William's six-and-a-half minute account (2002a: 4). In this way, the media templates used in the newspaper coverage afford a certain 'closure' (see Kitzinger, above) on the Trnopolje image by making it iconic through comparison and reducing the story from one medium to another to its instantly recognizable visual essence. This also works on an ongoing iterative basis. For example, the same still image was repeated in television news' secondary reporting as a visual anchor or even amplified larger-than-life on a studio wall behind the newsreader.

However, the increasing role played by journalists as witnesses to events (explored earlier in chapter 4) also extends the shelf life of both media templates and the stories to which they are attached. A further point arises here: in the reporting of genocide and other atrocities, journalistic witnessing can accrue a legal dimension, particularly over the identification of the prosecution of perpetrators, and in this case where the claims made over the reporting itself were subject to legal challenge. In fact, journalists can become synonymous with a given event or events on which they report to an extent that it comes to define their career. The former BBC war correspondent Martin Bell, for example, became an advocate for what he called a 'journalism of attachment', as well as becoming an Independent Member of Parliament for a term and a UNICEF Ambassador. In relation to reporting of the Bosnian 'concentration camps', *Guardian* journalist Ed Vulliamy became significantly involved in its afterlife as he accompanied Marshall and Williams (the ITN journalists) during their filming at Trnopolje and Omarska. Vulliamy testified in the war crimes tribunal at The Hague and also gave evidence in the ITN case against *LM*. Writing in the *Observer*, he refuted *LM*'s allegations that the images of Alic and others had been fabricated and also indicts the media storm around the whole issue:

> The BBC has been panting to get in on the act, with *Newsnight* trying to stage debates and its media correspondent Nick Higham brandishing Deichmann's

arguments, insisting that ITN's compelling and honest shot was a 'misleading image'. *Scotland on Sunday* called, asking me: 'Do you approve of ITN taking legal action?' This is becoming a *Late Show*-ish burlesque about the role of TV and the particulars of a fence, blurted largely by people who have never set foot in Bosnia, let alone the camps. The genocide is trivialised, its victims insulted. (Vulliamy, 1997)

Indeed, it was Vulliamy and also the newspaper he wrote for, the *Guardian*, which refused to use the Holocaust template, unlike much of the British press. In a 2007 interview, Vulliamy characterizes the world's response to the news coverage of the camps as twofold:

On the one hand there was this sort of Belsen 1992 thing because of the resonance of these images. That was not particularly useful because I found the . . . invocation of Auschwitz really detracted from the horror of what we found rather than emphasised it. But then of course there was this outrage – I gave 54 interviews the day after it happened. . . . [P]eople across the world who saw this thought, 'my goodness this is happening a couple of hundred miles down the road from Venice in Europe in our lifetime', and everybody was shocked. (Vulliamy, 2007)

In fact, Vulliamy was very reflexive about his own use of a Holocaust template. He even sought the advice of the then Director of the Holocaust Memorial Museum in Washington, DC for an appropriate lexicon for describing the camps: 'And I asked Walter Reich if the word "echoes" would be permissible and he said "echoes, loud and clear"' (ibid.). (Interestingly, this is the same phrase that Sontag uses (above) in describing the photographic templates of the Bosnian camps.) From these ongoing accounts and interventions across a range of media, one can see how Vulliamy is invoked as a witness to the Bosnian camps at a number of intersecting levels. At some points he put himself forward for this role. This provides an instructive example of the *post*mediation of war, how the long tail of contemporary genocide and other forms of warfare are interwoven with media data and the shifting accounts of those connected to the original events. However, does the invocation of the Holocaust and the past through implicit or explicit templates actually inhibit responses to contemporary atrocities, as Vulliamy suggests, 'detracting' from the horror of the moment rather than highlighting it? Put another way, we can return to the question we posed earlier: with all the layering and interweaving of the past into the present and the imagined future, what are the prospects for response and intervention in preventing and stopping atrocities? To consider these issues further we now turn to briefly consider the intersecting work of three influential contemporary commentators on the ethics of representation and response in the mediatization of atrocities and warfare, namely Judith Butler, Susan Sontag and Barbie Zelizer.

5. Towards an Ethics of Images

In Chapter 2, we considered accounts of the nature and function of recycled images of suffering on audiences, policymakers and other actors. Elsewhere we

argue that the prolonged near civil war conditions defining a difficult operational environment for journalists, and the exhaustion of stories from Iraq (and
now Afghanistan), all conspire to create a remote and thus critically disengaged
Western news discourse on these prolonged conflicts (Hoskins and O'Loughlin,
2007). Television news reporting of warfare is trapped between the inuring of
audiences through the repetition of certain types of images – particularly over
the extended Western interventions in Iraq and Afghanistan – and a credibility
gap opening up between broadcastable material and the 'reality on the ground'.
This results, we argue, in a 'moral crisis' for mainstream news reporting, with
television in particular caught somewhat paradoxically between saturation and
sanitization (ibid.). We return shortly to consider this theme. But the media
logic of premediation and the routine deployment of media templates also
work to filter out the responsibility for response and action in the present. For
example, in her comprehensive work *Remembering to Forget*, Barbie Zelizer
argues that earlier atrocities may be powerfully maintained in memory so that
current ones are displaced from it. On atrocity photographs from World War
II, Zelizer argues: 'Their recycled appearances in the discussion of contemporary atrocities constitute a backdrop for depiction that neutralizes much of
the potential response to other ravages against humanity' (1998: 220). In this
way, Zelizer's approach is implicitly (but also explicitly elsewhere in her work)
Sontagian in seeing habituation and repetition as a barrier to compassion and
to action (see Sontag 1979/1977, 2003, and below). But with media templates
of the Holocaust and other atrocities that have become iconized through their
recycling and remediation, it isn't just the exhaustion of habituation that inures
responses to them or to emerging events over which such templates are inter-
pretatively placed. Zelizer argues that such a familiarity of images may breed a
helplessness to action in response to viewing contemporary atrocities because
'we already know what they look like' (1998: 226). In other words, premediation pre-empts the potential for surprise and for shock in response, since the
present is contained through a persistent anchoring of the past.

However, it is not just the way journalists, editors or viewers recognize
and accord value to Holocaust images in themselves that is significant in the
premediation and templating of contemporary genocide and other atrocities.
Zelizer identifies different dimensions to this process: 'The Holocaust cues
atrocity memory in three ways – through the words that guide us through the
images, through parallels in the images, and through a pattern of substitutional
representation' (ibid.: 221). For instance, in relation to the first and second of
Zelizer's framework, the headlines and editorials in the UK print coverage, and
the images of the emaciated figure of Fikret Alic and others imprisoned behind
barbed wire outlined above, were explicit in their combined embedding of the
news story of the Bosnian Trnpolje Camp in a Holocaust aesthetic. The notion
of substitutional representation is perhaps more interesting. Zelizer gives the
example of the *New York Times*'s use of a photograph of the Nuremberg trials
to anchor a story on the Bosnian war crimes tribunal under way in the Hague
in November 1995.[4] But the cueing of atrocity memory through substitutional
representation can also be deployed to premediate events – in other words to
frame the story before the event even begins. For example, Hoskins (2004a)

identifies a 'pre-emptive template' used on 14 February 2003 by the UK's *Guardian* newspaper with its entire 'G2' supplement devoted to images of 'The unseen Gulf war' published just a few weeks before the opening of the 2003 Iraq War. This included images from the Basra Road, notorious as the 'Highway of Death' because of the destruction of retreating Iraqi forces at the very end of the Gulf War, caught exposed by coalition air forces, without the means of defence, surrender or escape. At the time (29 February 1991), and for a considerable time afterwards, no images of the victims of this attack were broadcast on television or gained wider publication. The exception was the publication on 3 March 1991 in the UK's Sunday newspaper, the *Observer*, of a single image, taken by Ken Jarecke, of a charred Iraqi soldier still upright at the windscreen of a burnt-out vehicle. (This photograph has since become iconic of the Gulf War and was also reproduced in the same *Guardian* supplement referred to above.) This template was used as a substitutional representation to graphically premediate the potential of the 2003 Iraq War to cause similar horrific bodily injury and death. Moreover, this occurred in the context of, first, the dominant political and military coalition discourse on the waging of the 1991 Gulf War as a 'precision' and thus ethically superior war; secondly, the sanitized (body-less) mainstream Western news coverage of this war; and third, the disjuncture between these mediations and the much more indiscriminate weapons actually deployed at the time. In Zelizer's terms then, atrocity photos from even comparatively recent warfare are used to link, frame and pre-empt the nature and impact of those not even yet begun. The *Guardian* G2 templates may be interpreted on the one hand to undermine the building of the legitimacy of Western (UK/US-led) military intervention in Iraq, by reminding readers of the nature and consequences of the previous war with Saddam Hussein. (Perhaps one can also add that such a publication might be much less palatable if printed during the mediated event time of the Iraq War itself and deemed unpatriotic if not insensitive in relation to national collective sensibilities at times of war.) On the other hand, the very publication of these images at this juncture could be seen to preclude the need for later reminders of 'what war looks like', to paraphrase Zelizer, above.

However, it is a photograph taken by Peter Turnley and reproduced in black and white in 2003 in the *Guardian* that provides a Holocaust template. The photograph shows an American bulldozer and soldiers burying the bodies of Iraqis on the road to Basra. Hoskins (2004a) argues that this image evokes another much more famous black-and-white photograph, of the burial of the dead at the Bergen-Belsen Nazi concentration camp (and which commands a significant presence in the permanent Holocaust Exhibition in the Imperial War Museum, London). The iconic image is that of a 'post-liberation' scene of a driver with his nose and mouth covered, bulldozing an entanglement of the emaciated limbs and torsos of those for whom liberation had come too late to save their lives. The cueing of Holocaust memory through the parallels in images, in Zelizer's terms, above, has a resonance that can be read at a number of levels. The invocation of the Bergen-Belsen camp in Turnley's photograph not only provides a retrospective template over the 1991 Gulf War, but simultaneously premediates the Iraq War. In this way, atrocity and other images of war can be said to be remediated in new times, contexts and conflicts.

As we demonstrated in chapter 2, the work of Susan Sontag is pivotal in grasping the shifting relations between still and moving image representations of distant atrocities and warfare and the responses these generate. We explored her claim that '[p]hotographs may be more memorable than moving images, because they are a neat slice of time, not a flow. Television is a stream of under-selected images, each of which cancels its predecessor' (1977: 17–18). However, Sontag's contribution to these debates spans the broadcast and post-broadcast eras, most significantly marked with her pioneering *On Photography* (1977) and the increasingly influential *Regarding the Pain of Others* (2003). This period is significant because it marks the transition from a pre-satellite, pre-digital and time-delayed mediation of distant suffering with tightly controlled iterations of terrestrial news cycles to the globally saturated immediacy of today's new media ecology. This trajectory of mediation also parallels an accumulation of atrocities previously unthinkable in a post-Holocaust, late twentieth-century world, in Bosnia, Rwanda and Darfur, for example. Are the relatively diminished, attenu-ated responses to such events due to their regimented, templated serialization, in other words their familiarity as 'atrocity' or 'genocide', or a familiarity with the endlessly repeated soon-iconic representations of these events, including that of prisoners behind barbed wire in the Trnopolje camp? What can be said is that over this time, the velocity, or potential velocity, of the image in its global circu-lations and remediations has massively increased. There is an increased likeli-hood of the viewing of a given image, particularly an iconic and/or controversial image, in a range of contexts. And these contexts may matter, as Sontag argues:

> Even those ultimate images whose gravity, whose emotional power, seems fixed for all time, the concentration camp photographs from 1945, weigh differently when seen in a photography museum . . . in a gallery of contemporary art; in a museum catalogue; on television; in the pages of *The New York Times*; in the pages of *Rolling Stone*; in a book. (2003: 119–20)

In *Regarding the Pain of Others* Sontag also questions the claims she made in *On Photography* over the inuring impact of the repetition of even harrowing images:

> As much as they create sympathy, I wrote, photographs shrivel sympathy. Is this true? I thought it was when I wrote it. I'm not so sure now. What is the evidence that photographs have a diminishing impact, that our culture of spectatorship neu-tralizes the moral force of photographs of atrocities? (Ibid.: 105)

As we set out in chapter 2, for Sontag and for many commentators on the relationship between mediation, compassion and action, it is television that is the context seen as most important. This seems to be the case despite the spectrum of positions over whether the medium creates and maintains obliga-tion for action through what it depicts and how and when, or whether it merely facilitates a vacuous or disconnected conscience, no matter how dramatic the images. As we suggested in chapter 3, the notion of an excess of images of suffering causing 'compassion fatigue' is a hypothesis not a proven fact. For example, Stanley Cohen places the images of the Bosnian camps[5] in a series of 'unforgettable icons of suffering' but nonetheless writes: 'For some people, such images have a nagging, reproachful quality ("I can't get those photos out of my head") as difficult to erase as an advertising jingle running through the mind. But they do leave the mind, and the media regime is ill-suited to remind us of them' (2001: 174). From this perspective, attenuation is the inevitable result. The images may have an uneasy persistence, yet they also appear to diminish in media and human memory.

However, images of genocide do possess a status that is critical in their postmediation that differentiates them from other representations of warfare, notably in terms of their potential use as legal documents in the identification and prosecution of the perpetrators of the crimes they depict. In fact, the labelling of events as genocide or as instances of other crimes against humanity may carry with them an assumption as to their documentation and corroboration. Sontag, for instance, argues that 'the very notion of atrocity, of war crime, is associated with the expectation of photographic evidence' (2003: 84). However, in *Frames of War*, Judith Butler provides a fairly extensive critique of Sontag's work, and challenges this idea amongst others. Butler argues that if the photograph is incorporated into the notion of atrocity, in other words if photographic evidence is obligatory to demonstrate that an atrocity has occurred, then photography is necessary for 'the case made for truth' (2009: 70). For Butler, this position misunderstands how non-verbal/linguistic media 'make their "arguments"' (ibid.) Instead, she argues:

> Even the most transparent of documentary images is framed, and framed for a purpose, carrying that purpose within its frame and implementing it through the frame. . . After all, rather than merely referring to acts of atrocity, the photograph builds and confirms these acts for those who would name them as such. (Ibid.)

In this way, Butler advocates a more inclusive and also meta-level analysis. By understanding how the war photograph is organized ('how it shows what it shows'), Butler claims we can reveal how it also organizes our perception and our thinking (ibid.: 71). In this way, her position parallels that of John Taylor, contained in his substantive work: *Body Horror: Photojournalism, Catastrophe and War*. From an analysis of the coverage of the 1992 Bosnian camp story and its subsequent trajectory (including the role of Ed Vulliamy), Taylor concludes:

> The case is a clear example of how the evidential nature of imagery is bestowed upon it by practices and professions, and does not exist within it naturally. The evidential force of photography derives not from some 'magic' quality of the medium but from institutional practices and within particular historical relations. (1998: 63)

In summary, there is some consensus concerning what we call a 'premediation of the visual'. In other words, despite the apparent immediate and transparent relation to the reality of visual images, or 'truth value', the frame of interpretation they offer is always already compelling in some direction or perspective. Butler contends that this compulsion or pre-figuration of the frame is ultimately imposed by the state through its rendering of 'permissible perspectives' to which the visual news apparatus conforms (2009: 73). Ultimately, for

Butler, such political constraints 'undermine both a sensate understanding of war, and the conditions for a sensate opposition to war' (2009: 100). Yet, for Sontag, the sensate responses to war are at least partially driven by the potential power of the photograph to 'crystallize' sentiment (2003: 85). Moreover, the sudden emergence of a photograph or video may disrupt and challenge even meanings of events deemed relatively stable or fixed. Our analysis in chapter 2 of the 'emergence' of the mobile phone footage of the execution of Saddam Hussein exemplifies this possibility. As the proportion of the media data through and from which history is shaped increases, so do the prospects for such image emergence to transform interpretations of more distant events. Sontag, for example, observes: 'photographs help construct – *and revise* – our sense of a more distant past, with the posthumous shocks engineered by the circulation of hitherto unknown photographs' (ibid.; emphasis added). So, perhaps Butler was too hasty by suggesting such images will always fall within the category of state pre-figuration of 'permissible perspectives'? Yet, there is a rejoinder to this argument: it is wrong to assume that even the mass circulation of images of genocide or other atrocities equates to their recognition and their capacity to transform the meaning of events for people.

We conclude this chapter by exploring the significance of the emergence of footage depicting the start of a genocide that was seen but that went unnoticed.

6. Emergence

On 11 April 1994, a praying man and a woman cowering beside him on a dirt road in Kigali, Rwanda, were hacked to death by a gang of men. The British journalist Nick Hughes captured this scene on video from the top floor of a building across a valley. This footage has since come to be seen to mark the beginning of the 1994 Rwandan genocide. Despite the rapid dissemination of these images across the global news media within a matter of hours of their recording, and their shocking singularity, they occupy an odd and terrible place in the history of the mediation of genocide. Bizarrely, it is as if the Hughes footage was never actually broadcast and witnessed around the world at that time, given that it entered posthumously straight into the history of the Rwandan genocide.

Allan Thompson (2009) has tracked the remediations of this film as it has become a template of the Rwandan genocide. Indeed, Thompson argues that despite its multiple iterations in news and documentaries and its dramatization in the movie *Hotel Rwanda*, the footage of the murder of a father and daughter on a dirt street in Rwanda haunts spectators today precisely because of its reminder of the missed opportunity to stop the killing of more than a million people. He employs a series of templates (Vietnam Napalm; Tiananmen Square, 1989; the 9/11 'falling man') as measures of the iconic status that Hughes's images should have immediately accrued. Instead, there is an almost anti-iconicity to the Rwandan images and Thompson confronts us with a terrible complicity through the imagining of what the emergence of this footage might and should have provoked:

[T]he images of the praying man and the woman who perished beside him on a dirt road in Rwanda are somehow different, more urgent, more haunting for what might have been.

The news footage of their deaths was captured in the first moments of a 100-day rampage, at the front end of the arc of a genocide that would overtake Rwanda in the months to come. If only we had understood what we were seeing – or cared enough to understand – Rwanda might have been different.

As their deaths were broadcast around the world, their unidentified bodies were hurled into the back of a yellow truck and dumped into a mass grave, forgotten by the world that also forgot their country. (Ibid.)

The story of the Hughes footage illuminates the disjuncture between the *potential* of emergence to transcend inaction in the face of genocide and the reality that even the mediatization of genocide is not sufficient to prevent or to halt it. Thus in 2009, in the context of the Twitter revolution following news of unrest after the Iranian election result, the British Prime Minister Gordon Brown epitomized this misunderstanding by declaring: 'You cannot have Rwanda again because information would come out far more quickly about what is actually going on and the public opinion would grow to the point where action would need to be taken' (cited in Viner, 2009). The myth of the CNN effect again looms large, as if the very existence and real-time delivery of images will lead publics to notice and force policymakers to act.

Although the Rwandan images were globally mediated very soon after their recording, they were not held up at the top of news programming agendas but, rather, soon dropped from the news cycle. Thompson writes that despite a small number of journalists risking their lives in attempts to beak the Rwanda story, most international news organizations misinterpreted the nature of the killing as tribal warfare, rather than genocide. This returns us to the issue we identified at the outset of this chapter: the difficulties in actually defining and intervening in and preventing genocide, given that its certitude is often only established posthumously. Indeed, as Thompson (2009) makes clear, other than the Kigali footage, there are virtually no other known images documenting the actual crime of genocide in Rwanda. The international media only reached a critical mass in recording the signs of the *aftermath* of the genocide, notably the 'bloated corpses, strewn at the roadside or choking Rwanda's rivers'.

In conclusion, genocide is increasingly defined through the media logics of premediation and postmediation, which perpetuate an axis of imagined retrospective and prospective intervention. As a result, emergence remains a muted threat to the politics of non-intervention and the status quo. So far, the potential chaos triggered by images of killing and suffering remains largely contained, so one can perhaps apply Butler's argument that genocide itself, like other images of war, is already pre-figured in the frame in terms of the shaping of 'permissible perspectives'. Following Shaw, the need for genocide to be crucially seen as a destructive *process*, rather than the completion of the destruction of life (2003: 38), is not permitted, despite the apparent intensity of our connective turn and the saturation of real-time news media.

6

MEMORY

1. The Diffusion of Media and Memory

Entangled in the transformations of our new media ecology is an emergent ecology of memory. How, what, and why individuals, groups and societies remember and forget is being shaped by technological, political, social and cultural shifts that interpenetrate memory and memories, their makers, deniers and their archives. This 'memory boom' (Huyssen, 2000) includes an array of shifting public and academic discourses and a wholesale readdressing of our temporal horizons and constituents of the past. At its forefront are a popularization of war memory and the remembrance and commemoration of the traumas and triumphs of conflicts and catastrophes (Winter, 1995, 2006; Sturken, 1997; Wood, 1999; Wertsch, 2002; Müller, 2002; Simpson, 2006).

The emergence of diffused war is marked by a shift to a diffused memory of warfare, notably memory that is sifted through the co-evolution of technology and perception. Not only do the technologies of witnessing, documenting, recording and archiving of the day, affect the legitimising, the contesting and the waging of warfare, but they also shape the prospects for future remembering and forgetting.

Just as we have argued that the connective turn of the second phase of mediatization has produced a more complex and uncertain world, so the value of the memory of warfare has renewed purchase in mitigating the radical indeterminacies of present and premediated threats. This, as with all processes of remembering, operates at a double logic. So, as discourses on the past are employed as key arbiters of current conflicts and as powerful 'blueprints of legitimacy' to promote and to contest nascent conflicts, highly selected ghosts (e.g. D-Day, the Tet Offensive, and 9/11) haunt our mediatized present and resurrect old trauma in a soothing narrative guise that strikes a delicate balance between therapy and amnesia (Keller, 2001). In other words, just as there is a modulation of the mediation of warfare, there is also an interconnected modulation of the mediation of the memory of warfare, and in this chapter we argue that diffused war is fought, legitimized and contested through a diffused memory of warfare.

The unprecedented archival accumulation and emergence of a 'hybrid memorial-media culture' (Huyssen, 1995: 255) raises both prospects and problems for future social and cultural memory of warfare. On the one hand, government and other elite institutions are seen as proliferating overbearing and hierarchically organized archives and producing a 'terrorism of historicized memory' (Nora, 1989: 14). On the other hand, the fluidity, reproducibility, and transferability of digital data, as we have argued, delivers a 'long tail' (Anderson, 2007) of the past (documents, images, video, etc.) marked by a shift 'from archival space' to 'archival time' (Ernst, 2004: 52), feeding new opportunities for the digital production and reproduction of war memories (for instance via the Internet). Some of these directly counter and ultimately undermine elite and organizational versions of events, such as soldiers' mobile phone images and videos sent from war zones or which may emerge years later to disrupt even well-established social and cultural memories. In this way, the technologies and media of the day directly shape what is remembered (and forgotten) of that era as well as simultaneously remediating and re-memorializing previous eras. This includes, as Steven Rose argues, the pre-dating of modern technologies and even the pre-dating of writing itself, namely oral cultures which have a different dependency on memory and particularly those charged as 'memory-keepers' in 'retelling' stories (1993: 61). Rose contrasts this idea of the malleability of human memory with the impact of technologies – and particularly when moving from the realm of the individual to that of the collective – in the 'freezing and fixation' of what he calls 'artificial memory' (ibid.: 97). Thus, Rose asks: 'Is it possible to create a space in which we can both assimilate into our own experience the meaning of the ever screaming, ever-napalm-burnt child on our television screens without simply freeze-framing it, fixing it for ever and thus losing the dynamic of real, biological memory' (ibid.: 97–8). This highlights the role of memory in debates that run through the model of diffused war we have developed here, and notably in terms of consciousness, witnessing and compassion. Furthermore, the idea of the resonance of the visual in memory adds another dimension, or perhaps complicates, Butler's (2005) argument in response to Sontag (explored in chapters 2 and 5) as to the already-interpretative force of the visual image.

The visual is also associated – at the very least metaphorically – with the endurance of memories, for instance the idea of 'flashbulb memory' referring to the 'photographic' quality of the recall of events owing to their apparent vividness and visual clarity. Consequentially, this feeds the idea that the institutions/organizations of broadcast and print news and popular media exert a certain influence in editing, shaping and mediating public images of events. However, in terms of the workings of memory and media, we take 'diffusion' as a much more appropriate and useful analytical concept than the idea of a static or fixed visual memory. Thus, as Rose (in more recent writing) articulates with reference to the working of memory of brains: 'they are distributed networks of cellular ensembles, richly interconnected, which between them create the illusion of coherent experience that we all in our normally functioning moments share. The enigma of memory, as with so many aspects of brain processes, seems to be that it is both localised and non-localised' (2008: 67). Thus, Rose traces the shifts in neuroscientific accounts of the brain to this more enigmatic model from a paradigm that previously held the brain as 'composed of discrete centres' with a 'super-coordinating centre' (ibid.: 66). We see this as analogous to the transformation needed away from the modelling of the workings of mass media *and* the notion of an institutional production or at least shaping of 'memory' through hierarchically organized archives, as mentioned above, and the sometimes distinct but sometimes associated variant of 'collective memory',[1] towards a more contingent and dynamic model of the 'diffusion' of media/memory (cf. Hoskins, 2011).

In addition to being situated in the second phase of mediatization, diffused war is also shaped through its emergence in what we are identifying as the 'third' modern memory boom, characterized by a diffusion of media/memory.

2. The Second Memory Boom

The historian Jay Winter identifies two 'generations' or 'booms' of memory. The first is drawn from the 1890s to the 1920s, when memory was central to the formation of national identities, which pivoted around the memorializing of the victims of the Great War (2006: 18). It is the remembrance of the Second World War and the Holocaust in the 1960s and 1970s which marks the second memory boom (ibid.)

The 'time lag' between the war and genocide of the mid- to late twentieth century and the second generation of memory involved a shift in 'the balance of creation, adaptation, and circulation' of memory (ibid.: 26), including 'when the victims of the Holocaust came out of the shadows, and when a wide public was finally, belatedly prepared to see them, honor them, and hear what they had to say' (ibid.: 27). Winter notes that a corollary of this process (rather than its principal driver) was the capacity for Holocaust survivors' testimonies to be recorded via the audio/visual technological advances of the 1970s. This includes the premiere screening of the Holocaust television miniseries on NBC in 1978 (see Shandler, 1999). Furthermore, in 1979, a project began to record Holocaust witnesses and survivors, leading to the establishment of the Fortunoff Video Archive for Holocaust Testimonies, a collection now holding more than 4,300 videotaped interviews at Yale. The Archive website describes their concept: 'The survivors and witnesses of the Holocaust are diminishing in number. Each year their recollections become more important, but each year moves them farther away from the original experience. This gives special urgency to the effort to collect as many testimonies as possible – now'.[2] Thus, the diminishment of 'living memory' as survivors and other witnesses to these events were dying out increased the need to preserve it, powerfully intersected with technological advancements in retrieval, capture and storage, to produce an emergent memorial-media culture – the second memory boom.

The nature and location of Holocaust exhibitions, museums and memorials, the marking and broadcast of 'Holocaust Day' commemorations in Europe, not to mention the claims relating to a 'Holocaust Industry' (Finkelstein, 2000) and the work of the film director Steven Spielberg, for example, have, in themselves, produced extensive public and academic debate. This acceleration of memory discourses in Europe and the US, according to Andreas Huyssen, are part of the extensive resonances of Holocaust memory, and he argues, 'one must indeed raise the question to what extent one can now speak of a globalization of Holocaust discourse' (2003: 13). And we set out the velocity and the ubiquity of Holocaust media templates, as part of this trend, in chapter 5.

The revisiting and revisioning of twentieth-century wars and other cata-strophic events of the second memory boom were also enabled in part by the 1989 revolutions in Eastern Europe, which permitted new and explicit dis-courses on pasts, particularly in Germany. More recently, the 60th anniversary of the Second World War – obsessively covered by electronic media – became more intense and overdetermined than even the marking of 50 years on had been. At various points during 2005, broadcast news and documentaries exten-sively commemorated '60 years after': the end of the Second World War (VE Day and VJ Day), the death of Hitler and the bombing of Hiroshima. These anniversaries are interspersed with an array of others, including, for example, documentaries marking the 30th anniversary of the fall of Saigon, and the 10th anniversary of the massacre of Bosnians by Serbian militia at Srebrenica. The second memory boom can also be characterized by the features we identified in chapters 1 and 2 of the rise of satellite television, enabling 50th and 60th anni-versary and memorial events to be televised live and simultaneously across those countries implicated in those events.

The mediatization of oral history was a key driver of this memory boom. By the 1970s, as Winter argues, 'new voices emerged with new memories. These were the new "remembrancers", the new carriers of memory; they form a new singular collective which we term the witness' (2006: 28). But the 1990s marked a pinnacle of this memory boom in terms of the high point of satellite televi-sion news in providing extended coverage of the 50th anniversary of the end of the Second World War, preceding the saturated commemorative culture of 2005 mentioned above. For example, in 1995 television news and documentary employed a plethora of oral histories from former Western POW's, to mark the 50th anniversary of the surrender of Japan at the conclusion of the war. On 12 August 1995, CNN International broadcast interviews with Morris Janis, a 'Former British WWII POW', prompted by the news anchor to recall his experience at the hands of his Japanese captors from 50 years earlier. The cov-erage included black-and-white film footage as an authenticating backdrop to accounts of images of Japanese POW camps. And recorded text in the form of archive film of the Second World War was proportionally twice the size of the frame of Janis recollecting (live) his experiences, thus positioning the archival version of memory as somehow larger than life. This was presented as a three-frame split television screen enabling the portrayal of archival footage alongside its audiovisual historical recollection in real time. This is matched simultane-ously in the larger CNN frame showing a video history – like a portrait of the occasion of this anniversary (with a patterning on the background of the CNN frame verging on the ornate) or a commemorative postcard.

This example, although perhaps unremarkable in terms of the complex new media ecology of today, is indicative of the development of global televisuality (introduced in chapter 1, after Caldwell, 1995) notably of the multidimensionality of the medium even prior to the advance of digital technologies. The full televisual frame constituted a new electronified mix, as a record of commemoration, available then to be used itself in other TV frames, stories and events. Television routinely combines individual memory and official public document in this way, always in 'new' instantaneous packages. But, this simultaneity of past and present past is doubly authenticating, in terms of the use of black-and-white film 'documentary' footage, and what historians still hold up today as a primary mode of history – oral testimony.

The latter became a routine but central element of mediatized commemoration, along with film footage. Television often combines these modes of historicization, bringing together visual and verbal accounts in a new frame. The medium routinely combines individual memory and official public document in this way in a new instantaneous package, at the same time imposing its own authority as storyteller and documenter of history in its own right. White and Schwoch (1999), for example, argue:

> [T]elevision's ideas of history are intimately bound up with the history of the medium itself (and indirectly with other audiovisual recording media), and with its abilities to record, circulate, and preserve images. In other words, the medium's representations of the past are highly dependent on events that have been recorded on film or video, such that history assumes the form of television's self-reflection.

Television's siege of late twentieth-century conflict is, then, partly attributable to the advances in audiovisual recording technology of this period which facilitated revision and repetition of conflict on the medium. It was the fusion of human and media memory that seemed to produce the ultimate history-in-the-present, with television taking on the mass recording, dissemination and, ultimately, preservation of oral testimony. These trends also impacted upon the representational strategies of the cultural memory of warfare and perhaps a greater hybridization of approaches in museums and exhibitions, for example. The popularizing mode of cultural memory of the screen is evident in its move from outside the domestic space of the home and its encroachment into public spaces. For example, the growth in the use of fixed television-style monitors in museums and other settings is part of the growth of what Anna McCarthy (2001) has called 'ambient television'.

3. Media and Holocaust Memory

According to Michele Henning (2006: 71), 'museums have become increasingly mediatic'. In the 'permanent' Holocaust Exhibition at the Imperial War Museum (IWM) in London, for example, there are numerous monitors showing personal testimonies to camera by Holocaust survivors. However, exhibition visitors often seem unsure as to when to stop viewing a piece of archive footage or an account by a survivor, as they simply do not know when it will end, or even when it began. The temporality of the moving image ensures that television's relationship with the past is problematic; television is 'always on' – even in the video loops in the Holocaust Exhibition (Hoskins, 2003). Again, in such representations, the distinction between the photograph (as an artefact), other artefacts and moving images looms large. The second memory boom saw a fundamental tension in the advance of the televisual in popular culture (apart from when it is treated both as historical object and subject) and its apparent antithesis in terms of a desire (perhaps driven precisely by the audiovisual saturation of the first phase of mediatization) for preserving, observing and being proximate to the materiality of the past, and the associated aura of 'original' objects of memory. Andreas Huyssen for example sees the ultimate triumph of the museum in this respect:

> The museum fetish itself transcends exchange value. It seems to carry with it something like an anamnestic dimension, a kind of memory value. The more mummified an object is, the more intense its ability to yield experience, a sense of the authentic. No matter how fragile or dim the relation between museum object and the reality it documents may be, either in the way it is exhibited or in the mind of the spectator, as object it carries a register of reality which even the live television broadcast cannot match. (1995: 33)

If the dominance of television has raised the expectations for the audiovisual in mediations of the past, it has also fed a desire to develop a counter-memory culture that resists associations with the ephemera and relatively low cultural status of television.

Indeed, the relentless advance of television in the cultural industry is part of a significant debate of the second memory boom. One of the central critiques made of television in this regard is that its inherent temporality, ephemerality, fleetingness, in addition to its association with the lowest form of popular culture, make it appear as a medium of forgetting as much as of remembering. However, as we have argued, what and how we remember the nodal events of the twentieth and twenty-first centuries are bound up in the technologies and media of their first mediation. By extension, a memory culture is thus also shaped through the ongoing technological developments that afford different modes of representation and mediation. This is particularly the case with the second memory boom in respect of television and the Holocaust. For example, Jeffrey Shandler argues:

> Holocaust television serves as an exemplary case study of the relation between historical event and memory culture it generates. Other forms of Holocaust representation – histories, novels, memoirs, documentary or feature films, paintings, dramas – already had established aesthetic boundaries, protocols, and conventions by World War II. But when television first dealt with the Holocaust, the medium was itself new. Thus, television and Holocaust memory culture have, in some ways, a shared history. (1999: xvii)

Yet, as Saul Friedländer argues of the Holocaust in *Probing the Limits of Representation*, 'we are dealing with an event which tests our traditional conceptual and representational categories, an "event at the limits"' (1992: 2–3). It is unsurprising, therefore, that the modes of representation most associated with television should be seen as both inadequate and inappropriate at a number of levels where history, memory and the cultural industries have an uneasy set of relations, with the latter even feeding a cultish 'Holocaust Industry' according to Norman Finkelstein (2000).

More evidently, the deployment of the Holocaust and other twentieth-century (and more recent) historical markers as tropes (and as we demonstrated in the previous chapter – media templates) for interpreting other events has reached saturation point. It is difficult to overestimate the impact of Holocaust discourses as a thematic for wider analysis and comprehension of social and cultural memory. As pivotal to the second memory boom, the popularizing of the Holocaust through its national and international mediations, however, presents a certain set of dilemmas in terms of the nature of modern mediatized public ceremonies and actual responses. For example, the eminent historian David Cesarani (2005), who serves on the UK Holocaust Memorial national ceremony steering group, writes of some of the 'incongruous aspects of the memorial events' but nonetheless concludes: 'Despite the patriotic kitsch and the platitudes, the essential message resounded clearly.' So, Holocaust memory been perpetuated through an intensely and extensively mediatized environment with a concomitant sense of a loss of the 'appropriateness' of some of these public articulations. In contrast then, over this period, it is the museum that is seen as a memory site where more control could be exercised.

It is against this background that the permanent Holocaust Exhibition at the IWM was opened in 2000. Its advisory group (including Cesarani) sought to establish more of a singular, fixed and 'purist' narrative, deliberately contrasting itself with Holocaust museums elsewhere in the world that had perhaps embraced a wider set of technologies and post-Holocaust representations and discourses in their curatorial scope. This visualizing of the Holocaust is geared to notions of what might be termed 'old memory' – of an event declared unique and incomparable and appropriate to representation through a relatively fixed, rather than fluid, narrative, whereas events (other genocides) witnessed in an era where television was an increasingly pervasive and dominant medium of history are more easily negotiable, as pasts that are subject to the relatively ephemeral vision and revisions of the electronic media (cf. Hoskins on 'new memory', 2001, 2004b). The exhibition's advisory group sought out authentic objects of and from the Holocaust to provide more 'real' signs of this event. Suzanne Bardgett (2000), the project director, suggests how the narrative of events was constructed from the objects they were seeking to assemble: 'We asked ourselves what our top eight artefacts would be, or how we would tell our story if we had to choose just eight photographs.' However, the exhibition reveals the tensions between the purist curatorial and design aims, 'which relied on authentic material to stimulate the visitor's imagination and curiosity' (ibid.), and the actually highly mediatized experience of the audiovisual which resonates throughout the museum. In other words, there are few spaces which are not intruded into by the audio and the audiovisual, which effectively serve to afford a mediatized simultaneity of experience. The fact that there are more than 30 televisual monitors and screens in the exhibition is indicative of the influence of the expectations of an audiovisual audience on Holocaust memorial culture. Moreover, the intersections between media in the second memory boom and Holocaust memory is a key focus for debates over the tension between, but also the blurring of the distinction between, 'popular' and 'professional' history (cf. Edgerton, 2001: 1).

In addition to the growing scarcity of living memory – of testimony and witness to the nodal and catastrophic events of the twentieth century – and the mediatization of this memory, the second memory boom is also marked by a seemingly growing desire on the part of the next generation to attempt to emotionally engage with these events – including and perhaps especially the Holocaust – of which they do not have a living memory. There are two key debates or positions around the idea of 'postmemory' for instance. The first is exemplified by the work of Marianne Hirsch, who writes: 'Postmemory describes the relationship of the second generation to powerful, often traumatic, experiences that preceded their births but that were nevertheless transmitted to them so deeply as to seem to constitute memories in their own right' (2008: 103). She goes on to state: 'Postmemory is not identical to memory: it is "post," but at the same time, it approximates memory in its affective force' (ibid.: 109). The second is a more pessimistic account of the prospects of 'postmemory' in terms of 'the unspoken desire of many people who have no direct experience of the Holocaust but are deeply interested in studying, remembering, and memorializing it (Weissman, 2004: 4). Weissman claims that these can only amount to 'fantasies of witnessing' (also the title of his book) which 'express a desire for the Holocaust to feel *more real* than it does in American culture' (ibid.). This is the actualizing of fantasies in an attempt to 'gain access' and 'remember' the Holocaust as a personal experience that eludes us, according to Weissman. What is interesting in relation to the limited scope of our account is that media of different kinds are influential in both perspectives, notably photography in Hirsch's influential *Family Frames* (1997) and video and film in Weissman's (2004) work. These are also implicated in different phases of response.

In terms of scholarly treatments of the Holocaust, Weissman highlights Langer's work and his identifying of a 'second stage of Holocaust response': 'The first stage appears to have been dominated by historians and their project of determining, through archival research, our historical knowledge of the event, while the second stage means moving from 'what we know' to "how we remember it"' (ibid.: 103–4). In other words, the latter stage extends beyond the limits of Holocaust knowledge, and involves 'to "remember" the Holocaust not as a distinct historic event, but as an immediate, personal experience' (ibid.: 107). There is a growing body of work to support this claim. Alison Landsberg for example, identifies what she calls 'prosthetic memory' which is produced 'at the interface between a person and a historical narrative about the past, at an experiential site such as a movie theatre or museum' (2004: 2). She claims that the individual does not merely engage with historical knowledge, 'but takes on a more personal, deeply felt memory of a past event through which he or she did not live' (ibid.). Landsberg's concept of prosthetic memory is liberating in its apparent transgression of the exclusivity that is carried by generational or living memory (and with historical knowledge, for that matter) in enabling new experiential connections with the past. It suggests a reflexivity about the unavoidable mediality of our experience of relating to the past.

These mediations of the Holocaust and other nodal events of the mid- to late twentieth century, including their use in debates about the possibilities and impossibilities of representing and remembering, all share the common context of the first phase of mediatization. The very prospects for remembering are transformed in the shift to the second phase of mediatization (as introduced in chapter 1), when mediation is the default condition and experience of late modern society. A corollary of this in terms of the relationship between media and memory is that *whereas, before, forgetting was the norm, remembering becomes the default condition.* Thus, it is our newly mobile recording culture – in which anybody and everybody routinely records events, personal and public, trivial and momentous – that feeds a new spectrum of diffused memory.

4. From Witness to Embodied Memories

Contrasting starkly with the Holocaust Exhibition at the IWM is the exhibition which opened in December 2002 on the floor above, the Crimes Against Humanity Exhibition (CAHE). This does not contain a single artefact or museal object. Instead, it provides a narrative of (other) twentieth- and more recent twenty-first-century genocides entirely through the use of a 30-minute documentary projection onto a large screen, and six touch screen consoles which provide access to a database. The exhibition is housed in a bright atrium of mostly white surfaces at the very top of the IWM. If, as we state above, the IWM's visualizing of the Holocaust is geared to notions of 'old memory' – of an event unique, incomparable and appropriate to representation through a relatively fixed narrative, then the CAHE is closer to 'new memory'. The latter's emphasis on ethnic conflict and genocide (including East Timor, Bosnia and Rwanda), originally mediated when television was a pervasive and dominant medium of history, thus seems more easily 'negotiable' than pasts subject to the relatively ephemeral vision and revisions of the electronic media. Again, as we argued in the previous chapter, this is in relation to their often posthumous acknowledgement and public and political (and sometimes legal) naming as genocide.

The CAHE documentary's narration is indicative of the growing influence and commodification of the testimony of media correspondents and other newsworkers as key to the 'new witnessing' of modern conflicts. The story of Nick Hughes's footage of the 'unnoticed' beginning of the 1994 Rwandan genocide and the subsequent work by the journalist/academic Allan Thompson (2007), referred to in the previous chapter, is part of this trend. And part of the CAHE documentary film is provided by frontline broadcast journalists Fergal Keane and Martin Bell. The growing portability of digital recording and broadcast equipment has enabled more immediate access and greater proximity to events by professionals and amateurs alike, all feeding shifting cultures of news and cultures of memory. This facilitates the mediatized record, reflexively shaping any later oral/audiovisual individual memory (see Thompson, 2009, on the Rwandan genocide). In this way there are multiple fusions of individual, group and mediated memory.

It is not just that those who have been bystanders to, or part of, historic events possess a certain authority to narrate an account of those events. The frequent fusion of personal testimony and audiovisual media also extends significantly to those who are the producers of that media. For instance, war correspondents inscribe their own remembering with similar degrees of authority to those who actually fought in or who were the victims of war, for they carry both the personal memory relationship to the event and the wider public/historical relationship as mediated to their audiences.

To mark the 30th anniversary of the fall of Saigon, Michael Nicholson produced a two-part radio programme, *Vietnam Notebook*, which was billed as a 'personal history' of the Vietnam War. At its conclusion Nicholson describes his own and his colleagues' relationship to their memory of Vietnam today:

> Should we be ashamed to admit that we remember it with – how shall I say – a certain fondness, but we do. Well you've been listening to us, didn't it show? I suppose we might, each in turn, in response to a critic's harsh words, try to excuse ourselves by offering this or that explanation of why. But you know, I don't think we would try very hard. To be honest, we were there, and we couldn't give a damn. (*Vietnam Notebook*, broadcast 3 May 2005, BBC Radio 2)

The journalist is a powerful narrator of personal and public, autobiographical and historical memory, as fused through the media in new times. The extract of Nicholson's narration includes his reflexive comment on the value and the validity of his nostalgia-tinged recollection of his experience as a reporter during the Vietnam War. Some may see it as inappropriate, overbearing and even arrogant. This war, like a number of contemporary conflicts, became partly synonymous with the journalists and the media that reported it. Much has been written, and rewritten, on the reflexive relationship between public and political support for the US involvement in Vietnam and its television news coverage at home (as we indicated in chapters 2 and 4). However, it is the subsequent documentaries, journals and memoirs, which constitute a significant discursive remembering, that are often addressed as a 'body of memory'. This tends to include a further fusing of personal autobiographical memory – that of war veterans themselves.

For instance, the BBC documentary *The Last Tommy* (2005) mapped the personal accounts and stories spoken to camera by the last few surviving British veterans of the First World War with film clips and photographic stills from the time. The series claimed some urgency given the state of health of the remaining handful of British veterans of the Great War, some of whom died before the programmes came to air over their two-year production period. One of them – Harry Patch – became a minor celebrity in the later years of his life, actively contributing and embodying memorializing of the First World War in the UK right up until his death in 2009. This programme also reveals a trend in the commissioning of documentaries of 'high recognition' past events containing powerful 'experiential' narratives. It is this form of narrative, then, that has particular value in modern memory, rather than accounts that are necessarily more easily verifiable and technically more 'accurate'.

Moreover, the diminishment of living memory of the Great War, as those who survived particularly catastrophic events or who were witness to them, inevitably continue to reduce in number, their bodily presence, their testimony – their memories – are afforded greater significance. Today, our memorial culture appears increasingly embedded in a shift towards both an embodied and an archival memory. The memory boom is also inflected in the representations, mediations and experiences of present events – they too are afforded memorial status, even though – as with the war on terror – they are ongoing and unfinished. It is in this way, and with the tensions and transitions between embodied and archival memory, that individual and public obligations to remember are negotiated or mitigated.

The idea that an individual, group or society *must* remember, or rather must not forget, is entwined with an ethics of the time. As Paul Connerton argues, the many usages of forgetting 'have one feature in common: they imply an obligation on my part to remember something and a failure to discharge that obligation' (2008: 59). These perceived moral *obligations* to remember something from the past are now frequently and easily employed in and conflated with the present, to powerfully obfuscate present actions – in this case in the war on terror – that offer the prospect of a haunting future memory. In other words, a marker of what we are calling an emergent *third* memory boom is a more acute and immediate concern for how present events may come to be memorialized and remembered in the future.

Yet, the *living* memory of warfare is also seen (and not seen) embodied in victims and in veterans themselves. So, Jay Winter, for example, defines 'embodied memory' as something that is shared by and in 'the body of the sufferer and in the gaze of the onlooker' (2006: 55). Winter writes of the shell-shocked bodies of veterans which not only bore the traces of combat but which also possessed 'internalized' memories; 'it is *written on* the men who fought – as though inscribed in them in a way which is not available to their direct or premeditated control' (ibid.)

For Winter, images and memories seem to live both embedded in these soldiers and yet also curiously detached from them: memory itself, or images of catastrophic events, appear to be free-floating powerful agents that somehow control the movements of the shell-shocked survivors. Bodies from this perspective seem to remember something – they have the past inscribed upon and within them. In Winter's examples of those suffering from shell shock, bodies engage in a kind of unwitting re-enactment which he claimed tended to defy both verbal expression and the urge to forget. This is another key way, then, in which we can distinguish between a generational memory, which is embodied in the rememberers of events, and the memory that exists beyond this, which is often seen as secondary and more dependent upon external mechanisms of memory, such as archives, monuments and media.

How society and media treats, accepts and denies the injured, wounded and shell-shocked bodies of conflicts, on all sides, is crucially part of a process of the discursive legitimizing of engaging in armed conflict – a consciousness and memory of warfare – that extends way beyond the temporalities of its beginning and end. This includes the rationalizing of the destruction of human life, which essentially also includes forgetting as well as remembrance. Elaine Scarry, for instance, writes on the 'structure of warfare', which, she argues, 'requires both the reciprocal infliction of massive injury and the eventual disowning of the injury so that its attributes can be attributed elsewhere, as they cannot if they are permitted to cling to the original site of the wound, the human body, (1985: 64).

The 'disowning' of injury or the way that it disappears from view, according to Scarry, is achieved in two ways: first, and simply, by means of 'omission', and, second, by way of an 'active redescription of the event: the act of injuring, or the tissue that is to be injured, or the weapon that is to accomplish the injury is renamed' (ibid.: 66). And this is very much the vicarious experience of much of the Western audiences of wars claiming to be fought in their name in modern times. A fundamental disowning of injury at the time was achieved and a crystallizing of memory around a belief in precision strikes and 'limited' warfare was evident in the first phase of mediatizaion. The totality of media coverage, for example, as we explored in chapter 4, did not evoke images of 'the original site of the wound, the human body' (ibid.)

Yet, the wars fought in the aftermath of 9/11, in Afghanistan and Iraq, are mediatized at this turn in generational memory of the nodal events of the twentieth century. Jan Assman (1995: 128–9) contrasts the dynamics of 'communicative' or 'everyday memory' with the fixity of 'cultural memory', the latter usually spanning a generation. What is significant about diffused war is that it involves a more pronounced struggle over memory, part of a third memory boom. Compared with the world wars, for example, more recent conflicts have a long tail of co-present witnesses, citizen survivors and veterans in their extensive mass of embodied memory, which is sometimes much more easily and immediately translatable into public discourses.

The digital ontology of memory must be accounted for. For instance, what happens when material posted online – such as soldiers' self-made videos and blogs – becomes the material of a dead person? John Durham Peters writes: 'Our bodies know fatigue and finitude, but our effigies, once recorded, can circulate through media systems indefinitely, across wastes of space and time' (2000: 140). The words, images and voices of those not just distant but departed can reach us. A certain percentage of soldiers' emails or blogs (milblogs) will be written by individuals who, by the time you read their words, are dead. Their presence endures. A YouTube video posted by a soldier who has died since the posting seems to be in limbo, his voice and appearance suspended in time. You can see and hear him. You can even appropriate the content, mash up the video into something new, 'steal' the soldier's apparition, reinvigorating him as you see fit. How do we deal with the ethical problems this creates? Who is to decide how such material is used? Can anybody know how the original personality of the soldier intended his communications to be used? A number of accumulating ethical and legal issues are generated by this long tail of digital archiving.

The war on terror and other conflicts of our age are also reconfiguring popular and medical notions of memory, or embodied memory, in other ways. The prolonged production of injured and wounded (rather than many more dead) Western and other veterans over the course of the wars in Iraq and Afghanistan has been partly facilitated by advances in modern medical science. Shattered bodies and minds that would have expired if subjected to the same injuries only 15 years earlier are now rejoined, prosthetized and rehabilitated. Although this does not compare with the numbers of civilian victims on all sides of the war on terror, it constitutes a mass of embodied memory in the West that enters into living or communicative narratives, that has recently become much more prominent in media assessments and reflections upon the cost of the some of the post-9/11 Western military interventions.

5. The Third Memory Boom

The memorializing of those who have perished in ongoing and recent warfare marks the third memory boom. The key difference between the second and the third boom is that the second was founded upon a certain forgetting – or at least an absence of remembering – involving, as Winter (above) argues, 'the balance of creation, adaptation, and circulation' of memory (2006: 26). In contrast, the third is characterized by the immediate, perhaps even hasty, marking and memorializing included as part of the politics of memory of the twenty-first century, notably in the legitimizing or deligitimizing of ongoing warfare and those with a 'long tail' (as with Iraq). This is afforded principally by the connectivity of digital media and one can argue that the memorializing of warfare, as with war itself, has become diffused in its digital archival form. Furthermore, this kind of memorializing and commemorating is also linked to offline exhibitions and events and not just contained in/by the digital archive. For example, the academic artist Joseph DeLappe directs the Iraqimemorial.org project, which seeks to commemorate civilian deaths since the beginning of the Iraq War in March 2003. Its stated aims include to:

- honor and commemorate the deaths of thousands of civilians killed since the commencement of 'Operation Iraqi Freedom' on March 19, 2003;
- establish an Internet archive as a living memorial that will serve as a repository of memorial concepts;
- mobilize an international community of artists to contribute proposals that will represent a collective expression of memory, unity and peace;
- encourage the vigilance of contemporary memory in a time of war; to stimulate an understanding of the consequences and costs of 'the war on terror';
- support the moral imperative of recognizing the deaths of Iraqi civilians;
- create a context for the initiation of a process of symbolic, creative atonement. (www.iraqimemorial.org/mission.html)

The project is conceived as 'open and ongoing' and is thus indicative of the potential continuousness of digital memorial sites, archives and databases. It is the future-oriented perspective of digital memorials, the setting out of the possibilities of future memory of present and recent-past warfare and other catastrophes, that also signals a shift to what we call a third memory boom. Furthermore, as the second aim on the list above suggests, this project goes beyond the traditional parameters and functions of a memorial in that it seeks to probe and extend the very concept and its practices. This project includes a call for 'proposal concepts' to memorialize civilian casualties in the Iraq War, with more than 150 artists' works listed under the 'Exhibition of Memorial Concepts', which includes diagrams, plans for galleries, photographs, videos and mixed-media exhibits. In addition to invited 'internationally based curators and scholars', members of the public are also encouraged to view and rate entries on the site. There is a particular diffusion of those involved in this site as a node of memorial practice in the selection of a 'top ten' from each year's entries on a rolling basis.

The immediacy and also the hypothetical character of memorial culture in the third memory boom is also illustrated offline by the 'Memorial to the Iraq War' Exhibition which ran at London's Institute for Contemporary Arts (ICA) from 23 May to 27 June 2007. Even though the war was still ongoing, 26 invited artists from Europe, America and the Middle East were asked to 'imagine' what a memorial to it might or should be. Some of these were realized through installations or performances in the ICA's exhibition space, whereas others were published as text and images in the newspaper-style publication which accompanied the exhibition.

Part of the rationale for the exhibition was a response to a sense of frustration and exhaustion at the relatively meaningless television news images of the Iraq War and its aftermath. In one of the text pieces of this exhibition, Tony Chakar (2007) writes of television news reports: '[T]hey tend to obscure knowledge instead of providing it by focusing only on the spectacular. In fact, the only way for a person to make sense of all these television image-based reports is to actually turn away from them, to watch them with eyes wide shut'. In this way, some of the exhibits aim to challenge television news' reduction of narratives to simplistic sets of readily-assembled images through standard editorial conventions, and the diminishing of any potential for conceiving alternative explanations and outcomes. Moreover, in terms of the traditional memorializing of the first two memory booms, and particularly in respect of the permanent memorial object, once constructed news reports actually foreclose the memory of the event they mark, and it is no longer deemed necessary to remember something whose memory work appears to have ended in something material, solid, visible and permanent.

This is relevant to our analysis (especially in chapter 2) of the potential for still images or photographs to take on a monumental form and function as they fix (and fixate) and leach out meaning from an event through their often instant and mass-mediated repetition, circulation and overexposure. For example, the installation by Roman Ondák entitled 'Snapshots from Baghdad, 2007' explores the phenomenon that we have defined as 'emergence'. This exhibit consists of a single-use (disposable) camera containing an undeveloped film of shots from present-day Baghdad, mounted in a glass case on a plinth. The unexposed images trapped inside the unbroken camera permit an imaginable, unimaginable future, in relation to both what the photographs may contain and their impact, and the contingency of the indeterminable moment of their exposure. It is not even made known whether Ondák had recently visited Baghdad and taken the photographs himself or whether he had obtained this camera and its unexposed contents from someone else. In this way the intact camera challenges our highly mediated imagination of the 2007 aftermath of war in Baghdad, instead placing it as contingent upon the moment and context – the emergence – of the exposure and mediation of the unseen images.

The third memory boom thus intersects with the contingency of diffused war and involves shifts in the conceptualization of memorialization and commemoration, but also of memory itself. The second memory boom involved a relative convergence of the social and cultural memory of the nodal events of the last century. But the emergent and third boom in memory is characterized by its diffused nature. So, as Ann Rigney writes, 'the more time has elapsed between events and those who recall them, the greater the degree of mediation in the transfer of memories and . . . the greater the degree of convergence between them' (2004: 367). Perhaps then the divergence and diffusion of memories in this third wave will later converge and become more like the second memory boom. Yet Rigney herself argues for the need for memory studies to leave behind the unsatisfactory but common formulation, which she calls a 'plenitude-loss-restoration model of memory' (2005: 25). This is the assumption that memory is something that was once complete in the past and which frustrates attempts to fully recall it as it inevitably diminishes over time, and so preservation is employed as a strategy to somehow prevent its fading from memory. Instead, Rigney advocates a 'thoroughly cultural view of memory', which she sees as particularly applicable to 'artistic media': 'By virtue of their aesthetic and fictional properties they are more "mobile" and "exportable" than other forms of representation, whether in translation or the original, and certainly more mobile than actual memory sites' (ibid.) As Mark Sladen (ICA Director of Exhibitions), commenting on the 'Memorial to the Iraq War' Exhibition, concedes, some of the most effective exhibits 'have an absurd or impossible character', and all of the works 'are in one way or another paper monuments, and it is their hypothetical and provocative character which makes them relevant to the current moment' (2007). Thus, the multiple texts, performances and exhibits that constitute the memorial inhabit a kind of node, posing a cluster of 'connections' and 'transfers' – in Rigney's (2005: 25) terms – and mediations of memory between and beyond communities, times and places.

So, the ICA exhibition memorializes a present past, and projects this into an imagined future, not one perhaps expected by some curators, visitors and historians, nor one that affords an appropriately distant perspective of the past and that seeks order and completion, but instead a future in which the same complexities and chaos are acknowledged as constitutive of 'memory'.

In sum, we have argued that memory appears to be more diffused with its mediations in this third memory boom. The purchase of the memory of warfare, especially of those of fixed duration and of unambiguous conclusion (Paul Gilroy even identifies a 'postcolonial melancholia' (2006: 27) in this respect), has increased with the second memory boom. That these have become even more significant against the backdrop of the seemingly perpetual and horizon-less diffused wars that mark the opening of the twenty-first century may also be the case. Yet, recent conflicts and warfare are at once already networked, in their initial mediation and as plugged into a memorial culture. And it is this memorial culture – constructed and contested more immediately and more continuously through its digital diffusion – that is part of the third boom in memory. This is not to say that the second boom of memory is finished, but it itself is challenged by the third. Whether and to what extent the opposite eventually occurs, that even the social and cultural memory of the first decade of this century and beyond will converge and become more like the second memory boom, remains to be seen.

7

VECTORS

Writing in the aftermath of the 1991 Gulf War in which CNN enabled global round-the-clock coverage of a war for the first time, Mackenzie Wark borrowed the term 'vector' from social theorist Paul Virilio (1986) to describe the shape of communications enabled by satellite broadcasting:

> It is a term from geometry meaning a line of fixed length and direction but having no fixed position. Virilio employs it to mean any trajectory along which bodies, information, or warheads can potentially pass. The satellite technology used to beam images from Iraq to America and on to London can be thought of as a vector. This technology could link almost any three such sites. . . . It could just as easily link Beijing to Berlin and Sydney, or quite a few other combinations of points.
>
> This is the paradox of the media vector. The technical properties are hard and fast and fixed, but it can connect enormously vast and vaguely defined spaces together and move images, and sounds, words, and furies, between them. (Wark, 1994: 11–12)

In the early 1990s, news was transmitted by journalists in Iraq via satellite to CNN's studio in Atlanta; the live news broadcast was then relayed via satellite to other broadcasters, such as the BBC in London; and indeed to viewers anywhere in the world where CNN's coverage was available. As Wark notes, such a pattern of communication – such vectors – could be generated from any point on Earth where the technology was available. Thirty years after Marshall McLuhan wrote of a 'global village', finally a live visioning of the globe was possible: 'Its tendency to become an abstract geometric space across which powerful vectors can play freely' (ibid.: 13). Today, thanks to Global Positioning System (GPS) and mobile technologies, we can create our own vectors; indeed, we need them in our everyday lives. Citizens plot and coordinate their movements in relation to their friends, family and work colleagues. And as the field of vision of war becomes increasingly expanded through digitization and surveillance on and above the battlefield, all movements can be tracked.

The first axis of diffuse war concerns the potential for more chaotic patterns of vectors and greater connectivity, bringing us into unforeseen relations to distant others, as witnesses, spectators, citizens and, possibly, soldiers. However, as we go on to explore how this affects long-term public diplomacy and short-term responses to the sudden emergence of new images from a war or conflict, we see how these vectors have the potential to disrupt or reinforce the control and continuity of framing or discourse around a war or conflict that actors might seek. This chapter demonstrates how the three axes of diffused war interconnect.

Wark spoke of 'furies', and vectors are both a cause and effect of asymmetry – the notion that an actor with preponderate military power or kinetic force can be undermined or defeated by a weaker actor, such as a terrorist group – and the hypersecurity introduced in chapter 2. If communication could be limited to those with the economic and political power to sustain media institutions that broadcast regulated content in a linear, predictable and orderly manner to audiences, then asymmetry would be difficult. However, the chaotic nature of vectors and the speed of connectivity in our new media ecology means terrorists and those with minimal kinetic resources are able to gain publicity for their actions and to contest the claims and legitimacy of major powers.

Wark suggests a paradox whereby the properties of a vector are fixed, but the shape it forms is fluid and malleable. A second paradox when thinking about the new media ecology is that the sum of all lines of communication add up to a vector – a space or shape which could be plotted on geometric axes – and as such is *topographic*; yet this geometric space creates *topological* experiences; that is, it disrupts notions of distance and proximity by bringing geographically distant phenomena into our presence (Rosenau, 2003; Tomlinson, 2008). Distant events can seem 'close to home'; we can be 'touched' by suffering that is geographically remote (see chapter 3). NGOs or Al-Qaeda, for instance, try to assemble publics in topological ways: 'It does not matter where you are, support us.' People can be brought together in unpredictable ways to act in concert from dispersed topographic locations. And what counts as 'local' is no longer given, for, as Gitelman writes, 'global media help to create a world in which people are not local only because of where they are or are from but also because of their relationships to media representations of localism and its fate' (2006: 17).

Take what it means to *go to war* now that remote military robots and aerial drones are part of warfare. Peter Singer suggests:

[F]or the whole concept of the individual 'going to war', whether we were talking about ancient Greeks going to war against Troy or my grandfather going to war in the Pacific in World War II, that phrase 'to go to war' meant the same thing. It meant to go to a place where there was such danger that you might never see your family again. . . . For the Predator Drone pilots, to go to war is literally: they wake up in the morning, they commute into work, they sit behind a computer, and, as one of them put it, 'you put missiles on targets'. And at the end of the day you go home, and 20 minutes after you were at war, you're talking to your kids about their homework at the dinner table. (Cited on BBC World Service, 2009)

Does it make sense to think of going to a situation one is connected to electronically, and what are the practical and ethical consequences of such changes?

This chapter explores the vectors triggered by and through war and media. Even since Wark wrote in the 1990s, the nature of vectors have transformed in crucial respects. First, many vectors are less linear, less of a *flow* from one point to another and more of a scattered *flux* whereby individuals at many points (not so much three points as three million) send content back and forth, acting and reacting to one another and creating unforeseen patterns and feedback loops. This is made possible not only by the proliferation of technology but also by its convergence, since digital information can be recorded, stored and transferred across media (Hanson, 2008: 2). Second, the content of these vectors is not a fixed message that is relayed, but is rather something fluid and formed or constituted through these millions of communications. Messages change through processes of translation, interpretation and re-use.

We proceed in three parts. First, we situate vectors of war and media within the broader conditions of globalization and the manner in which there is increasing 'structural global vulnerability' in economic, cultural and political processes which add to the uncertainties and dynamics of military processes.[1] In these conditions, the basic units central to war and media appear to be in a state of transformation. We examine how nation-states, borders and publics are becoming diffuse. In the next section, we look at how government and military actors try to control communication vectors in these conditions through the use of media in public diplomacy strategies. Finally, we introduce four case studies in which 'chaotic' vectors have emerged in ways beyond anybody's control. These are the open letter posted on the Internet by Iran's President Ahmedinejad to US President Bush in 2006; a clip recorded by MSNBC-embedded journalist Kevin Sites of US marines shooting an apparently unarmed man in Fallujah in 2004; images of the US journalist Daniel Pearl being executed in 2002, in which his body became the site of claims and counter-claims by actors in Pakistan, the US and further afield, while other beheadings and bodies went unremarked upon; and, finally, we look at the treatment by British media of 'radicalization' apparently triggered by the Israeli attacks on Gaza in December 2008 and January 2009.

1. Vectors and Globalization

The diffusion of states, borders and publics

The things traditionally fought for in war are diffusing. Nation-states' borders, as well as their internal composition (social, economic, political), are becoming diffuse, spread out, no longer distinct and fixed or stable. 'The people' in whose names war is fought can less easily be counted on. In Britain, for instance, a 'military covenant' exists as an unofficial bond between the society and its military: 'Soldiers will be called upon to make personal sacrifices – including the ultimate sacrifice – in the service of the Nation' (www.bbc.co.uk/ethics/war/overview/covenant.shtml). But the things constituting a nation, such as its people and its borders, are diffusing. Hence our understanding of war must be connected to the broader conditions of globalization: '*a process (or set of processes) which embodies a transformation in the spatial organization of social relations and transactions – assessed in terms of their extensity, intensity, velocity and impact – generating transcontinental or inter-regional flows and networks of activity*' (Held et al., 1999: 16; emphasis in original)

Globalization is not a mere hypothesis. Each of these measures – extensity, intensity and velocity – can be measured, qualitatively and quantitatively (though assessing impact is problematic: see the second section of this chapter and also chapter 10). In the context of war and media, the extensity of social relations is evident from the number and importance of live connections made between war zones and distant audiences. The intensity is evident by the regularity of such connections – they are not sporadic but regularized, steady streams. New media technologies can increase the velocity or speed of exchanges. And the impact of this interconnectedness is evident from events such as 9/11 or the Abu Ghraib photos, whereby particularly communities are affected and mobilized, leading to war and insurgency in these respective cases.

It is not that we necessarily had an age of nation-states *then* a new media ecology. Relatively new and peripheral states had no choice but to adopt the already established grammar of nationhood – including national anthems, national sports teams and national broadcasting systems – in exchange for visibility on the world stage. Yet, dressing up as a nation-state for outsiders tells us little about the exact ways in which the grammar of nationhood was implemented within a particular state and its media system. Once we turn to multinational states, communist federations or ethnically mixed areas and border regions, it quickly becomes clear that concepts such as 'nation-state' or 'national public sphere' do not have universal applicability.

Yet where coherent nation-states do exist, global issues create external pressures on the state. Processes become more complex and interconnected, resulting in more diffuse relations of cause and effect, making decision-making and the exercise of power to impose solutions on often transnational problems more difficult. Let us examine three examples: global warming, poverty and nuclear proliferation. The management of global warming is potentially the biggest problem we face, since it can disrupt our biosystem which, in turn, will disrupt our social and economic systems. We see conflicts over energy now, conflicts over water likely to become more frequent and the possibility of rising sea levels bringing mass migration as certain cities and regions disappear. There is no agreed international framework even for how we talk about it, never mind reach solutions. Similarly, on the matter of poverty, there has been little progress towards the Millennium Development Goals, agreed by the UN in 2000 (to eradicate extreme hunger and poverty, provide universal primary education, empower women and achieve gender equality, improve health, combat AIDS/ HIV, ensure environmental sustainability, and reach a partnership for development). Targets for these goals were agreed on, but so little progress has been made that the dispiriting effect of failed efforts may outweigh the benefits achieved. Finally, if we look at nuclear proliferation, more and more countries are developing nuclear capabilities. New nuclear and dirty weapons are being developed. The questions of accountability, regulation and enforcement of laws regarding nuclear and other weapons are completely open.

These three problems – global warming, poverty and nuclear proliferation – map onto basic puzzles concerning how we can survive on earth. Global warming – how can we sustain and share our planet (nature)? Poverty – how can we sustain and share our humanity (culture)? Nuclear – how can we sustain and share some rules and laws (order)? Nature, culture and order are like three legs of a stool: if one collapses, they all do. David Held labels this condition 'structural global vulnerability': 'The paradox of our times can be stated simply: the collective issues we must grapple with are of growing extensity and intensity and, yet, the means for addressing these are weak and incomplete' (2006: 157). The second axis of diffused war, unsettled relations of cause and effect, leads to the third, uncertain decision-making and less precision in the exercise of power to create intended effects. These axes appear to characterize humanity's relation to global problems beyond war alone. Indeed, Bauman argues that these pressures or forces have become detached from politics and control:

> Having leaked from a society forcefully laid open by the pressures of globalizing forces, power and politics drift ever further in opposition directions. The problem, and the awesome task that will in all probability confront the current century as its paramount challenge, is the bringing of power and politics together again. The reunion of the separated partners inside the domicile of the nation-state is perhaps the least promising of the possible responses to that challenge. (2007: 25)

Structural global vulnerability is the product of the interconnection that is being driven by several of the factors we have already discussed, namely the second phase of mediatization and the changing infrastructure of global communications; the development of global markets for goods and services; new migration patterns; that reaction to the spread of Western values following the end of the Cold War, captured in Benjamin Barber's (1995) book title, *Jihad vs. McWorld*; a new form of global civil society and perhaps a global public opinion. All these developments add up to a new dynamic or logic, one of *emergence*.

Policymakers respond by trying to prevent or pre-empt future threats before they have emerged. But since they cannot know the form these threats will take, knowledge is a problem. There is an imperative to act, but to act on what basis? Following 9/11, the US and UK advanced a notion of pre-emptive foreign policy, proposing that war in Iraq and potentially Iran would be justified on the rationale that each regime could potentially cause problems later. Saddam Hussein could sell WMD to non-state terrorists, and Iran could use its nuclear capacities for weaponry as well as energy generation. Here was one attempt to manage the structural problems generated by the diffuse vectors we associate with globalization.

Indeed, we can also speak of emergence internal to states and societies. Appadurai (2006) argues that the notion that a nation-state should map onto a national 'ethnos' or ethnically homogenous people is a fundamental danger because, given contemporary (and indeed historical) patterns of migration, there will always be an internal minority who is not of that ethnos. This creates a continual uncertainty about who is 'us' and who is 'them', and indeed what 'us' means. Appadurai calls his study of 'the *anxiety of incompleteness*' (ibid.:

8) *Fear of Small Numbers*. In many towns and cities around the world the link between people and territory is fundamentally uncertain; some metropolitan cities contain people born in every region of the world – what Vertovec (2006) labels 'superdiversity' – and in many countries it may be almost impossible for a government to carry out an accurate census. For some there is a temptation to respond by searching for certainty through purity. Uncertainty about social and individual identity can interlock with economic and political uncertainty (who gets what and who gets to decide). Violence as ethnic cleansing is a logical consequence, for, as Gourevitch wrote of Rwanda, 'genocide, after all, is an exercise in community building' (cited in Appadurai, 2006: 7). We explore how self/other categorizations are deployed in chapter 9.

The way in which politics mobilizes in the new media ecology may contribute an unpredictability to these dynamics. Western societies such as the US have moved to a condition of 'accelerated pluralism', argues Bimber (1998), in which class- or interest-based party politics have shifted towards more fluid issue-based group politics. This not only affects the coherence of institutions, such as representative parliaments and assemblies, whose members may not align straightforwardly with the fluid and shifting issue-based groups who make up their constituents; it also coincides with shifting forms or mechanisms of political mobilization, particularly through the use of online tools. Chadwick writes: '[P]osting messages to online forums and collaboratively maintaining data repositories, e-mail lists, and blogs in which the information and communication resources required for mobilization are *"happy accident" outcomes* of countless small-scale individual contributions' (2007: 290; emphasis added). Accelerated pluralism or the flux of issues and groups, combined with new technologies, disrupt the linearity of politics and make cause-and-effect less predictable. If, for Appadurai (2006: 11–13), part of the fear of small numbers is that minor differences can become major because they symbolize a potential slippage away from purity, then, today, minor differences can be communicated and become public very quickly; equally, attempts to 'deal with' difference became public too, notably violent video clips posted and circulated on the Internet.

Having explored emergent forces that are external and internal to the state, we must note the diffusion of *borders*. Borders are necessarily central to warfare in its traditional sense of dispute over territory. However, borders no longer correspond to sovereign territorial boundaries in many cases, but are found 'wherever selective controls are to be found' (Balibar, 2002: 84–5). As Rumford notes (2008), the dispersal and diffusion of borders has come into focus particularly following 9/11, as nation-states have tried to find new ways to monitor and regulate the movement of people and material things in the name of security. These are political processes: 'they do not work *in the same way* "equally", for all "people", and notably not for those who come from different parts of the world' (Balibar, 2002: 91; emphasis in original). The variable effects of diffuse borders may lead to grievances, particularly if some groups are 'profiled' while others move more freely.

Finally, we shall explain why publics are diffuse (see also chapter 4). Publics are intrinsically unknowable. It is only through opinion polling and elections that we can speak of 'public opinion' and the 'public's decision'. By representing a public, opinion polls and electoral counts bring that public into existence, even while suggesting that such a public pre-existed these acts of representation. This is not to say a public does not exist, only that it cannot exist 'without a certain medium' (Derrida, cited in Barnett, 2003: 24). Publics can be 'called', but they assemble themselves. They don't have predefined geographic limits or boundaries, which means that metaphors such as public sphere, public domain and public realm are not necessarily helpful (though they can be): '[P]ublicness is a process: it's something people *do*, rather than a space they inhabit' (Barnett, 2008b). Modern publics cannot be created by a state or other authority; to an irreducible extent, publics are self-organizing and sovereign. This can make it hard for some to have confidence in a public. If you are a political leader or policymaker, or in a minority position in a society, it can be disconcerting to confront the existence of a public that is once real yet elusive, felt yet ultimately unidentifiable. A little misrecognition is inescapable, but even a little misrepresentation can appear antagonistic to those feeling powerless or victimized. The very category 'public' generates the uncertainty described by Appadurai above.

For a public to exist, attention must be sustained. There can be no public of a single address or text; a public is generated through a chain of texts, such as newspapers, television news broadcasts or regular addresses by leaders. To assemble public support for a war, a series of political speeches and complimentary news reports is required. Publics assume there are texts that preceded and that will follow, so that more than fleeting engagement with an issue is possible. What links this past, present and future is sustained interaction between leaders and an indefinite audience; the former cannot know in advance who will listen and respond. A public 'can only act within the temporality of the circulation that gives it existence' (Warner, 2002: 68). When the circulation is predictable and on punctuated cycles, it would seem that publics are more able to act. The punctuation allows decisions to crystallize, as with elections or referenda. It allows members to understand themselves as belonging to a historically situated sociopolitical entity; to be comfortable with, and oriented to, a commonsensical temporality of decision, evaluation and reconsideration.

To summarize, through sustained communication, the definition of issues, problems and associated facts, communication infrastructures and forms of coordination, various publics are generated with various spatialities (Barnett, 2008b). It will be a struggle for policymakers, including militaries, to treat publics as diffuse. Bounded publics have a hold on our imaginaries, on our administrative and legal systems, and the way in which states mobilize support for war.

2. Controlling Vectors

Even in today's new media ecology some military authorities are able to prevent flows of information. In August 2007 Israeli jets breached Syrian air space to carry out then-unidentified operations. A month later, a BBC News headline ran: 'Israel's Syria "raid" remains a mystery' (Marcus, 2007). Such attempts themselves run the risk of becoming a negative news story for those Western authorities. The US military did not allow journalists into Fallujah when they attacked the city in April 2004, but, as Tumber and Webster note, 'when rumours leaked out of large-scale civilian deaths and of disproportionate and vengeful US force being applied, these were widely reported round the world. The conclusion that it is generally a mistake for military forces to exclude the media, however bothersome their representatives may be, is hard to avoid' (2006: 21–2). The Internet has not led to a borderless world (Goldsmith and Wu, 2006); it is structured by commercial and government actors, such that citizens in some geographic locations cannot access certain websites, for instance in China, Iran and Burma. Indeed, the very notion of secrecy requires scrutiny. Mark Danner writes in the context of the US-led war on terror and its global rendition locations:

> [W]hat is 'secret' exactly? In our recent politics, 'secret' has become an oddly complex word. From whom was the 'secret bombing of Cambodia' secret? Not from the Cambodians, surely. From whom was the existence of [US] 'secret overseas facilities' secret? Not from the terrorists, surely. From Americans, presumably. On the other hand, as early as 2002, anyone interested could read on the front page of one of the country's leading newspapers:
> **US Decries Abuse but Defends Interrogations: 'Stress and Duress' Tactics Used on Terrorism Suspects Held in Secret Overseas Facilities.**
> (2009: 69; bold in original)

The new media ecology is the condition for ambiguity about such phenomena; news is public *and* secret; it is for domestic audiences, not overseas; it may be contained now, but images emerge later. To explore the challenges such conditions pose to governments we look in this section at the role of media in public diplomacy. Public diplomacy refers to government attempts to communication with foreign publics.

Public diplomacy since 9/11

While diplomacy in general terms refers to communication between state representatives, public diplomacy refers to 'official communication with foreign publics' and non-state groups in other countries (Melissen, 2007: xvii). Many of the central questions of this book concerning credible representation across emergent transnational vectors apply to the study of public diplomacy; indeed, Paul Sharp defines public diplomacy as 'the process by which direct relations with people in a country are pursued to advance the interests and extend the values of those being represented' (Sharp, in Melissen, 2005: 106). Sharp's definition is not restricted to communications by officials or state representatives. Corporations, NGOs and cultural and educational institutions are all capable of public diplomacy, and public diplomacy strategies may operate through the cooperation of several such types of institution. Public diplomacy is not necessarily connected, therefore, to foreign policy: a nation's presence in the world is made up of its economic, social and cultural activities and relations, not just its political and military ones. We might also question whether public diplomacy entails communication with only foreign publics; the formulation of an acceptable, persuasive or legitimate foreign policy may involve engagement with both domestic and foreign publics (Dizzard, 2001: 5–6). For instance, the British Foreign Office engages with Muslim organizations in the UK and overseas as it attempts to win consent for policy towards the Middle East (Melissen, 2005: 13). As we explored earlier, in an era of 'superdiversity' it becomes less easy to distinguish 'foreign' and 'domestic' publics. As with our conception of diffuse publics earlier, a member of a public is defined not by their geographical location but according to whether they are addressed and respond to a chain of texts. Hence 'the American public' may include people outside the US, and people living inside the US may at times belong to other national publics, particularly immigrants who follow events in their country of origin as well as their country of residence.

The end of the Cold War challenged the demand in the US for public diplomacy programmes. A relatively isolationist US Congress shut down American centres around the globe and reduced staff levels at embassies; US presidential candidate Ross Perot said: 'What do we need diplomats for? Just send a fax' (Finn, 2003: 16). However, others were starting to recognize that communications technology was having an increasing impact on the environment in which policy was being made (Dizzard, 2001; Gilboa, 1998, 2001; 2002; Potter, 2002), brought into focus by the CNN effect debate in the 1990s (see Robinson, 2002; Gilboa, 2005; Hoskins and O'Loughlin, 2007; Miller, 2007). Discussion of the concept of 'soft power' brought to attention government use of media to project information and values to target publics (Nye, 2004); making one's country appear attractive – 'nation-branding'[2] – can have economic benefits, attracting investment and workers.

With the attacks of 11 September 2001 in the US and the resulting 'war on terror', the US administration fell back on an apparently successful Cold War strategy and set about trying to influence the 'hearts and minds' of Middle Eastern and Muslim publics. Charlotte Beers, appointed Under Secretary for Public Affairs in the aftermath of the 9/11 attacks, stated her goals: '[W]e promote US interests not only through our policies but also in our beliefs and values. Never have those intangibles been more important right now' (quoted in Kennedy and Lucas, 2005: 317). However, early attempts to do so began to highlight the difficulties the US administration would continue to face. An attempt to use a travelling exhibition of photographs of the 9/11 attacks launched in 2002[3] showed confidence in the universality of the American message:

> We needed to depict – not in words, but in pictures – the loss, the pain, but also the strength and resolve of New York, of Americans, of the world community to recover and rebuild on the site of the World Trade Center. . . . A message that – without words – documents that the World Trade Center was not a collection of buildings or a set of businesses – but a community, a way of life, a symbol, a place of the living and now also, the dead. How do you do that? How do you tell such a sad, grim, shocking, and ultimately uplifting story? You do that in pictures. (Beers, cited in Kennedy, 2003: 318)

However, it seems this confidence was misplaced. As the exhibition travelled, the images engendered unpredictable responses from audiences that interpreted them from their own social/historical standpoints (Kennedy, 2003). At times, it had the opposite of the desired effect. Demonstrations in Bangladesh highlighted the ill-will generated by American claims to embody universal human values. The interaction between projected image and foreign policy action in forming public opinion, and the sceptical nature of what Melissen terms 'assertive postmodern publics' (2005: 14) was captured by one demonstrator: 'What is outrageous is how the US government is capitalising on the tragedy [of September 11] . . . when the Israeli government is carrying out genocidal programs against the Palestinians. This Meyerowitz exhibition is obviously a ploy to elicit sympathy and as such is calculated' (Kennedy, 2003: 325).

The issue was credibility. This episode illustrated the manner in which local interpretation cannot be predetermined or controlled by the producer of the message/projection.

The rise of the Anglosphere

In recent years a new set of transnational news media have emerged with the potential to reconfigure relations between policymakers, publics and media. The raison d'être of these mainly Anglophone news channels, such as Al Jazeera English, Press TV (Iran), CCTV9 (China), France 24 and Russia Today, may be to challenge the predominance of BBC World and CNN International. A global environment marked by new migration patterns, shifting geopolitical distributions of power, and a new media ecology offer new possibilities for media and policymakers to reach publics overseas – a battle for 'hearts and minds' in new conditions. Are these transnational Anglophone media to act as conduits for policymakers to legitimate foreign policy objectives – a new 'media diplomacy'? Do these media together constitute a new 'Anglosphere' in which English becomes the language of public diplomacy? Can these media be considered political actors themselves? What is the relation between the Anglosphere and transnational media organizations that broadcast in other languages, such as Al Jazeera Arabic or Venezuela's Telesur?

The development of media diplomacy strategies will be constrained by a nation-state's institutions and history. Each of these transnational broadcast institutions emerged in particular historical circumstances which will shape its trajectory and the parameters of think-able strategies. We already witness a contradictory dynamic: a variety of institutional strategies growing out of varied cultural and political roots, alongside convergence of norms of journalistic credibility and presentational forms and aesthetics. Hence the exercise of 'soft power' (Nye, 2004) is played out across an uneven 'playing field', where material factors (oil and gas funding for Russia Today, Telesur and Al Jazeera), levels of political intervention and regulation, technological capacities of producers and consumers, and audience tastes and demands, may help determine how different actors can engage in new forms of 'media diplomacy'.

Is the proliferation of transnational television channels in the early twenty-first century a mark of continuity in the field of public diplomacy? Many transnational media are part of for-profit corporate organizations and driven by norms of professional journalism, and channels may be used to create or sustain connections to diasporic audiences and generate and maintain transnational identities. However, a major purpose of these channels may be to augment national prestige and/or to assert an alternative political perspective in an increasingly crowded but politically uniform news marketplace. These channels appear to offer nation-states a means to project their voice, their policies and their interpretations of events onto polyphonic global media publics (Rai and Cottle, 2007). So, different conditions, same purposes?

However, new media technologies allow more diverse use of media. Not only have we witnessed the recent proliferation of English-language transnational television *channels* such as Al Jazeera English, Press TV, France 24, Russia Today, and CCTV9, alongside BBC World and CNN International, but many of these media organizations also provide *platforms* and interactive features allowing for forms of public participation and conversation, such as the BBC's 'Have your say' message boards. Hence, these media organizations act as tools for traditional public diplomacy – the transmission of content to overseas governments and publics – but also allow new 'bottom-up' public diplomacy by enabling publics to interact and, perhaps, 'influence' each other independently of government communications, with 'soft power' reconceptualized as horizontal and dispersed. We explore this next.

Do new, dispersed or 'networked' forms of power enabled by new media technologies imply a fundamental transformation of public diplomacy? It is possible that interactive, participatory platforms of both emerging and established transnational media offer a user-led 'bottom-up' form of public diplomacy in which media consumers and publics could engage in, and even take responsibility for, practices of persuasion with overseas publics. Such horizontal, 'networked' power would demand a reconsideration of the concept 'soft power'. Additionally, the terms of debate around media 'impact' would be altered if media content is co-produced or partly user-generated.

These trends offer opportunities and risks from a public diplomacy perspective: an opportunity to generate understandings in ways not obviously directed by government media management, but the risk of users challenging government policies, agendas and discourses through open and, perhaps, democratic dialogue (Bennett, 2003; McNair, 2006). User-generated content may be a means to 'harness' 'collective intelligence' – a principle of a Web 2.0 environment – but such processes carry risks. 'Harnessed' by whom, and to what? Such processes could be a political tool (Jenkins and Deuze, 2008: 6). There is a need for empirical analysis of the extent to which traditional public diplomacy practices are being superseded by forms of 'media diplomacy' appropriate to a world of horizontal communication networks and distributed user-generated content; not a world of coherent messages being sent *to* target audiences, but one in which shifts in political values and beliefs are generated *through, by and with* globally dispersed publics.

Following the examples of failed US public diplomacy since 9/11, it is now recognized that public diplomacy experts can no longer work according to models that assume passive audiences yearning to be liberated (Robin, 2005). Mission statements now place emphasis on listening and 'mutuality' (Leonard et al., 2005: 46–9); former US Secretary of State Condoleezza Rice stated that 'our goal should be to have a dialogue with the world, not a monologue' (in Hughes, 2007: 34). However, the question remains: even if the metaphor of 'conversation' is applied through media diplomacy, for instance through interactive features, chatrooms and even transparent explanation of editorial decisions, how can any impact of dialogue be measured and the performance of these 'media diplomacy' strategies demonstrated?

To illustrate our analysis of media and public diplomacy, we now present two case studies.

CENTCOM

Our first case study is based on an interview with the Media Engagement Team of CENTCOM, Dubai (the US Central Command base for the Middle East).[4] This is a key case for several reasons. This team was very significant, standing at the nexus of US foreign policy and engagement with Middle Eastern leaders and publics. The CENTCOM staff saw themselves as being at the cutting edge of public diplomacy in the new media ecology, stating that they are 'changing the rules of the game'. On a theoretical level, the team represented a form of networked power, but at a meso-level, playing 'nodal' roles between political sponsors, media organizations and the 'Arab street'. The case is also important because there is a need for primary empirical data in the field of public diplomacy, and access is often limited given the political sensitivities involved.

Captain Frank Pascual and Captain Eric Clark told researchers about their practice since 2005 of being available '24 hours a day' to engage in rapid rebuttal on Arabic television channels. Their primary focus was not on the content of their own messages, but rather on ensuring a visual presence and offering an opposing perspective to show the provisional basis of political claims made routinely on these channels.

FP: We've had people come out from the Pentagon and look at this and say 'wow', really that's been the word used because they realize how far forward we're leading. There are times when, we basically have toothpaste and a toothbrush and not a lot more because things happen so quickly . . . I can't allow Al Jazeera or any other of the news media to get the high ground if we can seize it. Even if all I have is a piece of the information, or even if I don't have anything to be able to say: 'we're investigating', 'we're looking into that' and at least give them something to go with, you know in the case of something that might be an allegation of innocent civilians hurt, killed whatever the case may be, to say: 'we will look into that and if there was wrongdoing, we're not [confirming?], but what we're saying is that if there was, that we will hold our people accountable for it and you can rely on that, but if there's not, if this is a case where there's not a story, we would expect to have to opportunity to come back and talk about it.' And that has happened. So, that's very important and by having, the American comedian Woody Allen said: '80 percent of life is showing up', and that really is the word presence for us: being out there.[5]

Constant contact allowed trust to build up between the CENTCOM officers and Arabic news channel staff, such that not only did Al Jazeera offer CENTCOM a space on a show to speak, but they turned to CENTCOM as a source to verify facts about an incident. According to Pascual and Clark, relations became more than just transactions, but were based instead on trust and informal contact. They felt Arabic media staff were hungry for their US perspective:

> EC: Anecdotally, a week from last Thursday we did our 1,000th first media engagements, we're [. . . name] on Al Jazeera so in ten months of work, we've done 1,001 media engagements, just from a sheer quantitative perspective and then you look at the quality of it. It was almost like a *dry sponge* where we were, we were, we got there, we were getting full page and two-page full spreads of essentially Q & A. . . . Everywhere we went we were gaining an incredible amount of coverage, we sent that back to America: 'holy shit', getting one or two pages of coverage is remarkable for them, but because they've not been engaging, these people were like a dry sponge.[6]

In this respect, they claimed to have 'changed the rules of the game' for political discussion on Arabic media and developed a new form of media diplomacy that reached the 'Arab street' in contrast to conventional diplomats acting as 'monks' attending only formal diplomatic meetings or issuing statements:

> EC: We walk a very, sometimes a precarious precedence being military guys, but also serving a diplomatic function. We, I think, have far better relationships with the pan-Arab media than our diplomatic friends. They sit in their secure environment in the middle of the city, heavily guarded, heavily fortified, but they don't get outside the boundary and work. They're monks. Our friends in the pan-Arab community are actually putting a finger on the pulse, what their perspective is, what the man on the street, whether it's an Iraqi street, Lebanese street, UAE street, what they're thinking, not what the diplomats are saying in public or on-the-record to news organizations. But what the man on the street is thinking. We take that information and we feed our leadership.[7]

Pascual and Clark have attempted to insert themselves into how a (pan-Arabic) society represents the world and itself to itself. They acknowledged this may be a slow process and their temporal horizons for success appeared long term:

> FP: What we are concerned about, the issues that we've talked about and that I think are important are the ones that you know we keep raising with them and engagement is the only way of dealing with it. There are a lot of people in our own government both on the military side and on the diplomatic side who would tell you: 'what are you guys doing, you're wasting your time with them'. It's not wasted, the fact of the matter is that at least we got to say something on the air, live, and in fairness to them again it was not just 30 seconds, it was about five minutes of conversation, so it's a real

engagement, *the ball gets moved very slowly* sometimes and sometimes agonisingly slowly and I would argue that that's the case here,
but it's moving.[8]

Yet even this may not have the desired 'effects': Studies of Arabic TV audiences
show 'increasing levels of attention to coverage of the United States leads to
stronger anti-American attitudes' (Nisbet et al., 2004: 32). Whether stories are
pro- or anti-US, many viewers watch Al Jazeera through a 'perceptual screen'
(ibid.: 21) or dogmatic stance, whereby they use media to confirm their existing worldview. For the US, is all publicity bad publicity? Perhaps the work of
Pascaul and Clark simply struck audiences as a modified form of traditional
public diplomacy and US military press operations. Hence, as those charged
with media diplomacy strategies adapt to audience data that shows such
'awkward' conditions for 'impact', we might expect more innovative media
diplomacy strategies, enabled by new technologies.

Pascual and Clark worked to a ritual model of communication rather than
a transmission one (Carey, 1989). Their aim was to become a presence in the
daily news, the content of their message being secondary to achieving visibility.
Presence *was* the message, showing a human face for the US, and bringing a balancing voice to debates. They sought to become a visible, trusted node in these
mediation networks, yet, to the extent that they had a message, that message
was still top-down, state-led. This points to an avoidance of dialogic public
diplomacy. Pascual and Clark did not show that they were willing to take other
opinions into account. They did not offer a mode of diplomacy that is more
contingent, circuitous and cumbersome, but one that 'takes into account' and
is open to being 'taken into account' (Moss and O'Loughlin, 2008). So could
they expect to be heard if they did not demonstrate they were willing to listen?
A principle of mutuality has to define public diplomacy, of talk among equals.
Mutuality and trust become the basis for persuasion.

These contradictions are perhaps to be expected in a multi-layered public
diplomacy environment in which several strategies or hybrid strategies can be
pursued simultaneously and officials are themselves uncertain about what form
of communications will be effective in the second phase of mediatization.

The YouTube war

Our second example of networked public diplomacy is the US Department of
Defense decision to use YouTube as a platform for video clips it prepared, as
examined by Christian Christensen (2008). It launched its YouTube channel,
MNFIRAQ (Multi-National Force – Iraq), in March 2007, with the following
rationale:

> Multi-National Force – Iraq established this YouTube channel to give viewers
> around the world a 'boots on the ground' perspective of Operation Iraqi Freedom
> from those who are fighting it. Video clips document action as it appeared to per-
> sonnel on the ground and in the air as it was shot. We only edit video clips for time,
> security reasons, and/or overly disturbing or offensive images. (http://youtube.com/
> profile?user=MNFIRAQ)

MNFIRAQ is in many senses traditional public diplomacy or propaganda because, although it draws on some footage shot by (mainly) US troops, it is top-down, systematic, strategic and institutionalized. Hence many audiences may reject it out of hand 'simply because it was created by the USA' (Christensen, 2008: 161). The clips fall into three categories: street fighting and gun battles, which are sanitized, only showing coalition soldiers calmly firing weapons, with no human casualties visible; surgical warfare, in which coalition troops again destroy targets, but at a distance; and 'good deeds' clips, in which coalition troops are seen interacting peacefully with Iraqi civilians.

What the US Department of Defense appeared not to appreciate was that searching 'Iraq + fighting' or 'Iraq + US marines' in YouTube brings up uncensored video footage from Iraq alongside the MNFIRAQ clips. Furthermore, much of this graphic and disturbing footage is filmed *by coalition troops* recording their own atrocities, such as the killing and injuring of unarmed civilians and the shooting of injured 'targets' (in apparent contravention of the Geneva Conventions) with often joyful voiceovers. Christensen labels this juxtaposition of public diplomacy material with uncensored material '"propagandistic dissonance": moments when overt propaganda is placed side-by-side with material that renders such propaganda impotent' (ibid.: 172). The new media ecology creates a trap. If you support US military engagement in Iraq, the uncensored material may gain credibility and authenticity simply by being next to the US Department of Defense clips, but these, correspondingly, lose credibility and authenticity by being next to atrocity footage. Or, if you oppose the US intervention, the MNFIRAQ clips lose credibility by being associated with the DoD clips, and reinforce the connection between the US military and atrocity.

Summary

The emergence of networked media diplomacy, the efforts of CENTCOM and the role of YouTube all demonstrate that the second phase of mediatization offers nuanced and complex ways in which major powers and publics will relate to one another, always with a chaotic aspect in which the outcome of communicative exchanges cannot be foreseen in advance.

A central question to be asked by scholars as well as the policymakers and journalists involved is how the 'impact' of media diplomacy can be conceived and even 'measured'. One might expect any media channel to have a means to identify and measure its performance in primary strategic areas such as reaching and satisfying certain types and numbers of audiences/markets, for fear of otherwise appearing mere 'vanity projects' (Painter, 2007: 24). Today, for example, the BBC World Service (BBCWS), stating its aim to 'bring the world to the UK and the UK to the world', is required by its charter to measure its performance in 10 countries. For the BBCWS, demonstrating positive impact on audiences is potentially a powerful argument for the channel to retain funding in future charter reviews. But how can such impact be demonstrated? Similarly, Al Jazeera English (AJE) aims publicly to 'give voice to the voiceless'. While it is relatively straightforward to examine whether 'the voiceless' are represented in the channel's content through analysis of on-air representation of different groups, it is unclear how AJE will demonstrate that either voiceless or already-voiced audiences are paying attention and engaging with the channel, and hence that AJE has any 'effects' on target audiences. And while some transnational media have extensive audience research capacity (e.g. CNN, BBC), it is only since 2008 that emerging media such as AJE and Press TV of Iran have allocated budgets or recruit staff for this purpose.

These questions have political significance. From a liberal pluralist perspective, one could argue that a media ecology featuring an ever-diversifying range of broadcast and online media offers an impetus to processes of democratization and conflict resolution. Critical scholars argue that new transnational media simply offered governments and militaries new tools for conducting traditional propaganda, even 'softening up' target publics for war (Sreberny, 2007). Additionally, those who would seek to uphold ethics of journalistic independence may resist the notion of media playing a consciously political role. Many would fiercely contest that transnational media have political 'uses'; Nigel Chapman, Director of BBCWS, has asserted that if the values that the Foreign and Commonwealth Office wish to project and BBCWS programme content happen to coincide, then that is what it is: a coincidence.[9] Yet such debates centre largely on intentions. Notwithstanding current studies of individual transnational media organizations (Painter, 2007; Zhang, 2007; the AHRC *Tuning In* study[10] of the BBCWS; and the current *Al Jazeera English* study[11]), for instance, there is a lack of comparative study in this field, which is striking given claims made as to the importance of transnational media in the 'post-9/11' security order.

There is also a danger that studies of media and public diplomacy are too US-centric. Jan Melissen begins his edited collection *The New Public Diplomacy* by noting:

> [I]t is equally interesting to look at big, medium-sized, small and even micro-states, and also to analyse the way in which non-democratic countries explore this new form of "outreach" in foreign relations. The strong emphasis in the United States on homeland security, the "war on terror" and "winning hearts and minds" in the Islamic world does not mirror the concerns and interests in public diplomacy that are articulated in many other countries. (2005: xviii)

The question of how officials communicate with foreign publics is a universal one. Officials everywhere must both react to events that pertain to their country's reputation and form forward-looking public diplomacy strategy to build an attractive image over time. For instance, countries in transition from one form of regime to another (authoritarian to democratic), or having to rebrand their country's purposes within a changing regional power balance, or desperate for overseas investment, all have an interest in media diplomacy (ibid.: 9–10).

Finally, a subset of questions about new transnational media networks remain. What are their *institutional histories*? How do the different histories and institutional trajectories of specific transnational media explain different (or converging) journalistic and public diplomacy practices today? What are their *journalistic practices*? What explains the practices and decisions of news-makers in the representation of critical security events? How is the role of transnational news media affected by temporality of the news event – breaking, orchestrated or ongoing? What is the relation between *technologies* and *publics*? How does technological change allow new conceptualization of, and forms of engagement with, transnational audiences? What uses do viewers/users make of 'interactive' services? Can and do news organizations monitor who partici-pates? Who moderates and who sets the agenda and parameters of discussion and what counts as 'political'? Is there coherence in agenda between a news organization's transmission and dialogic spaces? How can we conceive of *audi-ences and impacts*? How is performance measured by different transnational media organizations? (How) do those organizations explain this 'impact' to sponsors and audiences? Finally, questions remain about *journalistic ethics* and *diplomacy*. How do these media manage tensions between independence and credibility? Do newsmakers work according to total, editorial or operational independence? What forms of state censorship still be effective in the new media ecology?

3. Emergent Vectors

The fragmentation of news production and consumption has created 'cultural chaos', writes Brian McNair, which is pluralist and fantastic. Nobody can control news agendas or information flows around the world, so we are facing a free market of ideas. 'Contagion' is one term regularly used to describe this chaotic process, with ideas spreading like viruses, stealthy and unstoppable. An alternative metaphor, from a policymaker's point of view, is that of con-taining a raging fire. The following quote is from General Rupert Smith, who was Commander of the United Nations Protection Force (UNPROFOR) in Sarajevo in 1995. He is speculating about how he would have handled the Abu Ghraib controversy had he been in the US military:

> You're in damage control, make no error, and my whole action would be to isolate the incident, in time and space, within the organization of things and be seen to be dealing with it as clearly as one can, and *shut it down . . . just as you would a fire in the hull of your ship*. The difficulty of actually doing that would be great, and you've now got this multi-level audience, because, at the very least, you've got your own people at home, you've got your own army, you've got your allies at home, and the collection of their armies in the theatre. Because *you don't want this to spread in that direction*, of course.[12]

Can the raging 'fire' of communication be contained? Does such a metaphor make sense in the first place? In the final section of this chapter we present four short cases of apparently chaotic vectors triggered in situations of war, conflict or international hostility. In each case the second phase of mediatization creates the condition for a loss of control which authorities and news organizations have responded to in diverse and often surprising ways.

Example 1: President Ahmedinajad's open letter to President Bush

On 8 May 2006, President Ahmadinejad of Iran sent a letter to President Bush of the US. It was the first official communiqué from the Iranian government to the US since diplomatic ties were broken in 1979. This 18-page letter was delivered by Swiss go-betweens, and it was also published online. President Bush did not reply to the letter.

Annabelle Sreberny (2008) points to an analogy between this letter and Edgar Allen Poe's story *The Purloined Letter*, written in 1845. The idea of a private letter is a modern invention (Peters, 1999). We did not have pre-paid postage stamps until 1840; the envelope was not patented until 1849, and public post-boxes arrived then too. Hence, Sreberny notes, Edgar Allen Poe could write *The Purloined Letter*, in 1845, about the transit of a letter. The story is summarized by Sreberny as follows.

The Queen receives a letter and, while being visited in her boudoir by the King, her evident embarrassment and attempt to hide the letter is seen by the Minister, who contrives to replace the letter with a substitute, to the knowledge of the Queen, who can do nothing for fear of attracting the King's attention. After 18 months of frustrated police attempts to find the letter, Dupin the detective arrives at the Minister's office, only to discover it is in the most obvious place, hanging in front of the mantelpiece, whereupon he substitutes it for another letter unknown to the Minister. However, Dupin's letter has a message in his own handwriting that will make his act known to the Minister if and when he opens the letter.

The story offers a number of plays about who sees what, who has power over whom, about interpersonal politics and the deceits that are performed. This has led to a dispute among more linguistically minded philosophers, Sreberny documents. Lacan writes: 'The letter always arrives at its destination.' Derrida replies, in *The Postcard*: 'What happens if it gets lost? A letter does NOT always arrive at its destination.' Finally, Zizek has argued that Derrida misread Lacan: wherever a letter arrives, he writes, 'it always arrives at its destination, since its destination is wherever it arrives'.

Returning to Ahmedinejad's letter to Bush, for whom was it intended? As an open letter freely visible on the Internet, in English and Farsi, everybody received the letter, and many people responded. Commentators, journalists, experts, politicians: the letter was responded to in countries across the world, on Internet message boards. The world became a 'hall of mirrors', people responding and reacting to each other, a momentary global public sphere. As one satirist wrote: 'At the White House, aides said that writing a letter of such length to President Bush, who is known for his extreme distaste for reading, was the most provocative act Mr Ahmedinejad could have committed' (Borowitz, 2006).

US spokespeople dismissed the letter as 'rambling' and as a 'meandering screed', while Bush told reporters: 'It looks like it did not answer the main question that the world is asking, and that is, "When will you get rid of your nuclear program?"' (cited in Goodall, Jr. et al., 2008: 99). However, this was not what the international press was asking. Instead, the letter was reported as a rare chance for communication (*The Jerusalem Herald, Mideast Mirror, BBC*

Monitoring, and Lebanon's *The Daily Star*) and a case of US dismissal of diplomacy (*Agence France Presse*, *Xinhua News Service*). The US response was framed negatively as 'dismissive and somewhat unsophisticated', suggest Goodall, Jr. et al. (ibid.: 101). They write, as US scholars:

> The letter, and the official US response to it, should serve as a case study in failed strategic communication. By misreading the intent and ignoring most of the content of the message, by failing to adequately interpret the letter within known intercultural and religious frameworks, and by refusing to respond to the significance of the communiqué even after world opinion chimed in, the US lost an important opening for dialogue and further tarnished our image on the globalized world's mediated stage. (Ibid.: 109)

This case study is instructive in several respects. It illustrates how a 'global public opinion' can emerge and that governments must find ways to respond that take that into account, as well as taking domestic public opinion into account. The communiqué was also a risk for Ahmedinejad: he could not anticipate how the letter would be received around the world, or how Bush and his officials would respond. The case also illustrates that what is significant is not necessarily the content of a communication, but its circulation or mediality.

Example 2: Kevin Sites and MSNBC embed in Fallujah

During the joint American-Iraqi offensive in the city of Fallujah in November 2004, an incident took place in a Fallujah mosque which became subject to international attention. During a 'sweep' for insurgents, the MSNBC journalist Kevin Sites, embedded with US troops, recorded footage of a US marine shooting dead an injured and apparently unarmed man lying on the floor of the building. NBC broadcast the footage two days later. It was then picked up by news organizations and Internet commentators around the world (see also Gillespie et al., 2010, Matheson and Allan, 2009).

Western and Arabic media differed in their presentation of the incident in terms of defining those involved and in terms of defining the context of the incident. Western media labelled the man killed an 'insurgent', while Arabic media used the term 'wounded unarmed man' (see table 7.1). Most Western media referred to the context of the incident: that the marine was in a stressful situation, that he had just lost a member of his group, that he was himself shot in the face only a day earlier, and that an Iraqi insurgent's corpse was booby-trapped shortly before the incident. Such context shapes perceptions of whether the marine was justified in shooting the man on the floor. Western media such as Associated Press wire service and the *Guardian* provided this context:

> Charles Heyman, a senior defence analyst from the Jane's Consultancy Group in Britain defended the Marine's actions saying it was possible the wounded man was concealing a firearm or grenade. 'In a combat infantry soldier's training, he is always taught that his enemy is at his most dangerous when he is severely wounded.' If the injured man makes even the slightest move, 'in my estimation they would be justified in shooting him', said Heyman. (AP)

Table 7.1 Media Coverage of the Fallujah Killing

Wording	Media channel	Date
A US marine filmed shooting an **unarmed and injured insurgent** in a Falluja . . .	*Guardian*	16-11-04
The video then showed him raising his rifle towards a **prisoner** lying on the floor		
The images of the alleged point-blank shooting of an **Iraqi insurgent**	BBC	16-11-04
It must explain, he [BBC correspondent.] says, whether **wounded combatants** were abandoned, or killed, illegally.		
The U.S. military is investigating the killing of a **wounded and apparently unarmed Iraqi prisoner** inside a mosque **during combat operations**	CNN	16-11-04
Lieutenant General John Sattler, Commander of the 1st Marine Expeditionary Force: "The First Marine Division is investigating an allegation of the unlawful use of force and the **death of an enemy combatant**."	US Army spokesman (AP)	16-11-04
Arabic Media Channels		
The Iraqi government and Arab League yesterday condemned the **shooting of an unarmed and wounded** [man] in a mosque in Fallujah by an American Marine.	Al-Sharq Al-Awsat	18-11-04
The provocative pictures of a US marine killing a wounded man inside a mosque in Fallujah . . .		
. . . the US Army is investigating the killing of **an unarmed and wounded** [man] by a US marine . . .		
TV channels broadcast a clip of US marines entering a mosque where there were several lying dead. When one of them [marines] discovered there was one **Iraqi** amongst the dead still breathing, he immediately shot him dead.	Al Jazeera	18-11-04
A US marine shot dead **an unarmed wounded man** in a mosque **without any reason**.	Al-Sabah (local Iraqi paper)	20-11-04

US marines rallied round their comrade, saying he was probably under combat stress in unpredictable circumstances. (*Guardian*)

Where Western media focused on the *immediate* context, Arabic media omitted that and instead focused on a perceived *broader* context, that of US violence towards Iraqi civilians:

'What happened is not groundbreaking given what happened in Abu Ghraib. This is more of a confirmation of Arab suspicions than a revelation.' Sharif Hikmat Nashashibi of Arabic Media Watch.

'Both the Sunni Clerics Association and the Iraqi people are fully convinced that it is in the habit of the American troops to kill the injured', Omar Ragib, a member of the Sunni Clerics Association, said in a press conference. (AP: 16 November 2004)

A writer called Rania Al-Zubi on the Al-Shabab (Youth) site defined the context in terms of US revenge for prior attacks on US contractors:

> Some experts and monitors say that the true purpose behind this US offensive on Fallujah and the bad conduct of US soldiers is revenge for the four US contractors killed there and the fact that the American forces have so far not been able to subdue the city and its people. That is why American troops are overwhelmed by their desires for revenge, say monitors. (Cited in Awan et al., 2010)

The posting, which went on to describe the situation in Fallujah, allegedly reported to the writer by insiders, received many supporting comments, all agreeing that US troops were seeking revenge. Blogs also highlighted that American troops violated the sacredness of the mosque, which is a place of worship, also failing to mention that some fighters did take mosques as combat bases.

Some Arabic blogs suggested that the fact that US media would broadcast such footage indicates they must be hiding more violent crimes by US troops. The Shabab website wrote: '[T]he broadcast of this clip/ images by American media channels themselves raises suspicion that there may be images and clips more horrific than this that did not find their way to the public.' Hence, even the choice of American media channels to make public the clip was eyed with suspicion and indicative of concealment of graver crimes.

In 2005, six versions of the clip were shown to military policymakers and to audiences in the UK by researchers.[13] The policymakers were worried that in the news reports from which these clips were taken, no context was given as to the type of operation or the rules of engagement and that this would add to the mounting negative reporting on military operations in Iraq. From the immediate perspective of the UK military, audiences might infer the same conclusions as many Arabic media: that this was the unjustified killing of an unarmed man, part of a wider 'crusade' against Muslims. However, UK audiences' perspectives were not so one-dimensional. Several respondents expressed surprise that they had not registered this particular incident at the time of its occurrence but agreed that this was probably because it fitted a dominant narrative news pattern of US abuse and atrocity ('we have heard so much of what goes on in Iraq of this nature'). But judgements depended on the way the film footage was anchored. Some interviewees automatically judged the incident to be an act of 'murder', based primarily on what they saw, and what they thought that meant. Others problematized any easy equation between seeing and knowing, and showed a high awareness that there might be contextual information which had been omitted from the report. Some pointed to other factors in the situation which might have made the marine's action justifiable, such as 'the (Iraqi) guy was just about to explode a grenade'.

This case shows how news acquires particular trajectories depending on how it is framed by different media systems, but that audiences are diffuse and their responses less predictable than policymakers would assume. UK audience responded in ways that resonated with both Western and Arabic media treatment of Kevin Sites's clip.

Example 3: Daniel Pearl's body

On 23 January 2002 the *Wall Street Journal* reporter Daniel Pearl was kidnapped in Karachi, Pakistan, by the National Movement for the Restoration of Pakistani Sovereignty (NMRPS). Pearl had been investigating the connection between Richard Reid, the 'shoe bomber', and Islamic organizations. A month later the US consulate in Karachi received a videotape of Pearl making a confession and then being executed. The video became the focus of political and media statements around the world. In particular, Pearl's body itself became the object around which different actors made claims and counter-claims (Grindstaff and DeLuca, 2004; see also Scarry, 1985). Beginning with Pearl's 'confession', through torture the kidnappers were able to make him say what they wanted. The confession itself signifies the power of the torturer, who is able to appropriate Pearl's voice through harm to his body. Pearl's voice is used to speak words that would validate the kidnappers' ideology. For instance, he speaks of being a Jewish American, whose great-grandfather was a founder of the Israeli state. His voice has an American-English accent. The video switches between shots of Pearl, and shots of Muslim, Arab and/or Palestinian bodies, in particular of children's bodies, thereby connecting Pearl to policies of the US and Israel that had apparently caused this suffering. Pearl's body is used to stand for both the US and Israel, and to legitimize the kidnappers' purposes.

The video became a matter of public debate in Pakistan and the US. As Grindstaff and DeLuca document, the Pakistani press was divided between those who condemned the killing but remained opposed to US policy, and those who simply used the event as the platform to express grievances against the US. Pearl's body was also the focal point of Pakistani politics. The President, General Musharraf, supported the prosecution of the executors so as to signal to domestic and international audiences his government's opposition to Islamic extremists. Meanwhile, in the US, political debate centred upon the role of Pearl as a heroic agent in the 'war on terror', as a servant of the American nation, but also Pearl's body became used as a justification for retaliation not only against the group responsible but also against 'terrorists' generally. The media response was mixed. Only CBS News, the Ogrish website, and the *Boston Phoenix* published footage of the video. Dan Rather of CBS News argued in the broadcast, on 14 May 2002, that it was the responsibility of media to show such footage so audiences could be aware of the kind of propaganda terrorists were producing. Others, including Pearl's family, asserted the need for a blanket ban on the video, on the grounds that seeing it did not make audiences any more aware of the issue, and because making the contents of the video public was what the video's producers would want – CBS News was providing the 'oxygen of publicity'.

What received less publicity were some events triggered by the video of Pearl's execution. Grindstaff and DeLuca note: 'In the same week as Pearl's murder, a 10-year old Pakistani named Abdullah was shot and killed by an 11-year-old American boy because Abdullah was Pakistani. Instead of an international outcry, there was deafening silence across the globe' (ibid.: 316). There was an outcry in Pakistani media about the lack of outcry elsewhere compared to the attention devoted by politicians and journalists to the death of Daniel Pearl. The very invisibility of the story elsewhere could only have added to anti-US sentiment in Pakistan and the success of Islamist, anti-Musharraf political parties. Hence, through an exchange of dead bodies, one intensely mediatized, the other gaining insufficient media coverage for some, we see unfold a complex web of political communication.

Example 4. The 'furies' of radicalization triggered by Gaza

Our final example of a vector concerns the mediatization of 'radicalization', based on an analysis of British television news. On the 27 December 2008, Israel begun a military assault on Gaza in response to rocket attacks, which continued for 22 days and resulted in a disproportionate Palestinian death toll relative to Israeli casualties, and which left tens of thousands homeless and also left a great deal of the Gaza Strip in ruins. Although most journalists were denied access to the conflict zone by Israelis, there was no shortage of images and footage of injury, death and destruction being replayed in news media across the globe and available online. Here we consider how politico-public responses to this coverage were amalgamated (through an example of a mainstream 'in-depth' news programme) as indicative of the prevailing logics of 'hypersecurity' in the UK, which we introduce in chapter 8, triggered by a conflict far away and for which the UK government was not necessarily to blame.

On Monday 12 January 2009, around the peak of the intensive mediatization of the 22-day assault on Gaza, the lead item of BBC2's *Newsnight* programme focused on speculations about the 'radicalizing' effects of the ongoing coverage of the conflict on British Muslims. Notably, despite the intensity of the Israeli military action and the accumulating civilian injuries and deaths, there was a sense that the UK government was, if not tacitly supporting Israel, at least seen to be acting without due purpose in attempting to bring about an immediate end to the conflict. This, it was suggested, would function to 'radicalize' 'vulnerable' individuals in the UK in terms of their potential for violence and terrorism. *Newsnight* opened with the programme's anchor, Kirsty Wark, talking over footage of blood being hosed from a street in Gaza and a covered body, presumably injured or dead, being carried away by several men: 'The bloodshed in Gaza is being used by extremist Islamist groups in the UK to radicalize British Muslims. How dangerous is this?' Following the introductory programme theme and graphics, Wark, standing in a studio, continues: 'Tonight, here in Britain, are fears of the radicalizing impact of the conflict in Gaza. *Newsnight* has uncovered evidence of propaganda and recruitment efforts. The Communities Secretary tells us of her fears.' This sets the tone for the entire lead item, which constructs a causal relationship between conflict in the Middle East and the increased risk of radicalization in the UK. However, it does so through the connection of a varied set of texts, events and commentators, which together produce the 'intangible, tangible' phenomenon of radicalization. Ultimately, no 'radicalized' violence was committed.

Newsnight's narrative is packaged in a report by journalist Tim Whewell, who begins: 'For two weeks now they've been seeing images like this [close up of injured child with bloodied face being carried in the arms of a man] and now protestors at London University are outraged that the death-toll in Gaza is still rising.' Following vox-pops with some of the student protestors the report builds a chronology around a series of statements and events as supportive of the programme's thesis:

- Tuesday 6th January: The Head of the British security service MI5 'warns that Muslim extremists in Britain would use the Gaza crisis to radicalise individuals';
- Wednesday 7th: Muslim advisors on counter-terrorism wrote to David Miliband [UK Foreign Secretary] to warn about: 'possible repercussions of the serious on-going conflict in Gaza';
- Friday 8th: Tony Blair on *Newsnight* stating that there was 'no justification' for those in the UK to 'commit acts of terrorism' in response to events in the Middle East.
- Saturday 9th: 'angry scenes' in London between protestors and police.

Whewell then talks with Usama Hasan (Imam, Masjid al-Tawhid) and legitimates his contribution by stating: 'He understands the psychology that leads young people into violent jihad. Years ago he himself went to fight in Afghanistan, and he's seen renewed attempts to promote jihad here in recent days.'

This media event demonstrates the transnational vectors triggered by an event: the Israel–Palestinian conflict is continual, a constant presence in the global media ecology, but with this violence a sudden upsurge in (latent) feeling is made public thousands of miles away. As Wark wrote, the new media ecology 'can connect enormously vast and vaguely defined spaces together and move images, and sounds, words, and furies, between them'. It appears that the transnational vector fed into local social and political problems, entwining global and local frames of interpretation, and journalists played a key role in enabling these connections to be made.

4. Conclusion

The proliferation of digital media devices, global news networks and ever-expanding space of the Internet contributes to an evolving dynamic between control and chaos. This is not simply because vectors of communication emerge in unforeseen ways, but because there is an ever-present possibility of new images emerging at any moment. This coincides with the condition of 'structural global vulnerability' as economic, environmental, political and cultural processes feed into one another and into war and conflict in complex ways, while the basic units through which war has been legitimized in the twentieth century – nations, borders, publics – are becoming increasingly diffuse. All these trends make the control of communication about war and conflict more difficult, yet the mediatization of war also offers ways for states to manage these vectors by quietly nudging or harnessing citizens' own communications and user-generated content in strategically useful directions.

Today's emergent vectors offer novel ways for actors to further their interests. Why did Ahmedinejad make his letter to Bush public, and why was Daniel Pearl's beheading made public but a copycat beheading not? What functions are served by US CENTCOM officials appearing on Arabic news networks or the BBC's *Newsnight* adding to speculation about the possible threat of 'radicalization'? And for each of these decisions, how did those communicating know what effects they had, upon whom? Alongside these questions of power and effects, the emergence of vectors of war and conflict create ethical dilemmas too. For instance, how do we gain the literacy and understanding to move between public spheres or cultures, to receive and respond to vectors originating elsewhere?[14] Can we – as readers, bloggers, citizens, producers of texts – minimize the potential for conflict by showing we are reflexive about our mobility and take into account our own failings in communication?

8

RADICALIZATION

Radicalization is a phenomenon that exemplifies how media become a weapon for those engaged in warfare. In media reports, government statements and military doctrines, radicalization is invariably linked to the rise of the Internet and to fears that this medium offers an untrammelled potential for seeding, harbouring and delivering terror. For instance, a US intelligence survey from April 2006 stated: 'The radicalization process is occurring more quickly, more widely, and more anonymously in the Internet age, raising the likelihood of surprise attacks by unknown groups whose members and supporters may be difficult to pinpoint.'[1] In this quote we see three of the key dynamics of the politico-media-military discourse on the threat of modern terrorism: speed, extent and unknowability. These are readily fused in accounts that elevate the Internet as the medium of unlimited opportunity for twenty-first century terrorists.

There is nothing new about 'radicals' in a society advocating political, economic or religious ideas contrary to the mainstream, nor about groups and individuals taking up violence against a state or society. There is a long history of resistance, insurgency or terrorism around the world, and volumes of academic and policy studies offering explanations. Yet in the years since the 11 September 2001 attacks on the US, the term 'radicalization' has emerged as part of a discourse for describing the process by which individuals come to hold ideas considered extreme or radical and advocate or commit violence in the name of those ideas. Radicalization has become associated in particular with Islamic extremists claiming to be undertaking 'jihad', but the term has also been used to describe extremist violence from far right organizations and groups connected to anti-abortion, animal rights and ecological causes which undertake or support violence. Centres for the study of radicalization have been created. Government policies have been developed to prevent those already committed to violence from carrying out acts, and to prevent people from finding violence a reasonable course of action in the first place. Many countries have instituted de-radicalization programmes. Within a matter of years, radicalization has become a political problem and priority across many continents, and a whole set of discourses and practices have been generated both by 'radicalized' people justifying their beliefs and actions, and by governments trying to stop them.

Radicalization is a central theme in diffused war. There is great uncertainty about how and why people become radicalized, and the role of media technologies in the process. Can people be radicalized just by looking at websites advocating violence, or do people only visit such websites once they are already radicalized and find the message of these websites simply confirms what they now believe? As such, the threat thought to be posed by radicalization in government and media accounts is a diffuse one. With 'radical' ideas and media content easily available on the Internet, media technologies enabling coordination and mobilization between like-minded individuals scattered across the world, and violent disruption of modern societies relatively cheap and straightforward, it is easy to imagine that the threat could come from anyone, anywhere, at any time.

This chapter is structured around the three axes of diffused war, which are that (i) the mediatization of war (ii) makes possible more diffuse causal relations between action and effect (iii) creating greater uncertainty for policymakers in the conduct of war. We explore how radicalization is often considered a mediatized process, looking at how jihadist groups have constructed an adaptive media system to maintain members and attract new followers, while counter-radicalization agencies also use online tactics to achieve the opposite effect. Each confronts the challenges and opportunities of the second phase of mediatization, namely that Web 2.0 and the proliferation of digital devices enables a chaotic dynamic to communications, which radicalizing and counter-radicalizing forces attempt to control and manage to their advantage. At the same time, however, 'radicalizing influence' may also be felt by individuals in offline situations, and it may be that tracing the interaction of on- and offline communications is needed for a fuller understanding of radicalization.

This mediatization of radicalization creates extreme uncertainty about the causal relations involved. The second phase of mediatization, marked by Web 2.0 and the massive archiving and unforeseeable emergence of digital communications, appears to some scholars to be entwined with a shift to a 'new' terrorism: in place of 'old' terrorists who had explicit political goals, today's jihadists and other groups offer no viable demands with which to engage, only an apparently purposeless affinity for unpredictable acts of well-publicized violence. What radicalizes individuals to take such a stance is a matter of several factors such as ideology, personal experiences and social networks, but the time taken to become radicalized, the sequence of events in that process and the relative importance of these factors vary on a case-by-case basis, offering no 'model' of radicalization. Moreover, the rhetoric of jihad is so ambiguous and contested that anybody could interpret their actions under the rubric of this term.

These uncertainties make policies to prevent or counter radicalization extremely difficult. In the final section of the chapter we consider the idea that networked forms of organization adopted by terrorist and counter-terrorist agencies alter the 'logistics of military perception' by making some aspects of the radicalization process less visible but some more visible. Yet the effort to combat these diffuse networks has created a condition called 'hypersecurity' (Masco, 2002) in which fears about terrorism, technology and the movement of people merge into a generalized fear of the future itself. Despite the uncertainties surrounding the term and the process it is presumed to refer to, news reporting in recent years has instead tended to reproduce a government- and intelligence-led discourse of radicalization and insecurity in an uncritical manner, thereby contributing to hypersecurity by presenting radicalization to audiences as a known process that is now part of normal life.

Media and terrorism have long had a 'symbiotic' relationship, but the emergence of diffused war adds new layers, forms and dilemmas to this relationship. The three axes of diffused war – mediatization, nonlinear causality and uncertain decision-making – offer a lens for researchers to identify and understand the relationship between media and the radicalization phenomenon. This field of war has been subject to many overgeneralizations by politicians, journalists and jihadists themselves, because sustaining a discourse of ever-present radicalization and the uncertainty of technology-delivered threats may function to further each of their interests (Awan et al., 2010). In a field where, often, little data is available at all, where media content may cross platforms and languages, and where interactions between on- and offline dynamics must be accounted for, careful analysis is required.

1. The Mediatization of Radicalization

In Chapter 1, we introduced Paul Virilio's idea of the 'logistics of military perception': '*[T]he history of battle is primarily the history of radically changing fields of perception*. In other words, war consists not so much in scoring territorial, economic or other material victories as in appropriating the 'immateriality' of perceptual fields' (1989: 7; original emphasis). So it is for radicalization and terrorism: they work through the appropriation of perceptual fields. Radicalizing agents such as Al-Qaeda have media systems that commission, produce and distribute content that legitimates their worldview and actions, as well as media-monitoring websites that report on how their content is being reported on in mainstream Arabic and Western media (for a historical overview, see Awan and Al-Lami, 2009). Counter-radicalizing agents respond with their own content, and we explore these radicalizing/counter-radicalizing media struggles below, unpacking how each 'side' tries to win the 'battle for hearts and minds' of 'vulnerable' potential radicals. These struggles, facilitated by the media technologies of the second phase of mediatization – Web 2.0, mobile recording devices – build upon long-standing dynamics between media and terrorism. The emergence of mass media encouraged those committed to political or religious violence to seek the 'oxygen' of media publicity to create awareness and, possibly, fear, just as mainstream media have long faced the dilemma of how and whether to report on terrorist activities. The first phase of mediatization was marked by instances of the human and material destruction that national and global media so obligingly made spectacular, from the 1972 Munich Olympics to the attacks of 11 September 2001. But the manner in which radicalization and terrorism are now mediatized is not just a matter of the quest for publicity and propaganda success, nor the ability to use media technologies to sustain terrorist network structures and counter-terrorism organizational structures. The mediatization of radicalization also refers to the manner in which media technologies themselves, because of their association with extremist materials and other threats, become a source of insecurity. In this way, we see radicalization – and terrorism – as key constituents of diffused warfare, its dynamics exemplifying the latest stage in a continuum of the mutual transformations of mediation, perceptual fields and the waging of warfare.

Since the late 1990s a jihadist media system has emerged, adapting to new media technologies as they became available and to the need to stay one step ahead of law-enforcement agencies. For most of this period, Al-Qaeda has created and dominated a centralized, controlled, top-down approach to the production and distribution of the videos, speech transcripts, *nasheeds* (songs) and other content disseminated as a means to legitimate their cause. For example, if a militant group carried out a jihadist violent operation in, say, Iraq or Afghanistan, it would not post the video directly onto jihadist web forums. Rather, the video would be sent to one of a handful of media producers working with Al-Qaeda, such as As-Sahhab or Al-Furqan. Once the package is produced, it would be sent to a jihadist media agency, such as Al-Fajr, for distribution to trusted people or nodes in the jihadist media network. These trusted people would use their membership of jihadist forums to post the finished package. Such forums put up regular warnings against members posting videos they have made themselves, since a potentially chaotic influx of uncensored videos, whose quality and ideology may depart from the expected standard and line, could harm the credibility of Al-Qaeda's media system by association. Al-Boraq Media Institute, part of the system core, warned in September 2006 against 'Media Exuberance' – that is, the proliferation of unsanctioned material by users (Awan and Al-Lami, 2009). While assorted user-generated videos of jihadist-inspired rhetoric or violence have been posted on Web 2.0 forums such as YouTube, these do not appear in the core jihadist media system for the attention of members. Consequently, the jihadist media system has usually offered a relatively participation-free experience for users as those at the top of the hierarchy use the system to control 'the message'.

This is not always the case, however. The jihadist media system has modulated between centralization and decentralization depending on strategic needs. A centralized system allows for greater control of the form, content and timing of what is communicated, but renders the system vulnerable to disruption, since those centralized sites could be shut down by cyber-hackers or public authorities and the individuals administering the sites could be liable to criminal charges. The tools of the second phase of mediatization offered solutions, such as anonymous, distributed peer-to-peer networks, as Awan and Al-Lami describe:

> The glaringly obvious solution to both circumventing culpability *vis-à-vis* online content, and decentralising media efforts entailed little more than completing the transition to Web 2.0, thus delegating responsibility for user-generated content to a

suitably large and diffuse body of anonymous web users instead, who would ensure the longevity of the message irrespective of attacks on any single node. (2009: 58)

Supporters began to participate in moderate, non-jihadist forums such as Aljazeeratalk, an affiliated website of the Al Jazeera news network. Rather than preaching to the already-converted, jihadists had to engage in arguments with those sceptical of their worldview and face the possibility of being critically questioned, out-argued or simply dismissed altogether.

Following the closure of Al-Qaeda's main media operations on 10 September 2008, just prior to the posting of a video expected to commemorate the 9/11 attacks, a cyber-migration occurred as members sought new spaces for the posting and discussion of jihadist material. Indeed, on 10 December 2008 a leading member of one of the few surviving forums, al-Faloja, suggested that the movement should launch an 'invasion' of Facebook, 'not to introduce jihadi forum members to Facebook, but to introduce Facebook users to jihadi forums' (Al-Lami and O'Loughlin, 2009). A jihadist Facebook group was set up, but quickly shut down again. Since then, several core sites have reappeared; authorities may not want such sites closed completely as they are a source of intelligence about the current thinking of jihadist members concerning various issues and conflicts.

The jihadists themselves appear to believe that their online campaigns and virtual spaces are a means of increasing support for their worldview and of encouraging attacks in their name. In other words, radicalization can be cultivated at least partially online; it can be a mediatized phenomenon, inextricable from the media that enables the process to occur. This has led to attempts to trace how online radicalization operates (Awan, 2007; Conway and McInerney, 2008; Bermingham et al., 2009), how it might be countered (Bergin et al., 2009; ICSR, 2009) and the relation between on- and offline radicalization processes (de Koning, 2008; Sageman, 2008). Understanding these processes is incredibly difficult, as we discuss in detail in the next section. Enormous practical and ethical challenges confront researchers trying to identify exactly where online users might be in the world, their gender and age, what is going on in their offline life, whether a person is actually playing the part of several users, and so on. And to then discern what forces are having an effect on whether a person is being radicalized or not presents a further series of difficulties.

Online de-radicalization refers to the process of persuading individuals to renounce a particular worldview or ideology through online interactions. For example, the 'Tranquillity' campaign in Saudi Arabia employed dozens of *ulema* (Muslim scholars) to enter jihadist or Islamist forums to engage in dialogue with young (16–30-year-old) individuals holding extremist interpretations of Islam but yet to commit violence (Yehoshua, 2006; Ansary, 2008). In the UK, the Research, Information and Communications Unit (RICU), a communications team based in the Office of Security and Counter Terrorism (OSCT), was launched in 2007 with the objective of disrupting and discrediting Al-Qaeda's 'single narrative' (Cornish, 2008; cf. Roy, 2008) across various platforms, while government funding was allocated to a group called the Radical Middle Way to carry out de-radicalization engagement online. Yet such programmes assume a model of radicalization in which an individual acquires a worldview or ideology and then eventually carries out violent action. The problem is that many of those who commit violence in the name of jihad do not hold such a coherent jihadist ideology prior to their actions. Rather, the ideology may be acquired later, in prison, say, among those with more religious and political knowledge (Roy, 2008.). Gilbert Ramsey writes:

> [M]any of the most militant of 'jihadi' cultural items available from the Internet are highly ideologically promiscuous, referencing in turns a heady mix of half understood Islamism, Arab nationalism, Salafism, the Nation of Islam, conspiracy theories of the left and the right and so on. The logic expressed is not that of a well-worked out theological justification for jihad as a *fardh 'ayn*, but rather a loose, but emotive sense that Muslims (as an imagined community more than as adherents to a highly specific creed) are under attack and must be defended. While there may be a narrative behind such beliefs, it is emotive rather than intellectual and therefore not necessarily accessible to argumentation. (2009: 42)

Policies aiming to tackle mediatized radicalization require a greater understanding of the radicalization process itself, then; simply engaging through the correct media is not enough. But, as we shall see in the next section, understanding how radicalization works is difficult for a number of reasons.

2. Diffuse Relations Between Cause and Effect

The radicalization phenomenon must be understood in the context of recurring debates about the emergence of a 'new' kind of terrorism. The standard account here (Devji, 2005, 2008; Neumann, 2009) is that while 'old' terrorism was carried out in order to achieve political goals, 'new' terrorism is without purpose. The IRA, Tamil Tigers and Hamas resorted to violence in order to achieve political goals such as the control of territory. In their struggles, an end-point was possible because they had concrete demands, so either these goals were achieved or it became clear that it was impossible to realize them, and they either reached a political compromise or were defeated outright. What is called 'new' terrorism appears nihilistic: while Al-Qaeda may demand that Western forces leave the Middle East, and others demand the replacement of nation-states with a caliphate, such goals are so unrealistic that negotiations are impossible. For instance, Leman-Langlois and Brodeur differentiate between 'conventional' and 'new' terrorism:

> Conventional terrorism blended physical aggression with an explicit intention to convey its meaning and its implications. It was reflexive violence: it reflected upon its purpose, which in some instances had a certain level of complexity (e.g., political independence and social reform), and repeatedly tried to communicate this reflection. . . . The new terrorism, in most instances uninterested in conveying an articulate message, instead produces a form of expressive violence that signifies little beyond anger, frustration, and a desire to return to some mythical and glorious past. (2005: 132)

This is not to argue that the new has replaced the conventional. Rather, these two forms of terrorism map onto the two phases of mediatization and also exemplify shifts, although partial and uneven, from the ordered to the chaotic mediation of terror and terrorism, and what we set out here as their juxtaposition, interplay and modulation in our model of diffused war. As ever, caution and precision are needed with these topics. Following the perceived imminence and scale of the threat of contemporary terrorism by governments, security services and some journalists and citizens, the subdiscipline of terrorism studies has emerged at a pace that has raised concerns from some analysts over the conceptual clarity and coherence of these debates. For example, Neumann and Smith criticize what they judge to be the 'semantics' of terrorism and dismiss 'the promotion of terrorism as an omnibus term to cover a spectrum of violent activity [which] often leads to a confusing and incoherent debate about the actual nature of the threat in the current security environment' (2008: 2). There is some purchase in this assessment, not least as the contemporary study of terrorism is still rather fragmented. Major fields of study include, for example, the psychological accounting for behavioural influences in predisposing and shaping the actions of terrorists; the politics of strategic policy, prevention and response; and the significance of the perceptions and insecurities of populations in response to media representations of actual terrorist atrocities and the potential threats. However, despite Smith and Neumann's claim that terrorism 'constitutes a strategic practice' and their focus is on its 'military dynamics' (ibid.), they do not see *these* dynamics as mediatized phenomena. They make some very limited reference to 'the media' in their account, but do not consider even their main object of critique – the discursive realities that forge our very understanding of and responses to 'terrorism' and military activity – as first and foremost mediatized. Whether we classify contemporary terrorism and processes of radicalization as novel or not, the role of media must be accounted for if we are to understand how these practices work. It is the transformation and diffusion of media technologies that enable radicalization to take the form of an 'effect without cause', or, as we shall describe now, an effect whose causation is extraordinarily difficult to trace and build consistent theory or model around.

The central principle across the many definitions of radicalization is that it is 'a process of change, a transformation from one condition to another' (Al-Lami, 2008: 2). But what causes such a change? One of the difficulties with the term 'radicalization' is that it is a general term to describe a process which may occur in very different ways and for different reasons. In a survey of academic and policymakers' studies of radicalization, Al-Lami (2008) found that five factors were consistently referred to as causes of individuals becoming radicalized. We depict these five factors in figure 8.1.

Socioeconomic deprivation refers to a lack of economic opportunity or achievement relative to other members of a society. Western European Muslims are relatively poorer than other demographic groups, which may be a source of grievance and frustration. While those committing violence in the name of jihad have rarely been poor themselves, they may resent the economic inequalities affecting Muslims in Western Europe generally. Plus, as Al-Lami notes, even considerable economic wealth does not imply social integration. *The search for*

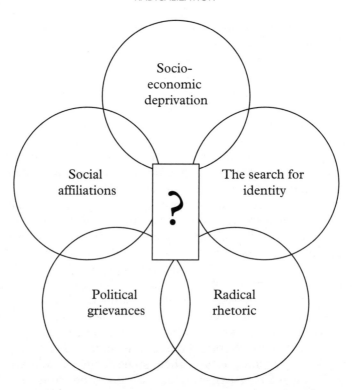

Figure 8.1   Factors Contributing to Radicalization
Source: Based on Al-Lami (2008)

identity is not exclusive to Muslims: sociologists have long argued that globalization destabilizes social traditions, identities and relationships as we are exposed to a greater diversity of people, culture, products and political and religious ideas. The issue is how these processes affect some Muslims and how they respond. For instance, studies demonstrate that young Muslims in the West have experienced a particular 'identity crisis' (Wiktorowicz, 2004) and sense of humiliation (Khosrokhavar, 2005). These local experiences are reinforced by the felt connection to Muslim countries and identification with Muslim societies, in which Islamic governments have failed to deliver peace or prosperity relative to other states. This leads to an apparently paradoxical situation in which Muslims born and raised in the West use a language of identity politics (Durodie, 2009) that originated in the West to assert their difference to the West by drawing on religious rhetoric or habits, such as wearing the headscarf or hijab, from Islamic traditions and countries about which they know little (Al-Lami, 2008). *Radical rhetoric* offers the basis for an appealing narrative about the possibility of fighting for change, and is easily found on the Internet as well as through offline communications from preachers, pamphlets and so on.

Political grievances refer not simply to disagreement with the policies of Western or Islamic governments, but also to a lack of opportunity for meaningful participation in politics at all and thus no capacity to influence events affecting the lives of Muslims. The foreign policy of Western governments is seen to harm the interests of Muslims around the world, while Islamic regimes in the Middle East and Southern Asia are deemed complicit. Consequently, only political action outside and against Western and Islamic regimes is thought to be effective; individuals must be radicalized against them. Finally, *social affiliation* is deemed the primary factor in some cases of radicalization. Marc Sageman (2004, 2008) has carried out analysis of the social networks of radicalized individuals and attempted to discern the difference made by particular networks. Individuals are not radicalized by consuming media containing radical rhetoric at their home computer or on their phone, but through face-to-face interactions with friends or acquaintances over time, although such interactions can be facilitated and extended through online communication.

Even if one could identify which factors are more likely to bring about the radicalization of individuals in a given society, the question of how the process would then play out is unclear. The change in a person's attitudes could take many years or happen in a matter of weeks or even days. It could be the result of a sudden, defining experience such as the death of a family member or an incident of racism, or it could be the result of a gradual shift in attitude or belief as a person consumes news or listens to particular clerical figures. There is no necessarily consistent sequence to the process: for some, a random encounter with the words of a cleric or an extremist website may be what sparks an interest in 'radical' ideas in the first place; for others, these words or websites may be the final 'tipping point' to violent action. A person may undergo many of the 'stages' of the process but then turn away from violence at the last minute. A 2008 report commissioned for the European Commission defines radicalization as: 'The phenomenon of people embracing opinions, views and ideas which could lead to acts of terrorism.'[2] This important term is 'could': it could not. Equally, however, a person could reject violence temporarily – for days or for years – and then emerge to commit a violent act. And should governments be concerned with those holding extremist ideas and sympathizing with those carrying out violent acts, but who do not commit violence themselves? What exactly is the threshold for being defined as 'radical': thought or action? How would a society arrive at agreement on this? Policymakers may speak of 'draining the swamp' of support for terrorism, but can liberal societies criminalize individuals merely for holding ideas? Many ultimately radicalized individuals are notable only for their normality (Home Office, 2006; NYPD, 2007), but liberal governments have not traditionally had the will or technologies to continually monitor all 'normal' people. Uncertainties about the radicalization process present a number of challenges to policymakers, then, in terms of preventing terrorism, but also in ensuring that efforts to prevent terrorism do not corrupt privileged social values of freedom of thought and expression. Paradoxically, if counter-terrorism policy is seen to override a society's values, this may contribute to radicalization by weakening the attractiveness of that society. Thus the difficulty of defining and understanding radicalization is entwined with apprehensiveness about compounding the problem by alienating the very people government wishes to prevent from turning to extremist violence.

These problems are exacerbated by terminological disagreement around the term 'jihad'. On the one hand, it is a term with a long history, having been subject to debates in religious scholarship for centuries. On the other, it is a term used loosely in media and by some self-proclaimed jihadists themselves. After conflict began between Israel and the people of Gaza in December 2008, Al-Qaeda and numerous Muslim clerics were quick to call for a *defensive* jihad, an obligatory struggle against an aggressive force. A joint statement was published by 100 Muslim clerics and theologians that argued: '[J]ihad in Palestine is completely legitimate and must be supported with lives, weapons, and money. Jews in Palestine are aggressors and therefore their lives and possessions are fair game.'[3] By 6 January 2009 Al-Qaeda's Ayman Al-Zawahiri had expanded the remit of this mission, calling for attacks against 'the Crusader-Zionist alliance worldwide' (Al-Zawahiri, 2009). The term 'jihad' appears to have sufficient ambiguity for different actors to use it to warrant different policies. At a conference devoted to addressing this confusion in September 2009,[4] Rudolph Peters, from the University of Amsterdam, suggested a series of levels of disagreement about the term, drawing in part on his 2005 book *Jihad in Classical and Modern Islam*. Here he unpacks the concept of defensive jihad:

1 If one can be clear on the difference between offensive and defensive jihad, what counts as a legitimate reason for defensive action? Outright occupation of one's country by another political power, aggression against one's country but not invasion, or merely oppression by one's own government?

2 If occupation, what counts as occupation? Osama bin Laden released a declaration in 1998 stating that the US was occupying Muslim lands. This referred to the presence of US troops in Saudi Arabia. But since the Saudi regime voluntarily accepted this presence, can it be classified as occupation?

3 Who counts as an occupier or oppressor? Is it just non-Muslims, or does it include Muslims who appear liberal or less pious than the jihadists themselves? Can enemies be divided into separate identity groups, or if one group is fighting a 'global' war on many fronts – Afghanistan, Sudan, Bosnia, Chechnya and so on – is there simply one enemy?

4 Once a response begins, what counts as legitimate application of violence? Islamic scholars and jihadists themselves are divided over whether suicide bombing is legitimate.

Not only is there disagreement on what a concept like 'defensive jihad' means, nor any clear definition or consistent usage in the Quran, but there is no agreement on who has the authority to decide the meaning, or a ruling authority to enforce its correct application. Hence, if a Muslim person wakes up and wants to know, 'What shall I do about X problem?', no single text or authoritative interpreter of the text can provide an absolute answer. This uncertainty represents a window of opportunity for groups and their leaders to offer interpretations according to their particular interests, including jihadist leaders seeking to enhance their own credibility, authority and following.

If the difficulty of defining and understanding radicalization and terminological disputes around the term 'jihad' are a problem for governments, then they are a problem for media organizations too. In the final section of this chapter, we address how decision-making has been affected, and some ways that governments and media organizations have responded to these uncertainties.

3. Uncertainty for Policymakers and Journalists Enables 'Hypersecurity' to Emerge

> Even the vocabulary of this war will be different. When we 'invade the enemy's territory,' we may well be invading his cyberspace. There may not be as many beachheads stormed as opportunities denied. Forget about 'exit strategies'; we're looking at a sustained engagement that carries no deadlines. (US Defense Secretary Donald Rumsfeld, 28 September 2001)[5]

In this section we argue that new media technologies enable networked forms of organization for radicalizing and terrorist groups. This form of organization would appear to make more difficult the identification and targeting of individuals that support or carry out violence, but as with the chaos-control dynamic running through many aspects of diffused war, it is not that simple: media technologies make people visible as well as allow them to hide. Such struggles in the field of perception, however, contribute to a condition of 'hypersecurity' (Masco, 2002). That is, in societies such as the UK the phenomenon of radicalization feeds into insecurities about technology, the movement of people and the impossibility of foreseeing exactly what threats may emerge in the future. The result is that the future may become framed in terms of an endless balancing of security and insecurity such that the containment of diffuse threats takes priority over matters of progress and acknowledgement that unforeseen risks are not in-themselves catastrophic. As Secretary Rumsfeld said, it no longer makes sense to think of 'exit strategies'.

The dynamics of accessibility and connectivity, the decentralization (Benkler, 2006) of *networks*, and the development of a 'network society' (Castells, 1996) (also linked with *flows*) are highly influential developments for the formulation of models accounting for the growth of and engagement with digital media. A network is a series or system of points or nodes interconnected by communication paths or channels. With the advanced and accelerated connectivity ushered in by digital and mobile forms and technologies, our new media ecology is partly constituted through overlapping and continuously available networks. For some commentators, networks are the organizational basis of a particular type of warfare, for instance 'netwars'. John Arquilla and David Ronfeldt consider that the 'information revolution' is:

> favoring and strengthening network forms of organization, often giving them an advantage over hierarchical forms. The rise of networks means that power is migrating to nonstate actors, because they are able to organize into sprawling multiorganizational networks . . . more readily than can traditional, hierarchical, state actors. This means that conflicts may increasingly be waged by 'networks,' perhaps more than by 'hierarchies.' It also means that whoever masters the network form stands to gain the advantage. (2001: 1)

Thus, the 'conduct and outcome of conflicts' for Arquilla and Ronfeldt are increasingly dependent on knowledge and thus information management (ibid.) And, as Arquilla in later work argues:

> The fact that a wide range of terrorists, rogue states, and transnational criminal enterprises have already gotten a head start in a new 'organizational race' to form networks – akin to the Cold War-era arms race – should galvanize our efforts to focus on building networks of our own to fight these darker forms. (2007: 1)

In this way, the security threat posed by networks is viewed as substantial. For instance, Al-Qaeda, the most notorious global terrorist group of the opening of this century, exhibits that which Samuel Weber claims are the 'underlying structural traits' of networks, notably 'dispersion and mobility' (2004: 15). As Awan and Al-Lami noted (above), the Al-Qaeda media system has in recent years responded to the threat of closure and prosecution by 'delegating responsibility for user-generated content to a suitably large and diffuse body of anonymous web users instead, who would ensure the longevity of the message irrespective of attacks on any single node' (2009: 58). Al-Qaeda's capacity to spread terror and its self-mutating generative capacity constitutes an 'enemy' against which it is extremely difficult to declare definitive 'victory' (Rid and Hecker, 2009: 10), hence the extended temporal horizons in Western political and military discourses to 'the long war' and 'the war on terror' (Westhead, 2006) and Rumsfeld's denial of the possibility of 'exit strategies'. In this respect, the network concept in itself does not seem sufficient to interrogate the complexities of emergent global terrorist groups and their impact, including their dynamic and fluid-like formations and re-formations. Network is a spatial concept, but there is a need to consider both spatial and temporal dimensions of radicalizing relationships. Social theorists have offered alternative formulations. John Urry (2003: 132) for example, observes, 'Al-Qaeda has been likened to a self-organizing system "on the edge of chaos"'. Thus, Urry identifies a 'complexity turn' in the social and cultural sciences as 'a shift from reductionist analyses to those that involve the study of complex adaptive ('vital') matter that shows ordering but which remains on "the edge of chaos"' (2005: 1). The point about being on the edge of chaos is that the system can tip, leading to a new form or structure unforeseeable in advance. Complexity may be a productive means of moving beyond a mere focus on networks to inform our account of diffused war because, like 'emergence', it describes a nonlinear development of relations, producing phenomena greater than the sum of parts, for example contagion and climates of fear.

Another formulation comes from Faisal Devji's analysis of Al-Qaeda. He points to a new form of political action, not simply the action of a coordinated network, but a network that harnesses the mediatized emergence of new events and stories. He writes:

> The Islam of militancy and offence occupies a global arena in which *it acts without being an actor*. That is to say militancy exists as a global agent by virtue of sacrifices that are *amplified* in the media and mirrored around the world without the benefit of political leadership and institutions. (2008: 206; emphases added)

This conceptualization of Al-Qaeda is supported in the analysis of Karin Knorr-Cetina, who suggests the 'world of Al-Qaeda appears to be fluid, processual and aterritorial':

> As the flow of events into which Al-Qaeda members are plugged is continuously reiterated, updated and extended, the various temporal and other coordinates of this world are continuously articulated and changed as operational goals are adopted, religious commentary and messages are interpreted, new decrees are issued, and the activities of various 'enemies' are observed and decoded. (2005: 222)

Al-Qaeda 'get' diffused war insofar as their members, dispersed and often hidden for security reasons, base their strategy on the expectation of continuous adaptation. At the same time, members fit any new events and media content into their longer-term narrative of a centuries-long struggle against a homogeneous, aggressive West.

As new media technologies enable groups to operate in this diffuse manner, making decisions about how to identify and disrupt their operations should correspondingly become more difficult. Arquilla and Ronfeldt, for example, argue that '[i]nformation-age threats are likely to be more diffuse, dispersed, multidimensional nonlinear, and ambiguous than industrial-age threats' (2002: 2). Thus, one of the key requirements for those in the business of containing and countering the networked threat, notably a tangible (identifiable, locatable and destroyable) target, is potentially undermined. This is a key challenge then for those charged with combating so-called 'netwar', as Samuel Weber argues in a response to Arquilla and Ronfeldt: 'There is still an enemy, and however acephalous or Janus-faced it might be, it must still be targeted – which is to say, located and subdued, either by being killed, destroyed, or rendered dysfunctional' (2004: 14). So does radicalization slip through the requirements for targeting in Weber's terms?

On the one hand, radicalization seems observable. The 'enemy' may be identifiable and prosecutable as those that preach 'radicalizing' views, such as Abu Hamza al-Masri (the Egyptian born Mostafa Mostafa) convicted of soliciting murder and inciting racial hatred in the UK in February 2006 and notorious for his use of Finsbury Park mosque as a powerbase for preaching and for radicalizing. Another example is the conviction of Mohammed Hamid in the UK in February 2008. Hamid had been found guilty of training men in secret camps in the Lake District and New Forest to prepare them to fight overseas. Those passing through his camps included the men who failed to detonate bombs on 21 July 2005 (the '21/7 bombers'). On the other hand, the spread of radical ideas or beliefs is not containable even by the prosecution and imprisonment of those identified as the principal 'preachers'. For instance, the ending of a BBC report of the Hamid conviction story provides one example:

> The men convicted alongside them were not the only ones to attend talks at Hamid's home and camps. Detectives think Hamid may have been making up to 10 new contacts a month during the period they were watching him. Many of these men would briefly listen to his theories and go on their way. Others would come to his home. The question is how many of those left believing what they had heard – and where did they go?[6]

These media representations of radicalization, and the periodic appearance of radicalization-related stories in mainstream news media, contribute to a condition of 'hypersecurity' (Masco, 2002).That is, in societies such as the UK the phenomenon of radicalization feeds into insecurities about technology and the impossibility of foreseeing and controlling the threats that technologies such as the Internet may bring.

In his authoritative ethnographic account, *The Nuclear Borderlands* (2006), Joseph Masco interrogates the cultural politics of national security in the US and describes how the Cold War obsession with the atomic bomb served to hide the wider and deeper impact of the 'nuclear complex' on everyday life in America. Masco defines 'hypersecurity' in this context as: 'an overdetermined effort to both mobilize and contain the nuclear referent through increasingly disciplinary structures of secrecy and threat' (2006: 279). He goes further to identify 'hyper-security in perhaps its purest form' in relation to the US-government issued warnings in the year following 9/11:

> These alerts were characterized by an absence of information about the source of the threat, the longevity of the risk, or the rationale for the warning. In essence, these state declarations of risk simply presented citizens with the category of 'threat' itself (i.e., the official message was: something terrible might happen, somewhere, any second now); the alerts provided citizens with no conceptual tools for evaluating or accommodating this new danger. It was danger itself purified and amplified as national discourse. (Ibid.: 286)

In a UK context, following the 2005 London bombings, a terrorist threat itself was 'purified and amplified as national discourse' in terms of radicalization. The targeting of the 'enemy' in Weber's description (above) did not seem to be a meaningful requirement for the constitution of a threat because, as we have discussed, authorities do not have clear data and models of how the radicalization process works. It is arguably more the case that the notion of 'enemy' has been replaced with threat itself, something that Frank Furedi, for example, considers is 'a threat beyond meaning' (2007: 77). Radicalization has quickly emerged as a threat that may be visible or invisible, feeding into a radical ambiguity of the construction of and responses to 'terrorism' in the UK and particularly following the 2005 London bombings. The policy implications of this ambiguous threat, argues Dillon (2007:8) has been a 'massive global security effort' invested in the 'war on terror' which itself has amplified danger and fear through attempts to 'make terror at least governable', if not to eliminate it altogether. As a consequence, Dillon argues, there has been a massive extension and intensification of security practices in almost every aspect of western life. Alongside Masco and Furedi then, Dillon's analysis points to the manner in which efforts to prevent radicalization and violence and maintain physical security in a society can lead to prescriptions and policies that undermine other forms of security such as the capacity to live without continuous fear. This echoes what Brian Massumi (2005b: 8) defines as an 'affective fact': 'Threat triggers fear. The fear is of disruption. The fear *is* a disruption'.

In this context of uncertainty, ambiguity and the prospect of endless counter-radicalization and counter-terrorism work, policymakers in recent years have focused attention on methods for forecasting likely future events. Richard Grusin (2004, 2010; cf. Baudrillard, 1994: 55) offers the term 'premediation' to describe how journalists, public officials and other 'experts' manage public expectations of future events through the broadcasting of various traumatic scenarios such that should such a scenario actually unfold, the experience is not shocking partly because it assumes a familiar form.

In Chapter 5, *Genocide*, we drew upon Astrid Erll's definition of premediation. To repeat from her excellent work: 'The American understanding and representation of 9/11 was clearly premediated by disaster movies, the crusader narrative, and biblical stories. Premediation therefore refers to the cultural practices of looking, naming, and narrating' (2008: 393). However, the strategic uses of premediation might be considered to amplify the condition of hypersecurity. In terms of security agendas, Grusin's analysis of this phenomenon is critical:

> [P]remediation characterizes the mediality [media practices] of the first decade of the twenty-first century as focused on the cultural desire to make sure that the future has already been remediated before it turns into the present – in large part to try to prevent the media, and hence the American public, from being caught unawares as it was on the morning of September 11, 2001. (2010: 5–6)

Premediation strategies contribute to the condition of hypersecurity by attempting to preserve against the potential shock of the future, the very prospects of that shock, and the anticipatory fear delivered through the articulation of those prospects. Through movies, documentaries, public statements and speculative journalist reports, possible scenarios can be imagined. It is a pressing research question to ascertain the extent to which these speculations amplify or contain uncertainties or provide useful guides for action and interpretation for policymakers, reporters and citizens living through diffused war.

Uncertainties about the nature and extent of radicalization processes are a problem for news journalists too (Hoskins and O'Loughlin, 2009b). On the one hand, radicalization events meet key criteria of newsworthiness. For journalists, 'radicalization' can anchor a news agenda, offering a cast of radicalizers and the vulnerable radicalized, and appear to warrant a government decision and policy response to such danger which journalists can then analyse. On the other hand, journalists may inadvertently reinforce prior myths and stereotypes about potential terrorist threats. In the UK, reporting of stories related to radicalization, whether major events such as the 7/7 London bombings, the 2006 transatlantic air plot or the 2006 Forest Gate raids, or routine reports on radicalization in prisons, have presented audiences with a 'clustering' of terms, phrases and associated discourses – for example, the term 'grooming' of 'vulnerable' young individuals has migrated from discourses around paedophilia and the Internet. By discussing radicalization in an unproblematic way, as if the term and process it refers to is widely understood (and we have seen, above, that it is not), journalists, policymakers and various 'experts' offer a false certainty (Hoskins and O'Loughlin, 2009a). The character of such reporting may be because security journalists rely upon official sources for concrete information about security operations and criminal cases related to radicalization, and such information is unlikely to be forthcoming in all instances in order to preserve the secrecy of the operations or not prejudice the case. Nevertheless, the ambiguous reporting that results may contribute further to the condition of hypersecurity since it represents radicalization as something both exceptionally dangerous and yet part of a 'new normal' (Massumi, 2005a), something we can expect to happen routinely and with no identifiable end-point or horizon.

4. Conclusion

The certainties once associated with the who, why, when, where and how of terrorism are scattered and obscured by the dynamics of our new media ecology. Often, certain knowledge cannot even be grasped retrospectively; communications data is deleted, relationships occurred face-to-face and former 'radicals' who do speak out in public may alter their story to lend themselves glamour and credibility. There is also a need to disentangle actual empirical studies *of* radicalization that, under scrutiny, appear valid and reliable, from claims made *about* radicalization, since the term itself may function in the interests of key constituents such as governments, assorted security 'experts', journalists and even terrorist groups themselves (Awan et al., 2010). In the study of the emergence of diffused war, then, analysis of radicalization presents two tasks and makes a double demand on us: to analyse how media is used to legitimize violence (radicalization as empirical fact, to the extent it can be verified), and to analyse how 'radicalization' as a discourse is used to legitimise certain policies, attitudes and fears.

Radicalization is often a mediatized phenomenon, so those seeking to research and understand how radicalizers communicate to persuade potential recruits, and the impact such communications have on those recruits and on wider societies, must adopt some model or approach to political communication. The reader may consider how the various conceptualizations of media frames, discourse and culture we survey in chapter 10, and the models or lines of causation they imply, might apply to jihadist media and de-radicalization programmes. Did Al-Qaeda create a media system to 'manufacture consent', as Herman and Chomsky (1994) propose Western governments do? How can we begin to map such diffused communications, distributed across the Internet and involving an unknown number of often anonymous users, let alone discern their effect? At present, Western governments have little idea how to assess the impact of their own counter-radicalization communications efforts (Wilton Park, 2008) – and no wonder: how can we discern the effect counter-radicalizing communications might have when a person is exposed to innumerable influences on- and offline every day? In chapter 9, next, we will see how actors involved in war legitimate violence, including the legitimations of the 2008 Mumbai attacks offered on jihadist forums. We also consider the role translation plays in the distribution of jihadist media content to audiences who lack Arabic, and how the gain and loss of aspects of 'the message' that is inevitable to translation might affect the legitimacy and credibility of that appeal.

9

LEGITIMACY

1. Introduction: Legitimacy, Representation, Discourse

War and conflict are sustained by legitimacy. If soldiers involved in a war think its conduct is morally unjustifiable and illegitimate, their morale will suffer and some may seek an exit by claiming to be a conscientious objector. If citizens do not believe a war being fought by their country is legitimate, they may elect alternative political leaders who will end the war, or resent paying taxes to fund the war. But to be able to give consent to a war, soldiers and citizens must have knowledge of the situation, including the factors that have made military intervention necessary, how the war will be conducted or is being conducted, and the consequences of the war for the affected soldiers and civilians. This knowledge is provided through media, by military and political leaders and by journalists, and even by civilians able to blog from war zones. Hence, the legitimacy of a war depends on how it is described and explained through media. In our introductory chapter we noted Virilio's statement that '*the history of battle is primarily the history of radically changing fields of perception*', and this is partly because legitimacy depends on how these fields of perception operate through media.

Legitimacy has become more difficult to sustain in the new media ecology. A leader or policy cannot be legitimate in itself; legitimacy is maintained through relationships. Legitimacy exists when a group of individuals consents, passively or actively, to obey a ruling body or set of policies. Legitimacy is not present or absent, but exists to an extent or a matter of degree (Beetham, 1991). Legitimacy must be analysed next to the concepts authority and credibility. Other actors and institutions such as clerics, scholars or news sources may not be seeking leadership over matters of war and conflict, but possess credibility to certain audiences in making political and/or religious claims and contesting processes of legitimacy. In the new media ecology there are many such credible sources and their authority may cut across territorial boundaries. As a result, processes of legitimacy and acts of consent entail complex, near-instant feedback loops between national, translocal/diasporic and global public opinion, all of which are diffuse to varying degrees and difficult to measure (by polls, surveys, data mining of blogs – see chapter 10). In addition, both the salience and the evidentiary basis for these claims and their evaluation by audiences can be plural and contested. Some audiences may consider a particular war to be irrelevant to them; others may find that war utterly salient to their sense of belonging or national identity. Some audiences may ask for statistical evidence gathered by medical units; others may judge a war by religious tenets. It would appear apparently impossible to convince all possible audiences or publics of the 'rightfulness' of certain problem-definitions and courses of action where war and conflict are concerned.

In the early twenty-first century, the legitimacy of the conduct of insurgency and counterinsurgency as forms of warfare has received great attention, particularly in the aftermath of the US/UK-led intervention in Iraq. Rid and Hecker argue that during an insurgency the population in the country concerned falls into three groups:

> [A] small and disenfranchised fringe group initially supports the insurgency; on the other side are those who want to see the counterinsurgent and the government succeed; in the middle between the two is the largest group, which is neutral, uncommitted, and apolitical. Both the insurgent and the counterinsurgent compete for this group's support, for their acceptance of authority, for legitimacy. (2009: 1)

The question is, what kind of claims or evidence would it take to persuade the uncommitted mass of the legitimacy of the insurgent or counterinsurgent's campaign? How should such claims be presented, using what media, and who would be the most credible voice to present the claims? Since they live in the country affected, local populations would find plenty of evidence in their daily lives, though they will also be addressed (by leaders on various sides) with appeals to religious or ethnic identity, to historical destiny, to the barbarism of the other side and so on. At the same time, the counterinsurgent force will have to appeal to audiences outside that country, in their home country and to international opinion. Is the object of war, the centre of gravity to be persuaded, the local uncommitted mass population or public opinion at home? In the US/UK-led interventions in both Iraq and Afghanistan, we have seen how the target of legitimation has shifted between the two as events have proceeded.

What makes a person offer legitimacy to war? Individuals' media consumption and discussions around media, with friends, family and colleagues, are critical to processes of legitimation. In the second phase of mediatization (see chapter 1), legitimation is further complicated by audience fragmentation, individuals' usage of a greater range of news sources and the existence of online private–public spheres or 'sphericules' (Gitlin, 1998) not necessarily seeking wider public engagement. Overall, this pluralization of possible constituencies, sources of claims and evidentiary basis of claims contributes to the condition of diffuse war, with its nonlinear, emergent and often unforeseeable dynamics.

If processes of legitimation of governments are to hold, more consideration is required for the presentation, content and basis of political claims, and more investigation into what makes counter-claims credible.

Legitimizing armed conflict entails representational 'work'. Shaw (2005) points to the rationalizing of the destruction of human life, and Scarry suggests authorities attempt to construct a 'structure of physical and perceptual events' based on the 'disowning' of injury or the ways that it disappears from view by means of 'omission' or by way of an 'active redescription of the event: the act of injuring, or the tissue that is to be injured, or the weapon that is to accomplish the injury is renamed' (1985: 66), for instance 'collateral damage' or 'targets hit'.[1] Equally, however, the legitimacy of war and military action and the rationalizing of human destruction are often challenged through discourses that put the experience of the ordinary person at the centre of our understanding of war: the dead or injured, the bereaved, the orphaned and so on. Highlighting the horror of war in graphic, detailed, human form becomes a media priority in its own right. Such highlighting intersects with a growing concern for the needs of civilian noncombatants who are the primary victims of contemporary wars (see Slim, 2007; Human Security Brief, 2006). Thus news media offers an apparently contradictory dynamic in the legitimation of war: it 'modulates between bringing the world's wars and catastrophes onto the West's horizon of responsibility and [yet partially] blocking them from view' (Hoskins and O'Loughlin, 2007: 131).

2. The Power of Representations

Decisions about war require public, intelligible justification by political leaders (Bellamy, 2005). Convincing arguments are required if a state is to achieve the people's consent to go to war or to negotiate for peace, or for secondary issues such as the decision to invest in weapons systems or decisions about how to treat captured enemies. Representation refers to the process by which an original object present at time/place X is made present again at time/place Y. The original object is represented, whether by a news report, a piece of art, or in our daily conversation. Representation is a process of copying that is never perfect, since some content or meaning is always lost and often something gained as the object being represented is copied from one context to another. How media represent war in one way or another makes a difference to the legitimacy audiences attribute to that war.

It is not simply that representations modify or selectively mimic the original situation being represented. It is a live research question whether and how representations might have a definite, identifiable effect on either those being represented or the audiences of those representations. Some discourse analysts argue that representations can *constitute* what is represented. David Campbell's (2007) analysis of the Darfur conflict demonstrates this well, and is worth introducing at length. Darfur is made up of between 40 and 150 tribes or ethnic groups, each numbering between a few thousand to more than a million individuals. The identity of social groups in Darfur cannot simply be reduced to north versus south, or Arab versus African: 'Darfur's Arabs are black, indigenous, African and Muslim – just like Darfur's non-Arabs' (de Waal, 2004, cited in Campbell, 2007: 363). However, from the late 1980s 'Arabism' became a political banner for some groups in Darfur and an organization was formed called Arab Gathering (*Tajamu al Arabi*) that demanded greater rights at the expense of non-Arabic indigenous peoples. This was granted through constitutional reform in 1994, leading to violent resistance and the formation of the Arab-only Popular Defence Forces – what became known as the Janjaweed militias. By 2003 they were at war with African tribes (see chapter 5). Yet neither the Janjaweed nor other groups were clearly defined or explicitly supported by the government. Some Arabs fight *against* the Janjaweed. Nevertheless, non-Arabs united to some extent, turning the pejorative label 'Zurga' given them by the Arab supremacists into a positive name. Coincidentally, most non-Arabs lived in the south. As Campbell notes, this political, often violent process since the 1980s has *produced* an apparent Arab-north versus African-south antagonism.

By 2003 international NGOs were reporting on the Darfur crisis, but media did not cover it. A peculiar vicious circle developed: 'When it comes to mass killings of civilians . . . [i]f editors do not see the story on TV, they do not believes it's news; if programme makers do not read it in the newspapers, they do not believe it's news. And if politicians and officials don't see it or read it except in reports thudding on to their desks from . . . NGOs, then that doesn't quite count either' (Crenshaw, 2004, cited in Campbell, 2007: 366). It became a story in March 2004 when, on the BBC, a UN spokesman called it 'the world's worst humanitarian crisis', which coincided with the tenth anniversary of the Rwanda genocide. Suddenly, news media had two frames, genocide and humanitarianism, which offer high news value: mass death (genocide) but the emotion of rescue and pity of suffering (humanitarianism). Photos of dead, injured or starving people in Darfur were suddenly contextualized alongside striking headlines on front pages (showing the importance of multimodality).

Legally, the crisis did not constitute genocide, however, because the violence was not motivated by ethnic, national, racial or religious difference. As stated earlier, the basic units of political identity in Darfur were tribes, of which there were 40–150. Yet the International Commission of Inquiry on Darfur (ICID) recognized that identities are constructions, not intrinsic or essential. If people in Darfur could see themselves as ethnic, national, racial or religiously defined, they could be protected. New representations of their identity could be legally recognized; in this way, the representations – Arab or African – came to constitute the identity of those in Darfur. People identified themselves so as to fit these legal definitions. Further, photographs in international news media seemed to *demonstrate* these identities *as* refugees or rebels, Africans or Arabs. 'The photographs that claim to represent genocide enact visually the reification of identity', Campbell writes (ibid.: 377). These external representations are then 'fed back into the political dynamic of the conflict itself' (ibid.). Groups fighting in Darfur, as well as international policymakers trying to solve the crisis, began to act as if these represented identities *really were* the identities: pictures bring the objects they purport to simply reflect into being' (ibid.: 379–80).

Just as mediation involves the loss and gain of meaning, representations offered in media reports or political speeches select-in and filter-out, make some aspects of the issue prominent and some invisible. Since mainstream media and party political leaders are the primary source of information or opinions about war for audiences (unless they are involved in a war themselves), then the representations offered by media and politicians may be the only version of the war that audiences know. Representations can have powerful effects, then, by suggesting to people *this is how the war is*; this is what preceded the war, this is what necessitates the violence.

Explaining the effect of political and media representations has been an important analytical task in international relations since the end of the Cold War. In the 1990s scholars at the Copenhagen Peace Institute began to write about security in a new way. Security was not simply a matter of the relations between nation-states, and whether shifting balances of power made states with increasing resources (nuclear weapons, armies, money) more secure than others. Instead, the Copenhagen scholars investigated how the naming of something as a security issue warranted treating that issue in those terms. Flows of money and of people (migration) were being talked about by policymakers as security issues rather than, say, issues of financial regulation or social welfare. Once these flows were named as such, then they had to be thought about as potential security threats and action had to be taken to secure them. These issues were securitized (Waever et al, 1993; Waever, 1995; Buzan et al., 1998). Securitization refers to the manner in which certain people, practices and things become considered objects to be secured, subject to security discourses advanced by states or security 'experts'. In this way, war was diffused; more phenomena became treated as security problems, crystallized in the 'war on terror', in which war against Al-Qaeda and the groups it inspired involved tracing flows of money (Biersteker and Eckert, 2007), people (especially at airports), and arms (especially chemical and biological weapons). One might ask also whose interests are served by securitization – the public interest or that of security firms that may profit from an expansion of social processes needing securing, a phenomenon Naomi Klein refers to as 'disaster capitalism' (2007).

The performative power of representations was understood by the George W. Bush Administration. An unnamed aide to the President told a *New York Times* journalist, prior to the 2003 Iraq War:

> The aide said that guys like me were 'in what we call the reality-based community,' which he defined as people who 'believe that solutions emerge from your judicious study of discernible reality.' . . . 'That's not the way the world really works anymore,' he continued. 'We're an empire now, and when we act, *we create our own reality*. And while you're studying that reality – judiciously, as you will – we'll act again, creating other new realities, which you can study too, and that's how things will sort out. We're history's actors . . . and you, all of you, will be left to just study what we do.' (Suskind, 2004; emphasis added)

Reality for the aide here is not given, out there, independent of humans who will find it, but created, authored, given meaning. For instance, through repetition over a period of many months, American citizens might come to believe the representation of Saddam Hussein as connected somehow to the 11 September 2001 attacks. For them, there was a real, actual connection.

Part of the power of representations and their relationship to legitimacy lies not in their content but in the manner of their circulation or flux. The *speed* of the emergence of vectors or flux of digital media content in the new media ecology would seem to further complicate legitimation, argues James Der Derian. The acceleration of communication, the reduction of time between an event and the global reactions to it, diminish the opportunity for 'the accountable leader, participatory citizen, the deliberative process' (2009: 252). Der Derian connects this complication of legitimation to the question of power: '[W]e have witnessed the emergence of competing sources and mediations of power: what I call a global heteropolar matrix, in which different actors are able to produce profound global effects through interconnectivity' (ibid.: 251). Power is diffused between terrorist groups, NGOs, activists and media-savvy citizens, but in a way that enables nonlinear dynamics that undermine the slow, patient deliberation we imagine democracy to require (Moss and O'Loughlin, 2008). Intelligence may suggest the existence of threats but government must convince citizens that such threats exist and that those threats warrant certain policy responses. Nevertheless, we can also observe the persistence and maintenance of discourses over decades; for example, the discourse of US exceptionalism – that the US is a chosen nation, the city on the hill, last best hope of mankind – or the discourse of victimhood among Arab or Muslim peoples, that, following colonial empires, oppression by the West continues through neocolonial projects (wars in Iraq and Afghanistan). We must therefore ask how these differing speeds or tempos contribute to the dynamics of control and chaos, order and disorder, and how this feeds into the legitimation of war.

Notions of 'pan-Arabism' or 'the West' show that discursive orders and identity groupings have never been limited to nation-state boundaries. A discourse is a persistent, largely coherent set of representations that presents a boundary of what can be communicated about a topic to make sense (Barad, 2007). A discourse may become naturalized, or it may be contested and seen as contingent.[2] In chapter 8, we discussed how a state-led discourse of radicalization has emerged in recent years despite little firm understanding or model of how the presumed process of radicalization actually works, and we suggested that this discourse may serve a function for states, counterterror 'experts' and reporters. What are the units of analysis within which we can analyse discourses 'at work' legitimating policy in this way?

The nation-state remains the primary democratic unit in world politics, a site in which power and authority can be held to account and in whose name most wars are fought. Important studies of the role of media in legitimating the Iraq war, for example, focus on national media in the US (Bennett et al, 2007) or the UK (Goddard et al., 2008). Yet one of the challenges for the study of war and media today is to devise research designs that take into account both national *and* transnational media, since citizens have access to media broadcast beyond their national borders, and journalists monitor how media in other countries report the same events as themselves. The role of translation becomes important here too (cf. Baker, 2006). Many global media events or 'accidents' (Der Derian, 2009: 204) in the past decade have involved communications to national audiences being consumed and interpreted outside the assumed target audience – for example, the Danish cartoon affair, the Abu Ghraib photos, or President Bush saying about Al-Qaeda, 'bring 'em on', a phrase with different resonance to certain US demographics than to audiences around the world. Achieving legitimacy for war or security policy has become more complex, then, involving communication through multiple media channels and platforms to multiple, unknowable-in-advance audiences, where meaning may be lost or gained in translation.

In the next section of this chapter we offer a framework to analyse representations and discourse based on a set of axes through which we can interpret the condition of diffuse war. These axes are based upon experiences of diffuse war: the experiences of military participants, elected officials, journalists and citizens-cum-audiences. Those attempting to legitimize military or security policy use these axes to present situations as problematic and warranting specific policy responses; those whose consent is sought must negotiate their own personal experience of these axes (for instance whether they feel panicked and feel threats are proximate) as well as interpret the representations offered by politicians and media.

Box 9.1 Axes of interpreting diffuse war

Justifiable death – Unjustifiable death

Routine – Exception

Patience – Urgency

Certainty – Risk

Us – Them

Through analysis of discourse in diffuse war situations, we can identify actors strategically representing a situation as one of routine unease or one of exception; a situation that calls for patience or for urgent decision and action; a situation of certainty ('known-knowns') or uncertainty ('unknown-knowns', or even 'unknown-unknowns'), safety or risk; a situation in which it is clear who 'we' are, and who 'they' are with whom we might enter conflict or cooperation; and, finally, since all war involves death, whether that death is justified or not. We could add others, too, for instance in chapter 3, we introduced the axis of proximity–distance, referring to the manner in which actors argue threats are distant or close-to-home. All these axes are matters of degree or extent, particularly in a new media ecology characterized by connectivity, emergence and contingency.

In the fourth section, we look at the reception of discourse and the problem of translation of media content and meanings. The majority of examples used to illustrate arguments in this chapter are taken from the 'war on terror', the conflict between Al-Qaeda and related groups and various governments that became a matter of global public importance following the attacks on the US on 11

September 2001. This chapter can be read alongside chapter 10 on methods to understand how we can analyse the discursive legitimation of war and conflict.

3. Diffuse War Axes of Representation

Justifiable – unjustifiable death

In chapter 7, we noted that the 'structure' of modern warfare included the rationalizing of the destruction of human life, as part of the legitimation of engaging in armed conflict, and cited Scarry's observation that this structure 'requires both the reciprocal infliction of massive injury and the eventual disowning of the injury so that its attributes can be attributed elsewhere, as they cannot if they are permitted to cling to the original site of the wound, the human body' (1985: 64). Such disowning can occur by omitting any mention of the injury, or redescribing it. We look here at a brief example of such omission and redescription, in the jihadist response to the Mumbai attacks of late 2009.

The Mumbai terrorist attacks of 26–29 November 2009 are typical of this (Awan et al., 2010). Across those four days, more than 170 people were killed by Pakistani-based militants from the Lashkar-e-Taiba group in coordinated attacks in several sites in the city, including a number of hotels favoured by Western tourists. On jihadist forums with ideological affinity to the group carrying out the attacks, discussion and celebration of the Mumbai attacks grew from the start of the initial violence. Praise increased especially following the resignation of Indian Home Minister Shivraj Patil on 30 November. It made the attacks seem justifiable, as the terrorists achieved something big, comparable to the '11-M' or '3-11' 2004 Madrid bombings in the sense that they led to political change (after the Madrid bombings, a new government was elected that removed Spanish troops from Iraq). In fact, memories of the Madrid bombings were explicitly revived, with one member posting gruesome pictures of victims and ending his posting with a 'Reminder' that the attacks had *'resulted in the immediate withdrawal of Spanish troops from Iraq'*. To legitimize the attack and establish its 'success', most of the postings made sure to mention that the head of the counterterrorism squad in Mumbai police was among the killed. There was very little mention of innocent civilian victims. Discussion of those killed in the attacks focused on Jews, Americans and Britons as 'legitimate' targets. When Indian victims were mentioned, it was always stressed that they were either members of security forces, who often persecute and torture Muslims or kuffar (infidel) Hindus 'who worship the cow'.

These jihadist interpretations of the Mumbai attacks involved strategic redescriptions of the victims by foregrounding Jewish, American and British victims and making Muslim victims invisible. This discursive work also involved redescribing the nature of the event, from the criminal and fairly indiscriminate killing to a legendary act of resistance within a larger jihadist strategy. An article called *Bollywood Movies & the Globalization of Jihad* by one of the prominent writers on jihadist forums, Abu Dujana al-Azadi, was highly publicized on some forums. The article compares the Mumbai attacks to 'fantastic/unbelievable'

Bollywood action movies, but adds, 'only the Mumbai events are real'. Stressing an (imagined) unity of Muslims and the globalization of jihad throughout his article, Azadi wrote:

> Our nations have had enough of injustice and conspiracies practised against them by the kuffar nations and can take no more. This is a war of all Muslims. Long gone is the time when only Arabs would shoulder the burdens of contemporary jihad alone [on behalf of all Muslims]. Jihad is now globalised.

Like other members, Azadi suspected, and seemingly hoped, that Al-Qaeda had some kind of involvement in the attacks. However, if it had not, 'the tragedy for the kuffar is even greater for it proves that the spirit of jihad has spread like wildfire amongst Muslims'. This is 'the era of global Islamic resistance brigades that started with the American embassy in Sana'a, through the Marriott Hotel in Islam Abad, to Mumbai today and only God knows where next.' Such a statement is ambiguous, perhaps usefully so for Azadi's argument: they did not know who committed the attacks at that point, and in a certain sense it did not matter. Rather, a chain of unforeseeable events presented a situation of 'effects without causes' (Devji, 2005), emergent without warning: the attackers arrived by sea, which Indian intelligence had not safeguarded against. Throughout Azidi's article, he gives a heroic, almost fiction-like narrative of the events of the Mumbai attacks. Demonstrating the mutual interpenetration of Western and jihadist media, his article relies heavily on testimonies of Western media and Indian officials regarding the sophistication, organization and dedication of the attackers. The jihadists reversed the intended meaning of those statements, editing them and recontextualizing them in order to justify the killings.

Certainty – risk

The war on terror as a vocabulary, strategy and set of policies both reflects and contributes to the uncertainty and diffuse character of contemporary warfare. Important conceptual and legal categories are treated as problematic rather than given, for example: civilian and combatant; collateral and non-collateral damage; the distinction between spaces of conflict and safety; and there being a clearly identifiable enemy whose goals a government can negotiate with or which can be identified and defeated.

If security policy is based on uncertain categories, then neither 'the conduct nor the outcomes of such acts are fully controllable' (Spence, 2005: 288). George W. Bush announced in 2002: 'If we wait for threats to fully materialize, we will have waited too long' (cited in Bumiller, 2002). This is an admission that the enemy was not known before action took place; the enemy was emergent, only becoming visible through the course of the war on terror. Policy was based on speculation, 'rather than demonstrable intentions, actions and capabilities' (Spence, 2005: 289). If there was no connection between Iraq and the attacks of 11 September 2001, the 2003 Iraq War created the conditions for Al-Qaeda to emerge in Iraq, and thereby created the enemy that justified the war.

Uncertain categories allow authorities to use ambiguous language as a tool. If a policy response can be warranted without certainty about what is being responded to, then policy is based on *interpretation* of data that *may* indicate *possible* threats. Layoun (2006) notes that the USA PATRIOT Act of 2001 defines domestic terrorism as activities that:

(A)   involve acts dangerous to human life that are a violation of the criminal laws of the United States or of any State;
(B)   *appear to be intended* –
    (i)   to intimidate or coerce a civilian population;
    (ii)   to influence the policy of a government by intimidation or coercion; or
    (iii) to affect the conduct of a government by mass destruction, assassination or kidnapping [*sic*]; and
(C)   occur primarily within the territorial jurisdiction of the United States.[3]

The benchmark of terrorism here is not the intention to spread terror, but the appearance of such an intention. Layoun draws attention to the ambiguity in this legislation: 'If intention is ascribed to appearance, then the distinction rests on the interpretive abilities of whoever decides what intention is indicated by what appearance' (ibid.: 49). For example, if a judiciary decides that looking at certain websites indicates an intention, then looking at the websites indicates that person is a terrorist. The definitional ambiguity gives scope to individuals in authority to decide what is or is not terrorism.

In early 2009 the British government responded to this situation of uncertainty about the identity of enemies by trying to force those enemies into publicly declaring their position (Dodd, 2009). Rather than leaving it for authorities to interpret whether actions demonstrate terrorist intent, a policy was announced called Contest 2 that stipulated a set of beliefs that indicate a person is an 'extremist':

- they advocate a caliphate, a pan-Islamic state encompassing many countries;
- they promote Sharia law;
- they believe in jihad, or armed resistance, anywhere in the world – this would include armed resistance by Palestinians against the Israeli military;
- they argue that Islam bans homosexuality and that it is a sin against Allah;
- they fail to condemn the killing of British soldiers in Iraq or Afghanistan.

While it is unclear what the circumstances are in which people would have to make public their position on these issues, the Contest 2 policy shows how governments may attempt to overcome uncertainty, in this case by forcing citizens to declare whether they are, in effect, a potential enemy or not.

Routine – exception

Since the attacks of 11 September 2001, the term '*new* security dilemma' has entered the public lexicon, based on a metaphorical 'balance' of security and liberty that signifies a policy problem. The pace at which such problems are solved – through debates in periods of calm reflection, or in the immediate aftermath of a terror attack or plot – points to the centrality of conceptions of time and temporality to the war on terror discourse. Huysmans and Buonfino (2008) argue that countries such as the UK have modulated between a *politics of exception*, where we ask whether the state and population is under threat, and a *politics of unease*, a general climate of risk that shapes how society deliberates and legislates policing techniques to manage migration, asylum, social cohesion and other matters apparently related to terrorism.[4] A slow pace can also mean anxiety if this implies waiting: waiting for the next attack, the next atrocity in the next city. Andrew Hill writes:

> In the Cold War, waiting constituted a central dynamic of this conflict for publics . . . awaiting the possibility of nuclear confrontation between the superpowers and their allies. Where the experience of waiting in the War on Terror differs from the Cold War is in terms of the degree of uncertainty . . . in regard to the form a future attack might take, where it might occur, its scale, and who might and might not be harmed . . . [and] an awareness that even if an attack does occur, this need not be final, with further attacks still possible. [This] gives rise to an endless process of waiting. (2009: 4)

Martyrdom videos from jihadist groups reach Western audiences and may contribute to such anxiety by creating a diffuse expectation of attacks, somewhere, some time:

> In June 2007 video footage purportedly shot that month appeared in the world's media showing a graduation ceremony for would-be suicide bombers, presided over by the Taliban's military commander Mansoor Dadullah, on the border of Pakistan-Afghanistan. The graduates had purportedly come from around the globe to attend the training camp and were to return to their countries – which included the US, the UK, Germany, and Canada – to carry out their missions. (The footage included excerpts of the graduates speaking in the languages of the countries they had supposedly arrived from about their planned operations.) (Ibid.: 74)

Hill argues that such videos begin a process of waiting. The martyrdom graduates are visible in the film, but then they disappear; we know what will have happened the next time they emerge into the world's media and our consciousness – an attack – and we know we are being *made to* wait, passively (ibid.: 81). Furthermore, the impression that *anyone* could turn to jihadist violence, not just 'Muslim-looking people', is something that jihadist networks have exploited. For example, the jihadist Global Islamic Media Front released a statement in 2005 by a 'Rakan bin Williams' that again put Western publics in a position of passive waiting, this time waiting for an attack by a Western convert to Islam:

> Al-Qaeda's new soldiers were born in Europe of European and Christian parents. They studied in your schools. They prayed in your churches and attended Sunday mass. They drank alcohol, ate pork and oppressed Muslims, but Al-Qaeda has embraced them so they have converted to Islam in secret and absorbed the philosophy of Al-Qaeda and swore to take up arms after their brothers. They are currently

roaming the streets of Europe and the United States planning and observing in preparation for upcoming attacks. (Quoted in Pargeter, 2008: 166–7)

Some politicians and policymakers have tried to frame and define the security context – and threats such as roaming jihadist converts – as signifying an exceptional situation, a departure from a previous normality: that 'the gloves are off', 'the rules have changed' and, as the UK Home Secretary John Reid said in 2006, those who disagree with this understanding 'don't get it' (Reid, 2006). Defining the situation as exceptional is a rhetorical device used to warrant a particular response, for instance policies that would be 'unthinkable' in 'normal' times. Indeed, some have defined the war on terror context as 'the new normal' (Massumi, 2005a: 31), superseding and displacing existing conventions and laws (Sands, 2005) and opening a space for new norms to emerge. A situation of apparent war with no 'exit strategies' (see previous chapter), without geographical boundaries, and without clearly enemies – diffused war – means war becomes the defining characteristic of society and all social, economic, cultural and political processes become framed in terms of 'security'. Once, Clausewitz wrote, war was the 'continuation of political activity by other means' (1976: 87). By contrast, the war on terror appeared to be organized around the principle that war determines politics, with the US and UK in particular defining themselves as in a state of diffuse and unending war. As a result, the way in which these societies are regulated and reproduced – by formal legislation and the evolution of social norms – became driven by a logic of securing, using available technologies to monitor, evaluate and gently guide conduct in ways that maintain order (Foucault, 2007; Dillon, 2008). The logic of this situation, however, is that there must be a threat against which to be at war. This could lead to the perpetual creation of undefined enemies and symptoms of dangerous disorder that must be targeted and combated. This was the central thesis of the BBC documentary *The Power of Nightmares*, broadcast in 2005 (Curtis, 2005).

Such scholars are identifying a logic in the war on terror discourse. A logic means: if this, then that. *If* we are in a state of emergency, *then* new measures must be taken. The analytical task is to identify these stages of the discourse. For instance, Huysmans and Buonfino (2008) draw attention to the manner in which disparate policy issues have been connected by policymakers. The British government, for instance, has made discursive links – a 'clear nexus' – between identify theft, immigration, terrorism and welfare fraud in order to justify identity cards. This creates a 'patchwork' of unease in which these issues are stitched together via a particular technology – identity cards – even though the only thing these issues have in common are the fact that government seeks to manage them all via identity card technology. The analytical challenge is to identify how distinct objects, issues and identities become connected through discourse and mediality into a single nexus, which can be analysed through nexus analysis, as described in chapter 10.

How much of a break with the past is required to define a situation as 'new'? Many security measures that seemed to exemplify the 'post-9/11' situation had actually been underway previously. Stuart Hall described the event of 9/11 as something 'both familiar and strange . . . a kind of unveiling of some of the

huge consequences of long-running processes that were always-already in place'
(2001: 9). The event therefore seemed a crystallization of slow, long-term processes, such as the emergence of networked terrorist groups and the need for an
organizing principle for Western security policy after the Cold War.

We need to be aware of our own use of terms such as '9/11' or 'war on terror'.
We have seen that many aspects of the war on terror were already in existence
before the 11 September 2001 attacks. But it is more problematic that this.
Following Obama's presidential victory in 2008, Angharad Closs Stephens
noted

> [I]f there is now a discourse on how the War on Terror might be coming to an
> *end*, then this is at the same time a discourse that re-affirms the *origins* of the War
> on Terror . . . Whether the claim is made from the perspective of a progress or a
> conservative politics, it keeps us tied to the idea that the War on Terror somehow
> represents a *break* or an exceptional departure from the dominant discourses of
> international relations, rather than an escalation of ways of seeing the world that
> were already present and available. (2009: 3)

A critical question, then, is how leaders in particular contexts can define or
frame an event as marking a crisis that signifies an entirely situation, such as
the manner in which the 11 September 2001 attacks became framed as signifying the arrival of a 'post-9/11' world in which war was the appropriate response
(Holland, 2009). Could leaders have framed the events in another way, to legitimize an alternative response, one not based on an unending war on terror?

Us – them

The experience and representation of identity groups as 'us' and 'them' or Self
and Other has long been analysed in the field of war and media (Picard, 1993;
Kolstø, 2009; Wright, 2009). However, it may be that this axis has become
more important for explaining the origin and conduct of conflict in recent
decades. Neumann (2009) argues that we have seen a shift from conflict driven
by 'universalist' ideologies such as communism, which sought dignity and
equality for all humans, to 'particularist' ideologies based on the supremacy of
a particular national, religious or ethnic identity. As a result, there has been an
increase in lethal violence against civilians who are deemed of secondary order
rather than part of a common humanity, such as Al-Qaeda's willingness to kill
non-Muslims or Muslims who do not follow Al-Qaeda's interpretation of Islam
(cf. Devji, 2008). In this section, we see how categories of time and morality are
ways of thinking through, and representing, differences between identity groups
and how these categories have been used to justify conflict.

One tool to distinguish between 'us' and 'them' in order to justify conflict or
cooperation is to claim a notion of historical progress that tells 'our' story but not
'their' story, to suggest that 'they' stand outside or attempt to obstruct historical
progress. The war on terror seemed an exemplary case of this, Closs Stephens
argues (2009). This was 'The Battle for Global Values', according to Tony Blair
(2007), between civilization and its enemies. As the US and its allies claimed
to make 'progress' in Afghanistan and Iraq, such a claim positions any actors

resisting this progress as being against progress per se. Closs Stephens argues that this notion of historical progress was described by Walter Benjamin early in the twentieth century: 'The concept of the historical progress of mankind cannot be sundered from the concept of its progression through a homogenous, empty time' (Benjamin, 1969: 261). Hence, the war on terror represents a stretching out into an empty temporal space ahead, to be filled in by a US-led progress synonymous with the progress of humanity per se. Such progress might include, we could infer, the enforcement of universal human rights (or, the universal enforcement of human rights) and perhaps even the achievement of 'freedom', however defined. The barbarians lie somehow outside this time and space. It is as though they hate our gods and customs, and that their gods and customs belong to a *different cosmos entirely* (Latour, 2004). Indeed in November 2001 the *New York Times* columnist Thomas Friedman (2001) effectively described Islam as having not yet reached liberal pluralistic modernity:

> Although there is a deep moral impulse in Islam for justice, charity and compassion, Islam has not developed a dominant religious philosophy that allows equal recognition of alternative faith communities. Bin Laden reflects the most extreme version of that exclusivity, and he hit us in the face with it on 9/11.
> Christianity and Judaism struggled with this issue for centuries, but a similar internal struggle within Islam to re-examine its texts and articulate a path for how one can accept pluralism and modernity — and still be a passionate, devout Muslim — has not surfaced in any serious way.

Judith Butler has argued that this assumption of Islamic pre-modernity translates into understanding the 2003 war in Iraq as a 'civilizing mission', 'to bring notions of democracy to those who are characterized as pre-modern, who have not yet entered into the secular terms of the liberal state, and whose notions of religion are invariably considered childish, fanatic or structured according to ostensibly irrational and primitive taboos' (2009: 14). Evidence for this, Butler suggests, is that the US Department of Defense assigned a text in the 1970s to officers called 'The Arab Mind', which proposed that anybody of a certain racial/ethnic category – Arab – would have certain social and psychological characteristics, including vulnerability to particular sexual forms of humiliation, which were put into practice through torture in Abu Ghraib after the 2003 Iraq War (ibid.: 15; Der Derian, 2009: 269–294). US soldiers put Iraqi prisoners into the position of living up to that stereotype by humiliating them in the way prescribed by the 1970s guidebook, which in turn justified the 'civilizing mission' itself. By forcing Iraqi prisoners into the position of being abased and treating them as less than human, the prisoners were, logically, in need of civilization: "[W]e embody freedom, you do not; therefore, we are free to coerce you, and so to exercise our freedom, and you, you will manifest your unfreedom to us, and that spectacle will serve as the visual justification for our onslaught against you" (ibid.: 18). Photos of Afghani women walking in public without the veil performed a similar role in legitimating US interventions, Butler argues, since such images demonstrate visually that Afghani women have been freed from pre-modern strictures and are now the equal of Western women; they have been allowed to 'catch up'. Consequently, conceptions of time underpinning categories of identity are used to justify progressive social change as well as violence against obstacles to such progress.

Alongside time, categorizations of us/them depend on moral distinctions. It is one thing to argue that Bush, Blair and bin Laden occupied a conflictual relationship that endured over time in the years following 9/11, another to say these actors were simply equivalents. Actors may or may not share a common space or time, but distinctions between 'us' and 'them' also involve moral discrimination. For terrorism is, in a very important way, *not* a communicative act. It rules out listening to the very people being killed. David Graeber writes: '[V]iolence may well be the only form of human action by which it is possible to have relatively predictable effects on the actions of a person about whom you understand nothing. Pretty much any other way one might try to influence another's actions, one at least has to have some idea who they think they are, who they think you are' and so on (2006: 7). While bin Laden and other leaders may show familiarity with Western cultures and societies, for those who carry out the terrorist acts, turning to violence is a point of ceasing to know the Other.

Indeed, Clive Barnett (2005: 4) argues that reducing Bush and bin Laden to equivalents prevents analysis and understanding, and that it is equally unhelpful to label one's enemies as 'evil' terrorists because it 'ultimately ends up absolving "terrorists" of responsibility', since they bombed because they were evil, and because they were evil they were always going to bomb (ibid.: 6; cf. Silverstone, 2007: 59). Clark and Jones write:

> [T]he Chechen rebels involved in the infamous Beslan school siege were undoubtedly aware that the very inhumanity of their actions would reap [media] interest (and, as a neglected global concern, those Chechen rebels would probably have gone unnoticed without such inhumanity). But that very inhumanity is what also, to the detriment of their cause, allows the continuation of a complete ignorance of anything which the terrorists are allied, insofar as it inevitably attracts opprobrium. (2006: 307)

To commit an evil act is newsworthy, but for an evil actor to commit an evil act is not political: it appears as natural, instinctive and therefore not a matter for enquiry. Clark and Jones quote the response of George W. Bush to the 9/11 attackers: 'They have no justification for their actions. There's no religious justification, there's no political justification. The only motivation is evil' (ibid.: 308). Clark and Jones characterize this description as 'certitude through lack of explanation' (ibid.).

Barnett adds that 'it is an act that disavows that such acts could ever implicate oneself: "I" am never evil; only "you" are' (2005: 30). Hence, it prevents consideration that oneself might have contributed in any way, reinforcing a black-and-white framing of events. For example, to those citizens who suggested a causal link between the allied invasion of Iraq in 2003 and the subsequent bombings in London in 2005, British Prime Minister Blair (2005) said:

> What I am really saying is this though, where does that argument lead you [because] that is the important thing. And what you have got to be careful of is getting into their perverted logic, which says even if people abhor the bombings in London;

well nonetheless we understand why it has happened because of what has happened in Iraq. No . . . we have got to be very careful that we don't enter into a situation where we think that if you make some compromise on some aspect of foreign policy suddenly these people are going to change. They are not going to change, they will just say right; they are on the run, so let's step it up.

Blair's predecessor as Prime Minister, John Major, infamously said: '[W]e should condemn a little more and understand a little less.' Though many scholars have characterized terrorism as a communicative act, Blair similarly tried to render the actions of the London bombers beyond political discussion, suitable only for abhorrence (Moss and O'Loughlin, 2008). The notion that Blair and 'us' could ever be implicated in 'evil' is foreclosed.

Yet as Roger Silverstone suggests (2007: 58), media bring us many instances of evil within 'us'. Abu Ghraib suggested an evil within American society, for instance. This makes any distinction based on us-as-good, them-as-evil, unsustainable. Both we and they are equally vulnerable to evil, so is there in fact any difference between us and them?

If labelling groups as evil prevents analysis and understanding, this is reinforced by the manner in which, in public debate, media and political leaders tend to focus on the perspective of the *victims* of violence, rendering the motive and context of the violent actor as irrelevant to the significance of the case. Yet it is striking that the notion of 'humiliation' is often used in terrorists' discourse. They see themselves as victims, and may list a series of provocations and irritations that led to their escalation and resort to violence. They had no choice, and thereby the responsibility was on the victim's side (Devji, 2008: 58). To explain violence is not to exonerate it; nor should it prevent recognition of victims' trauma and loss (Barnett, 2005: 8). Nevertheless, evil remains a concept or rhetorical term with a powerful silencing effect (Silverstone, 2007: 56).

Thinking beyond us-versus-them?[5]

We must develop forms of thinking about how groups represent themselves and others that are more empirically accurate and analytically useful than the binary oppositions often present in mainstream media or political addresses, while not discounting the continued purchase of those binaries on popular imaginaries. Any casual observer cannot help but notice that when global media events occur, a panopoly of perspectives and identities are triggered and made public. Take, for example, the Danish cartoon crisis of 2006. Many journalists and political and religious leaders immediately spoke of the event through binary categories, as if a 'clash' between a 'Muslim world' and 'the West' was occurring, while others sought to sustain, bridge or repair relations between what they too assumed to be binary groupings (Eide et al., 2008). At its most simplistic, such a dichotomy would have presented Muslims as 'under attack' or 'against free speech' and Christians/Westerners as 'ignorant and arrogant' or 'upholding free speech'. An analysis across 16 countries in a volume by Eide et al. (2008) demonstrates that many people did *not* start from the assumed Islam/West binary, and even for those who did, there were multiple points of view within those 'worlds'.

To conceptualize these identities, the authors draw upon Edward Said's notion of a 'contrapuntal reading' (Said, 1994). Contrapuntal is a term from music which refers to instances when more than one voice or musical line sound together, in concord or discord, such that they only have meaning together. Said noted that English novels from the eighteenth to the twentieth century excluded the narrative of imperialism which was the actual condition and context for the stories. To read contrapuntally, as Said tried to do, meant to read for what is absent as well as present, since the integrity of the meaning produced must include both (Silverstone, 2007: 86–9). We can analyse transnational media events in the same way:

> [They] collect the attention of a potentially global audience on a particular dominant theme. But at the same time, they open up a multitude of universes . . . from which other voices and experiences can be added. Moreover, voices parallel to the theme can be introduced, voices that change its meaning, and recontextualize it, and express the idea in a whole new key, sometimes offering consonant, sometimes more dissonant colour to the main theme – and sometimes even taking over the dominant theme itself. (Eide et al., 2008: 15–16)

Responses to the attacks of 11 September 2001 could be read contrapuntally. For one thing, there was greater variation in response within the United States than was apparent from media coverage. In chapter 10 we explore how various voices in New York City grew to resent the framing of 'their' event by national leaders as an 'American' story. The manner in which media construct some incidents, such as '9/11', as global media events, as history-in-the-making, live, appears contingent to some audiences, who question the prioritization and value attributed to some events over others. Moreover, the attacks that become known as '9/11' triggered immediate consideration in some diasporic UK audiences to *our* 'ground zeros', that is, the catastrophes and tragic events that had befallen people in the nations of their family and ancestors. Gillespie explains how these individuals compare news and events:

> Through comparing and contrasting different sources (e.g. the BBC, Al Jazeera and CNN), they construct their own narratives, which often contest and resist those put on the agenda by politicians and spin doctors. Such re-versioning of news relativises and reorders state discourses on security threats (in terms of sovereignty and military solutions) and brings into sharp focus alternative visions of security environmental, epidemics, poverty and crime. (2006c: 470)

These diverse, granular experiences do not fit simple historical narratives about war and conflict or binary identity categorizations used to legitimate new violence. Identifying, explaining and accounting for these diverse experiences and perspectives remains a challenge for policymakers, journalists and students of war and media, particularly when it is often in the interests of 'big' institutions to maintain simplified representations. The difficulty posed by the diversity of sources and audiences of news is exemplified by the issue of translation across languages and cultures. We explore the relationship between translation and legitimacy next.

4. Translation and Legitimacy

Many global media events in the past decade have involved communications to national audiences being consumed and interpreted outside the assumed target audience. That overseas audiences are reached may be deliberate, as with public diplomacy or psyops, or accidental, when political or military leaders say something offhand that is picked up by news wires and bloggers and scattered across geographical boundaries (see chapter 3). This presents problems and opportunities for leaders trying to legitimate military or security policy, for journalists trying to make sense of such addresses from other countries and for audiences trying to 'commute' between political and media discourses of multiple countries and cultures.

Two strikingly different responses to this challenge came from George W. Bush and Osama bin Laden. The discourse used by Bush around war and security was very culturally specific. He invoked 'Wild West justice' after 9/11, saying that bin Laden would be 'brought to justice', 'dead or alive'. David Campbell suggests this was an 'analogy that legitimates a revenge scenario' (2004: 175). This rhetoric brings one thing into the foreground: the need to kill Osama bin Laden. It also puts things in the background: 'Wild West justice' involved the killing of Native Americans. This discourse may have had appeal for some US audiences, but could easily be caricatured by overseas audiences and may even have contributed to anti-US feeling. Bush later appeared to have made some small recognition of this by apologizing: 'Saying "Bring it on", kind of tough talk, you know, that sent the wrong signal to people' (BBC News, 2006a).

In the same period, Osama bin Laden used a discourse that lacked cultural specificity. As Devji notes (2008: 111), bin Laden's language is a curiously 'archaic' and 'stilted' Arabic that isn't clearly intelligible to Arab-speakers. It anticipates or 'presupposes translation', for bin Laden knew he was talking to Muslims globally, who may speak many languages and may not speak Arabic. He offered 'a standardized technique made up of recognisable but not necessarily comprehensible words' ready for translation (ibid.: 112). The unifying rhetorical flourish used by bin Laden, in recognition of the globally dispersed character of Islam and Muslims, was a pagan discourse of pre-Islamic Arabia, of 'charging horses and fiery deserts . . . romantic images of virtuous knighthood' (ibid.: 113). Where Bush had a clear sense of his audience or domestic base, bin Laden addressed a diffuse public of potential sympathizers. However, Bush could not help but address that diffuse public too, exposing the national specificity of his discourse.

When news of war emerging from societies or cultures in another language reaches its audience, it is framed, remediated and translated. This may occur at the point of its original production, or by a news organization in our country that relays the original to us. By framed, we mean parts of the original are edited and recontextualized to re-present it in a way intelligible and appealing to the presumed audience. By remediated, we mean the original report or speech may be moved from one format to another, from the Internet to a television report for example. Finally, the translation of a war-related text from one language to another is relatively unexplored in academic research. Yet it is an increasingly important process. In this section we show how the loss and gain of meaning in the translation process can shape the legitimacy of political and military leaders. Our focus is the translation of speeches by jihadist leaders for Western, English-speaking audiences.

When Western news organizations present jihadist or Al-Qaeda media productions, such as speeches or beheading videos, the translation reaching the audience only presents what is presumed to be the main message in that production and completely ignores the other features that, while secondary, are very important to complete the overall meaning and message conveyed. Such secondary features include video clips before, during or after a speech, *nasheeds* (songs), citations from the Quran and *Hadith*, words of people other than the main speaker, poetry, images, prayers, introductions and comment on militant operations. Stripping a jihadist media production from all these secondary features, which occur in every production, makes full appreciation and understanding of the original text impossible. A main component of jihadist propaganda, like Arabic media and the Arabic language itself, is its literary, sensual and metaphoric nature. It creates meaning through words, songs and images. Sometimes the visual is the primary modality, relying on, for example, an image to illustrate the intended message. In Al-Qaeda's video commemorating the 7/7 London bombings of 2005, As-Sahab media production heavily relied on split screen images of Muslims being victimized in Iraq and Palestine accompanied with moving *nasheeds* to make its point. While the images had no comments, the viewer is supposed to understand immediately what they meant – an eye for an eye. This was Al-Qaeda's way of illustrating legitimacy for the London attacks. However, a non-Arabic speaker merely reading the English transcript of the video which says nothing about these images or the accompanying *nasheed* (which emphasizes that 'you have killed us and subjugated our people') will partly miss out on the means through which Al-Qaeda seeks to legitimize the attacks.

On 19 November 2008, Aymen al-Zawahiri addressed the new US administration by releasing a production entitled *Exit of Bush and Arrival of Obama*. The ensuing chain of (mis)communication usefully illustrates the misunderstanding or partial understanding of a certain message stemming from its incomplete translation. Al-Zawahiri's message caused controversy, as a majority of people seemingly only received the mainstream media version, highlighting his use of a racist term. The words that caused controversy were: "You are the opposite of honourable black Americans like Malik al-Shahbaz, or Malcolm X, God rest his soul. . . . Malik al-Shabaz, God rest his soul, was right to describe you and the likes of you such as Powell and Rice as 'house slaves'." This is immediately followed by a clip of Malcolm X (the third of him in the video) in which he talks about the difference between 'a house negro' and a 'field negro': 'You have to read the history of slavery to understand it. There are two kinds of Negroes: a house Negro and a field Negro.' Malcolm X goes on to explain that the 'house negro' was too obedient and submissive to his white master even at the expense of his own people, the 'field negroes'. By using this term, al-Zawahiri indicates that Obama will not be able to bring about the better change that the whole world is expecting of him, but rather he will be a slave to the White House and its global political agenda.

In fact, the meaning of the term al-Zawahiri used is 'house negro'. In Arabic, while it might sound insulting, it does not sound racist. It is a clear indication of the obedient stance al-Zawahiri thinks Obama will take – judging from his promise to intensify operations in Afghanistan and make a friendly visit to Israel, which al-Zawahiri first mentions – rather than an indication of his colour or race. The fact that the clip of Malcolm X, an African American himself who used those terms, is absent from English transcriptions of the message makes the words of al-Zawahiri, who is not African, seem racist. Mainstream media mostly ignored the fact that these were Malcolm X's words and focused on al-Zawahiri's 'racism'.

Examples of al-Zawahiri's message in the media

- *Washington Post:* Al-Qaeda calls Obama a 'house negro': Soon after the November election, Al-Qaeda's No. 2 leader took stock of America's new president-elect and dismissed him with an insulting epithet. 'A house Negro,' Ayman al-Zawahiri said.
- *The Guardian:* Al-Qaida leader uses racial abuse to attack Obama
- *BBC:* He also likens him to a 'house slave' – who had chosen to align himself with the 'enemies' of Islam.

On Western Internet forums, members were enraged by al-Zawahiri's 'racist words', especially those identifying themselves as African Americans. The majority of people only heard of al-Zawahiri's words from media or terrorism monitoring groups that translated the video, omitting the clips of Malcolm X's speeches. In fact, in this video, al-Zawahiri praised African Americans and called them to take example in honourable men like Malcolm X. However, this praise and all of this speech appeared to be overshadowed by the term 'house negro'.

On the al-Faloja forum, a leading website for jihadists, one member commented in English on the 'slur', saying:

> Once again, we find people misinterpreting something related to the current day Jihad in order to tarnish the image of the Mujahideen, which only goes in favor of the Crusader-Zionists. In Zawahiri's last speech, he said, 'And in you (i.e., Obama) and in Colin Powell, Rice and your likes, the words of Malcolm X (may Allah have mercy on him) concerning 'House Negroes' are confirmed'. In Arabic, al-Zawahiri used '*'Abeed al-Bayt*' which literally translates as 'House Slave.' However, he was using the word in a certain context to imply a much greater meaning. What was he implying? He was using the words in the context of Malcolm X's implication of 'house slave.' Malcolm X, however, used a much harsher tone of language by changing 'slave' to 'Negroes' and thus the usage was insulting but never racist. Its meaning was used for those who were close to the American Government and showed allegiance as well as love for the American Government when in reality, it is a corrupt and hypocritical Government.

This example shows the implications of incomplete description and translation of Jihadist messages. While ignoring certain clips and *nasheeds* may not affect the

What is said	What is heard	Possible alternatives
The dividing line is between terrorists and the rest of us	Can be a positive message, but only with a credible messenger and explained clearly	Ensure the context is clear
Communities need to stand up to/weed out terrorist sympathisers	Communities are to blame for extremism and are responsible for hiding terrorists in their midst	We all share responsibility for tackling violent extremism, and there are specific tasks
Struggle for values/battle for ideas	Confrontation/clash between civilisations/cultures	Idea of shared values works much more effectively
War/battle/clash	"Terrorists/criminals are warriors/soldiers fighting for a cause"	Challenge/threat
Radicalisation	"Terrorism is a product of Islam" (not easily understood or translated into Urdu/Arabic)	Brainwashing or indoctrination
De-radicalisation	As above, not easily understood or translatable to all audiences	Rehabilitation
Moderate/radical	Perceived as a means of splitting Muslim communities or stigmatising points of view/ lifestyles that are deemed to be less favourable to the government	Muslims (where necessary, mainstream Muslims)
Islamic/Islamist/Muslim extremism	"Extremism is the fault of Muslims/Islam"	Terrorism/violent extremism (including from non-Muslims)
Jihadi/fundamentalist	"There is an explicit link between Islam and terrorism"	Criminal/murderer/thug
Islamic/Muslim community/world, "the west"	"Muslims form a homogenous community/world (in opposition to 'the west')"	Highlight diversity, rather than reinforcing the concept of a homogenous Muslim world. Use national/ ethnic/ geographical identifiers or Muslim communities/societies
Islamophobia	Can be misunderstood as a slur on Islam and perceived as singling out Muslims (even though it indicates we are positively addressing their concerns)	Discrimination

Figure 9.1   British Government Handbook
Source: The Guardian, 4 February 2008

overall message in a certain production, in this case, the clip of Malcolm X was essential to the sense intended by the original author. By cutting it, the sense of the production is reversed and a new meaning and framing are made possible.

The British government has also had problems communicating with Muslims within its own borders and overseas. In February 2008 the British Home Office produced a table of phrases[6] or language guidelines for civil servants to use in order to make British policy more intelligible, to avoid accidentally offending Muslims, and with the overall objective of countering Al-Qaeda propaganda (see figure 9.1). The table is notable for acknowledging that 'what is said' by the British government is not 'what is heard' by Muslim citizens. The same words could mean different things to different people, indeed the very opposite of what was intended: when the British government spoke of 'Islamophobia' (fear of, or discrimination towards, Muslims) Muslim citizens thought use of the term meant the government was singling out Muslims. The task for the government was to find alternative words around which a common understanding could build.

The US government undertook a similar initiative, consulting a number of Islamic scholars and leaders to find alternative terms for describing potential terrorist threats. This resulted in a document published in January 2008, *Terminology To Define The Terrorists: Recommendations from American Muslims* (US Department of Homeland Security, 2008). Such an initiative indicates that the US government was aware that its own discourse was failing to achieve the desired effects. Specifically, the Department of Homeland Security document acknowledges that government language had lent glamour and legitimacy to groups such as Al-Qaeda that engaged in terrorism, that many Americans had come to understand the 'war on terror' as a war against Islam, resulting in a 'negative climate' for Muslims living in America, and that US government language would be translated in the new media ecology instantly and beyond their control: '[W]e must be conscious of history, culture, and context. In an era where a statement can cross continents in a manner of seconds, it is essential that officials consider how terms translate, and how they will resonate with a variety of audiences' (US Department of Homeland Security, 2008: 2).

This is an increasingly important and built-in aspect of media representation, and the default position for Big Media organizations and the military institutions of major powers will be for translation to be a standard feature of any strategic communication. Control of translation, and the capacity to offer multilingual communications, has become an important component of power.

5. Conclusion

There is a need to understand how the mediatization of war affects processes of legitimation. Media sources and audiences are characterized by both fragmentation and new patterns of connectivity. This complicates but does not make impossible the legitimation of warfare since it will be 'big' institutions – global news networks and the military structures of major powers – which have the resources to harness the proliferation of user-generated content and offer multilingual translations for diverse audiences. How the dynamic tension between control and chaos plays out in the case of each war or conflict may be determined not only by whether the information vectors and occasional leaks are managed by officials and editors, but also by audiences' assumptions about what they expect to see from a war. As we saw in chapter 3, individuals approach the same coverage in different ways, and may feel sympathy or condemnation from watching the same images.

The legitimation of war involves continual description or categorization of those involved. David Campbell's analysis of Darfur suggests how these categorizations or representations can have an effect on the conduct of war itself if participants think of themselves in terms of those categories. We introduced key axes through which the categorization and interpretation of those involved in war occur: justifiable/unjustifiable death, routine/exceptional situations, patience/urgency in response, certainty/risk in our knowledge of how war would unfold, and the basic us/them dichotomy which itself can be subdivided into categorizations by time (backward/modern) and morality (good/evil). Yet scholars have shown that people do not always think in such simplified terms; the work of Silverstone, Eide and Gillespie prompt questions about why individuals *might* come to hold simplified or binary views given that this is not the default or inevitable position, and the role media play in shaping these attitudes and understandings. If it is the case that media representations make a difference here, these are moral and political matters with significant practical consequences for the loss of human life. Is it necessarily the case that if media offered more nuanced representations of war, citizens would attribute less legitimacy to the conduct of war?

10

METHODS

Traditional concepts and their related theories and methodological approaches of mass media form, content and influence have imploded, because objects of analysis in the field of war and media do not stay still long enough for a coherent research paradigm to form. At least there is recognition by some war and media scholars that the frequently separated traditional modes of media content, audiences and practices need to be treated more dynamically and holistically (Philo and Berry, 2004). Yet, there seems a growing threat that the very categories and frameworks through which we could base knowledge run the risk of being outdated even by the time studies find their way through traditional academic publication processes. Moreover, claims for the manufacture of consent – the thesis that there are systematic factors that lead mass media to produce 'news' that favours a ruling elite (Herman and Chomsky, 1994; Ben-Shaul, 2007) – appear to be challenged at least by the emergence of networked, diffuse communication and participatory media. Just as relatively rigorous and substantiated concepts of framing (Snow et al., 1986; Gamson and Modigliani, 1989; Entman, 1993, 2004; Gitlin, 1980; Wolfsfeld, 2004; Chong and Druckman, 2007; Taylor, 2008; Archetti, 2008), indexing (Hallin, 1986; Bennett, 1990; Bennett et al., 2007) and effects (Nelson et al., 1997; Domke et al., 2002; Peterson, 2005; cf. Miller, 2007; Pfau et al., 2008) have been established in mass/political communication studies, so the new media ecology undermines the basis for their claims of generalizability and validity. And just as the study of media-security cultures and processes of discursive linking and differentiating and their performative effects is generating a body of studies (Altheide and Snow, 1979; Campbell, 1992, 1993, 2007; Mattern, 2005; Mirzoeff, 2005; Giroux, 2006; Hansen, 2006; Roselle, 2006; Altheide, 2007; Žarkov, 2007; Debrix, 2008), so it becomes more difficult to identify and track these processes because the potential for global connectivity and interactivity diffuses the practices through which a discourse takes place. Indeed, the diffused prolificacy of digital media seems to create a perpetually '*pre*paradigmatic' state insofar as there is no stable object around which a research paradigm could cohere (Hine, 2005; emphasis added).

We conclude this book by highlighting three challenges (among many) as we enter the second phase of mediatization. First, the challenge of identifying effects amid ubiquitous media. If media is environmental, is the research aim of identifying the effects of particular media content feasible? Can we identify the effects of simply living in a particular media ecology? Second, the challenge of analysing media practices. And third, how can we achieve an iterative analysis of these practices and their effects when they occur in real-time? We address each challenge in turn and propose a set of elements of a methodology for future research in this field.

1. Identifying Effects amid Ubiquitous Media

We have moved within a generation from the terminology of 'mass media', or 'the media', with debates about the monopolistic concentration of media power and dangers of pervasive manipulation . . . to the sense that media are now differentiated, dispersed and multi-modal. (Featherstone, 2009: 2)

With our mobile devices, the embedding of sensing machines in our environment, and increasing wireless environments, the conditions of connectivity, convergence and immediacy are or will transform all aspects of war and media, from the way in which military non-human technologies communicate with one another to how images of military conduct are recorded and remediated around the world. There are more empirical 'traces' of human and non-human activities. Not only is this happening, but we are aware it is happening, and this awareness feeds back into the processes themselves, a consciousness of mediatization; the strategies and tactics of militaries, political leaders and citizens all involve second-guessing how others will use or even manipulate this media ecology. In this context, how can researchers identify what media content, format or practice is impacting on what aspect of warfare (waging, justifying, viewing) and vice versa?

It is an indictment that Michael Carpini, Dean of the Annenberg School of Communication, one of the leading media and communication centres in the world, has recently noted that the field is losing ground on even as fundamental measure as exposure:

The sad fact is that even in the bygone era of many fewer media outlets and clearer (though always still somewhat ambiguous) lines between politically relevant and irrelevant genres, we have never been great at measuring individuals' exposure to information. And in the current, more complex, user-controlled environment, we are largely at sea on this topic. (2009: 55)

If you cannot identify which media people were exposed to that contained information about the 2003 Iraq War, for instance, it becomes impossible to justify claims about which media might have influenced their opinion about the war. Nevertheless, digitization may offer solutions as well as problems. As social life is lived through our 'ubiquitous' media ecology (Featherstone, 2009), then evidence or traces of our opinions, attitudes and relationships are increasingly transparent *as* digital media content:

> Instead of trying to extract information from a few thousand activists' opinions about politics every two years, in the necessarily artificial conversation initiated by a survey interview, we can use new methods to mine the tens of millions of political opinions expressed daily in published blogs. Instead of studying the effects of context and interactions among people by asking respondents to recall their frequency and nature of social contacts, we now have the ability to obtain a continuous record of all phone calls, emails, text messages, and in-person contacts among a much larger group. (King, 2009: 92)

In addition, it is possible to study real-time deliberations online rather than rely on post hoc accounts by participants (Price et al., 2006), and to study these deliberations in an unobtrusive way such that the presence of the researcher does not alter the situation. Online behaviour also tells us more about what people *do* in their monitoring of media coverage of war and conflict, compared to measures of exposure to radio or television broadcasts which might include people who happen to have the TV on while they're doing something else. Tewksbury writes: 'Television audience measurement can track the size and composition of program audiences, but it can say little about the news topics or stories that attract viewer attention' (2006: 327). Hence analysis can cover more communication yet be more fine-grained. Analysing this unprecedented volume and detail of information will require imaginative use of quantitative software packages, and the development of new tools to mine and code digital archives. King also points to the ethical dilemmas such research possibilities create. The boundaries of public and private online are fuzzy, and analysts could easily betray the trust and confidentiality of those they choose to analyse.

In the quote that began this section, Mike Featherstone wrote, 'media are now differentiated, dispersed and multi-modal'. This last aspect also presents analytical challenges. Communications scholars have difficulty conducting media content analysis of visual images. Rare is the study that analyses together the audio, visual and linguistic features of a soldier's blog or news broadcast from Afghanistan to see how meaning is constructed across the senses – let alone the tactile aspect of media. Furthermore, as well as the modalities of what we analyse, we must also think about the modalities of our own analysis. There is a need to think imaginatively about how we can represent the phenomena we are interested in. Can all experience of war be captured in representational modalities? In an ethnography of a military unit or audience community,[1] in which researchers engage in participant observation with the group being researched, can participants' experiences and feelings be represented in the modalities that we are required to present research *as*, such as books, research articles and student dissertations?

2. How Do We Analyse Media Practices?

In recent years, the social sciences have undergone a 'practice turn' (Schatzki, in Schatzki et al., 2001; cf. Bourdieu, 1977, 1990; Giddens, 1984; Latour 2005). Attention to practices shows how both structures and agents are produced, sustained and transformed; structures such as class, language and the balance of power, and aspects of agency such as rationality, subjectivity and capacity. The analyst can select a field of practice such as war, science or economics, and see, through analysis of the customs, routines and skills used in those practices, how ontological units such as structures, agents, institutions and processes are generated and and how they interact. It is through practices, Schatzki (2001: 5) argues, that order emerges, particularly as different fields of practice connect in mutually sustaining ways (as demonstrated in Bousquet's (2009) account of how scientific developments are used in designing and conducting war). Practices are the primary unit of analysis, rather than individuals or representations, because it is in practices that knowledge and power reside. It is only within practices that media representations 'acquire the property of being about something by virtue of how people use and react to them' (Bousquet, 2009: 12).

Two good examples of such an analysis focus on the practices through which the 11 September 2001 attacks were responded to in New York City. Abrams et al. (2004) used a mixed methodology: they conducted 50 in-depth interviews with New Yorkers not immediately caught up in the attacks, and these were triangulated through analysis of 200 personal accounts from blogs, radio programmes and published sources. The researchers found that the meaning of '9/11' emerged not from media but from people's everyday interactions in the city; strangers began helping each other, people began feeling unexpected racist attitudes towards Arab and Asian people, but, above all, people felt angry that their city, which for them represented 'the world', was appropriated by national politicians and media to represent 'America'. As far as they were concerned, official narratives lacked credibility. To demonstrate their 'New York patriotism', individuals began placing candles in windows. Abrams et al. offer an account of people's practices of local interactions and news consumption, and their use of objects to make public statements. Similarly, Sturken (2007) interprets the uses of snow globes to understand how US citizens made sense of 9/11. Snow globes are usually objects for tourists or children, a frozen moment and place to be rekindled with a shake. Sturken argues that it is through the buying, selling or gift-giving of snow globes that we can understand how Americans view their country as distant from the rest of the world, separate and innocent. Individuals are given a mediation of the event, a representation of the site of 9/11, which for them is 'an experience nevertheless' (ibid.: 9). Their relation to the event is a relation to its mediation, since media offer authenticity to sites: Ground Zero is not simply where people died, but from where iconic images emerged. The sudden sales of snow globes, Fire Department of New York (FDNY) teddy bears and I♥NY t-shirts results in history becoming something that is consumed, rather than responded to with a political subjectivity; citizens are not encouraged to engage in national politics to alter the foreign policies that 'enable' such events to happen, Sturken argues (ibid.: 13). Such studies of practices can illuminate the local explanations that cohere with the broader trends and shifts in relations between media, war and public opinion identified in studies such as that by Bennett et al. (2007).

A challenge for studies of war and media is to identify and analyse the media practices through which discourses are generated, sustained and distributed in different countries and contexts. A useful concept here is *mediality*, which refers to a relationship between media content or representations and our everyday media practices, and our ongoing relationship to 'the fact of mediation itself' (Crocker, 2007). There is a need for research of the 'medialogical significance' (Grusin, 2010) of media content and formats through which discourses emerge and perpetuate, in order to account for their status and impact. New Yorkers acquired a medial relation to 9/11 through what they did with candles or snow globes. Indeed, mediality can itself be represented. As our analysis of 'radicalization' and media in chapter 8 suggests, news media represent political and religious practices, but also the media practices of those radicalized or radicalizing – people's use of mobile phones, the Internet and other media technologies throughout the radicalization process. These reports show how life is mediatized, and that the lives of 'radicals' are mediatized in the same ways as 'our' lives. They have family photographs and self-made clips of themselves on their holidays, just as 'we' do. This potentially produces an additional insecurity: the inseparability of 'radicals' and their media practices from society per se from 'our' media.

It is through these practices, including their medial aspects, that emergence occurs – emergence of a post-9/11 'new normal' in New York communities, the emergence of the 'war on terror' through policy communities. But again, this is a very complex phenomenon, exemplary of the second phase of mediatization. What analytical tools might allow us to grasp it?

3. How Do We Analyse Discursive Linking? Nexus Analysis

A recent approach which may meet this demand is 'nexus analysis' (Scollon and Scollon, 2004; Awan et al., 2010). A nexus analysis maps the 'semiotic cycles' (the circulation of symbols, including media content) generated by actions taken in response to a mediated event or in the formation of a social network or institution such as a military or terrorist organization. It explores the past, present and future trajectories of meaning implicated in the sum of communications around the phenomenon. Scollon and Scollon later argued they arrived at this methodology after realizing, in a study of racism, 'that there was no single point at which we could address problems of societal discrimination, institutional structure, and social change with any sense that this point was the fulcrum point around which everything else rotated' (2007: 615). Across interviews with journalists and audiences, and through media content analysis, we can identify who responded to a key event and how they made sense of it. For example, images of a US marine shooting dead an Iraqi civilian in a mosque in Fallujah (filmed in 2004 by an NBC journalist, Kevin Sites – see chapter 7), provoked a set of interconnected semiotic cycles in different parts of the world.

In the UK, journalists and academics debated the ethics of broadcasting such footage. Across the Middle East, by contrast, Internet message boards and mainstream Arabic media interpreted the footage as demonstrating 'the truth' of US intentions. It was possible to compare the responses of citizens, journalists and policymakers within different semiotic cycles and at the nexus of cycles meeting.

As well as following clips, we can follow the response to political speeches about war and conflict. One could, for instance, follow the cycles of communication triggered by a speech by Pope Benedict XVI in September 2006 in Germany, in which he said: 'Show me just what Mohammed brought that was new, and there you will find things only evil and inhuman, such as his command to spread by the sword the faith he preached.' The speech provoked a response from Muslim populations around the world. Zimmerman describes how CNN covered that response:

> On CNN, a white male news anchor in a business suit occupied the center of the frame, flatly describing the reaction around the globe to the Pope's speech. Behind him, digitally composited images formed four quadrants from Indonesia, Gaza, Sudan and Pakistan. These images showed large groups of angry people with picket signs in different – but untranslated – languages. It was an image of chaos and of undifferentiation, of nameless crowds. (2007: 68)

CNN's depiction of chaos was actually containing: it reduced and simplified the responses of different groups in different countries to a mere mass of shouting. Additionally, that apparently uncontrollable mass is juxtaposed with the calm, Western news anchor who stands between 'us' and 'them'. This mediating anchor does not translate the specific claims and grievances of individuals in the crowds represented; those crowds are a mere object put on view for the audience. However, news audiences with Internet access could easily read Muslim responses themselves online.

Such a case study would exemplify the challenge of studying war and media in the second phase of mediatization. Analysis may have to be multilingual, may have to deal with complex feedback loops and may involve costly audience research to understand the practices through which people consumed and interpreted this story in different parts of the world.

The virtue of nexus analysis would be an openness to new and emergent phenomena rather than a reification of existing institutions and structures. A nexus is 'a group, whose unification is achieved through the reciprocal interiorization by each of each other' (Laing, in Urry, 2007: 94). Urry contrasts a series system 'in which each component is roughly like every other component' with a nexus system, in which the 'whole is only able to function if every component works' (ibid.: 94). Automobility is a series system: traffic stop lights might break down, but cars could probably still coordinate and keep moving. Air travel is a nexus system: if one part is wrong, a disaster occurs. Hence the focus of nexus analysis is the formation, operation, and the maintenance, transformation or unravelling of a nexus system.

Certain 'big' phenomena, or groups or systems in Urry's terms, have driven the study of war and media in the 2000s, and there will be similar big phenomena in the 2010s. We might think of such groups as 'post-9/11 security culture', 'war on terror' or 'transnational media diplomacy', major events such as 'the 2003 Iraq War', 'the cyber-attack on Estonia' or 'the 3/11 Madrid bombings', or social collectivities such as Al-Qaeda, NATO or the US 'military-industrial-entertainment complex' (Der Derian, 2009). All these phenomena are complex systems in which many actors, technologies and processes exist in relation to others to form a coherent whole. This is not to throw the baby out with the bathwater and ignore the role of institutions and structures. Empirically, we know that social complexity does not produce unidentifiable chaotic patterns. Research on social networks shows the Internet has formed into an aristocratic, near-hierarchical structure in which a small group of sites dominate, notably Google, Yahoo, Microsoft and the BBC (at the time of writing) (Urry, 2007: 215–19). Elements within a system may be fluid but the overall system might be quite stable (Knorr-Cetina, 2005), for instance as leaders in a terror network are killed but the network's ideology continues to generate new members. Digitization makes it possible to track the emergence of such phenomena in real time. We recognize this is a very difficult task, that will require research teams with diverse training and languages, but nexus analysis at least points to the kind of dynamic methodology required for our new media ecology.

4. Conclusion

We have articulated some of the main challenges facing the field of war and media, and surveyed some potential solutions. The problem of identifying effects demands we turn to new data-mining tools to understand our increasingly digitized communications, while being wary of ethical problems this may raise. The problem of analysing practices demands that we seek to identify links between subjects, objects and their relations – for instance, Americans, snow globes and a post-9/11 security climate – and implicate the medial dimension of these relationships. The challenge of doing such identifying and understanding or explaining such links demands approaches that do not take units of analysis as given, but take these phenomena as emergent, such as nexus analysis. What each demand suggests is that to generate useful knowledge for most research questions of any importance to the field, it has become necessary to *combine* methods through the construction of a *methodology*.

The growing volume and complexity of communication make this an exciting but also a daunting time for the study of war and media. With more of war, conflict and insecurity recorded, stored, transferred and broadcast, there are unprecedented opportunities to trace and map the dynamics of communicating war. Software is developing that allows us to track issues and communication networks automatically through the Internet. Scholars in various disciplines are offering nuanced analytical approaches for the interpretation of media content and practices. Yet, the danger with multiple shards of even excellent methods in the political and social sciences is that although their zones of interest may overlap and intersect, the prospects for dynamic interdisciplinary work are muted in disciplinary rituals and traditions. Rather, given the limitations of single-disciplinary studies, in the second phase of mediatization we must bridge the theoretical and methodological interstices and bring our subject matter into full view, thereby illuminating the multiple and contested dimensions of the phenomena identified here as diffused war.

NOTES

Chapter 1   Introduction

1 Britain, France, Turkey, and Piedmont-Sardinia fought in the Crimean War against Russia.
2 We find Fredric Jameson's influential definition of mediatizing, in his writing on the spatial turn of postmodernism, another useful starting point: '[T]he traditional fine arts are *mediatized*: that is, they now come to consciousness of themselves as various media within a mediatic system in which their own internal production also constitutes a symbolic message and the taking of a position on the status of the medium in question' (1991: 162).
3 For some, this account was never an adequate description of Western history in the first place. See Latour (1993).
4 Weinberger's work is indicative of a growing literature (cf. Lessig, 2006; Anderson, 2007; Leadbeater, 2008) that attempts to map the emergent terrain and fast-evolving consequences of the second phase of mediatization. Interestingly, this body of work has not emerged from the traditional academic disciplinary areas of media and communication studies, but from the fields of law, business, journalism and computer science, for example.
5 Satellite news-gathering (SNG) was developed in the 1980s but only became really significant at the end of that decade.
6 For an overview and critique of the key contributions to the significant body of work devoted to examining the nature and impact of the so-called 'CNN effect', see Hoskins and O'Loughlin (2007).

Chapter 2   Images

1 For example, Griffin and Lee, 1995; Fahmy, 2007; Fahmy and Kim, 2008; Moore et al., 2008; Silcock et al., 2008; cf. Rose, 2007: 60. However, we acknowledge that the exigencies of our not reproducing visual images on these pages could also be taken as problematic.

2 See Hoskins and O'Loughlin (2007) for an extended discussion on the persistence of this framing of British television 'standards'.

3 Shifting Securities, Strand A, AG3, para 42.

4 Ibid., SR6, para 105.

5 Ibid., SR5, para 134.

6 Ibid., SW2, p. 10.

7 Ibid., p. 8.

8 Ibid., SR5, paras 34–8.

9 Ibid., AG3, para 58.

Chapter 3   Compassion

1 The full title of the project is *Shifting Securities: News Cultures Before and Beyond the Iraq Crisis 2003*. The project was funded under the New Security Challenges programme run by the Economic and Social Research Council (ESRC) (Award Ref: RES-223-25-0063, principal investigator: Marie Gillespie; co-investigators: James Gow and Andrew Hoskins). Gillespie supervised the audience ethnography, in which the following carried out research: Ammar Al Ghabban, Habiba Noor, Awa Hassan Ahmed, Atif Imtiaz, Akil Awan, Noureddine Miladi, Karen Qureshi, Zahbia Yousuf, David Herbert, Sadaf Rivzi, Somnath Batabyal, Awa Al Hassan and Marie Gillespie. The news media discourse and image analysis was conducted by Andrew Hoskins and Ben O'Loughlin. The elite interviews were undertaken by James Gow and Ivan Zverzhanovski.

2 The term 'war pornography' is sometimes associated with the sensational, repetitive, faux-intimate coverage of disaster and suffering media can deliver. See Getachew (2008).

3 UN News Centre (2006)

4 Shifting Securities, Strand A, Interview OA2, paras 58–9.

5 Ibid., Strand C, Interview 15, para 20. Interview in London, September 2006.

6 Ibid, paras 16–18.

7 Ibid, para 22.

8 Henderson (2008). An excellent discussion of the role of celebrity in mediatized charity campaigns is Nash (2008).

9 Shifting Securities, Strand A, Interview 3, para 7. Interview in London, May 2006.

10 Ibid., Interview 12, paras 103–6. Interview in London, September 2006.

11 Ibid., Strand C, Interview 21, para 1. Interview in London, September 2006.

12 Ibid., Interview 19, para 8. Interview in London, September 2006.

13 Ibid., para 4. Interview in London, September 2006.

14 Ibid., Strand A, Interview OA2, paras 63–6.

15 See Boltanski (1999: 10-11) on vengeance and the satisfaction some viewing of suffering can elicit.

16 On interpretive repertoires, see Wetherell, and Potter, J. (1988). On 'interpretive schemas', see Richardson and Corner (1992). These media studies should be situated within broader sociological analysis of the repertoires available to individuals in particular cultures and nations. See Lamont and Thévenot (2000: 8–9).

17 Ellis here cites a phrase coined by Trevor McDonald, for many years the anchor of ITV's *News at Ten*, who, he explains, 'utters this remark as a justification of the activity of television news' (2002: 15, n6).

Chapter 4   Witness

1 This phrase, with its implied ownership of history, does not go away. See for instance this CNN transcript from 2007: http://transcripts.cnn.com/TRANSCRIPTS /0705/19/cnr.06.html.
2 See Cunningham's (2007) argument for the introduction of 'rhetoric reporters'.
3 On forms of realism see Chouliaraki (2006: 75), which she usefully applies through a series of case studies of war and disaster news-reporting.
4 We do not provide here a history of the war correspondent and attempts by militaries to control correspondents' coverage of the battlefield (see Knightley, 2003; Taylor, 2003; Paul and Kim, 2004; see also chapter 7, 'Vectors').
5 Speaking in the Channel 4 *Dispatches* documentary, 'Iraq: The Hidden Story' (2006), available at: video.google.com/videoplay?docid=2179700192640 504810.
6 Shifting Securities, Strand C, Interview 20, para 20, London, September 2006.
7 Ibid., para 88.
8 Ibid., para 78.
9 Ibid., para 80.
10 Ibid., para, 88.
11 Ibid., Interview 15, para 6, London, September 2006.
12 Ibid., Interview 4, para 32, London, May 2006.
13 These modes are derived from conversations with Marie Gillespie of The Open University. See also Gillespie, 2006b, 2006a. For an overview of post-war audience studies see Abercrombie and Longhurst (1998: 3–38).

Chapter 5   Genocide

1 Kitzinger's study principally examined the press reporting of what became known as the 'Cleveland scandal' in debates around sexual abuse in Britain beginning in the late 1980s. In addition to content analysis, the research included interviews with journalists and focus group analysis of 'audience reception' (2000: 62).
2 This tour was part of a programme of events for the workshop, 'On Media Memory: The future of mediated collective memory in an age of changing media environments', funded by the Israel Science Foundation, Yad Vashem, Jerusalem, 2 July. Available at: http://on–media–memory.org.il/. See also Hoskins (2011).
3 Sontag here identifies the 'Omarska' camp (rather than Trnopolje) as the location in which the defining images of prisoners behind a barbed-wire fence were taken. Although the Omarska camp was part of the same controversy and covered in both of the ITN reports with footage broadcast of prisoners therein, the iconic images of Alic were recorded at the Trnopolje camp.
4 The photograph anchored an article, Van Der Veen (1995); see Zelizer (1998: 225).
5 Cohen similarly names Omarska, rather than Trnopolje, see note 3, above.

Chapter 6   Memory

1 For the link made between 'media events' and collective memory, see Dayan and Katz (1992: 22).
2 www.library.yale.edu/testimonies/about/concept.html (accessed 12 June 2008).

Chapter 7   Vectors

1 Our treatment of globalization is necessarily brief. For more developed starting points, see Scholte (2005) and Sassen (2006, 2007).
2 A service offered by private companies such as Wolff-Olins and Placebrands.
3 The photographs are available at: www.joelmeyerowitz.com/photography/after911. html.
4 Shifting Securities, Strand C, Interview 7. Conducted in London in July 2006.
5 Ibid., para 10.
6 Ibid., para 48, emphasis added.
7 Ibid., para 35.
8 Ibid., para 25, emphasis added.
9 Address to the International Broadcasting, Public Diplomacy and Cultural Exchange conference, SOAS, London, 18–19 December 2007.
10 Marie Gillespie and Annabelle Sreberny lead the AHRC-funded *Tuning In : Diasporic Contact Zones* at BBC World Service: www.open.ac.uk/socialsciences/diasporas/.
11 Mohammed El-Nawawy leads the Knight Foundation-funded Al Jazeera English, *Clash of Civilizations or Cross Cultural Dialogue?* See www.ajerp.com.
12 Shifting Securities, Strand C, Interview 19, para 25. Interview in London, September 2006; emphasis added.
13 The policymakers participated in Shifting Securities, Focus Groups 3 and 14, Strand C, and the audiences participated in Interviews OA1, OA2, OA3, Z2.3, Z2.4 and Z2.5, Strand A.
14 We are grateful for Gillian Youngs for raising this question at the Politics: Web 2.0 conference at Royal Holloway, University of London, 19–20 April 2008.

Chapter 8   Radicalization

1 Declassified Key Judgments of the National Intelligence Estimate "Trends in Global Terrorism: Implications for the United States" dated April 2006. Available at: www. dni.gov/press_releases/Declassified_NIE_Key_Judgments.pdf   (accessed   August 2008).
2 'Studies into violent radicalisation; Lot 2 The beliefs ideologies and narratives', Change Institute for the European Commission (Directorate General Justice, Freedom and Security), February 2008, p. 7, note 3. Available at: http://ec.europa. eu/justice_home/fsj/terrorism/prevention/fsj_terrorism_prevention_prevent_en.htm (accessed July 2008).
3 www.almokhtsar.com/news.php?action=show&id=8357.
4 'Rethinking Jihad: Ideas, Politics and Conflict in the Arab World & Beyond', 7–9 September 2009. Details available at: www.casaw.ac.uk/conf/rj2009/about-the-conference.html.
5 See: www.defenselink.mil/speeches/speech.aspx?speechid=440 (accessed July 2008).
6 Dominic Casciani, 'Top extremist recruiter is jailed', BBC News online, 26 February 2008. Available at: http://news.bbc.co.uk/1/hi/uk/7231492.stm (accessed February 2008).

Chapter 9   Legitimacy

1 See also Butler's notion of an 'economy of grievability' (2008: 24–5) and the manner in which certain cultures may encourage the attribution of worthiness to some lives more than others.

2 A number of books have documented the 'war on terror' discourse (see e.g. Jackson, 2005; Lewis 2005; Croft, 2006; Faludi, 2007).

3 Title VII: Increasing Information Sharing for Critical Infrastructure Protection, sec. 802, 'Definition of Domestic Terrorism', cited in Layoun (2006); emphasis added.

4 See the research report of Jef Huysmans and Thomas Diez at: www.esrc.ac.uk/ESRCInfoCentre/about/CI/CP/the_edge/issue25/a_new_politics_of_unease.aspx.

5 The peace journalism school has examined practical techniques that could be used by journalists and editors to avoid binary categorizations. See Lynch and McGoldrick (2005).

6 Available at: http://image.guardian.co.uk/sys-files/Guardian/documents/2008/02/04/Phrasebook.pdf. The *Guardian*'s report is not available online. The hard copy reference is: Alan Travis, 'Phrasebook Diplomacy: Whitehall Draws Up New Rules on Language of Terror: Phrasebook Designed to Avoid Blaming Muslims for Extremism: New Rules on the Language of Terror', *Guardian*, 4 February 2008, pp. 1–2.

Chapter 10   Methods

1 Ethnographic methods have been used in recent studies of war and security, ranging from state-sponsored research such as the US Department of Defense anthropology programme, Human Terrain System (http://humanterrainsystem.army.mil/), to critical studies in which researchers are granted access to military environments, such as James Der Derian's interpretive explorations of training camps of the US Marines (2009).

REFERENCES

Abercrombie, N. and Longhurst, B. (1998) *Audiences: A Sociological Theory of Performance and Imagination*, London: Sage.

Abrams, C. B. et al. (2004) 'Contesting the New York community: From liminality to the "new normal" in the wake of September 11', *City & Community*, 3/3: 189–220.

Al Jazeera (2008) 'Al Jazeera English wins prestigious award', 14 June. Available at: http://english.aljazeera.net/news/europe/2008/06/20086150182634319.html.

Al-Lami, M. (2008) 'Studies of radicalisation: State of the field report', Politics and International Relations Working Paper, Royal Holloway, University of London. Available at: www.rhul.ac.uk/politics-and-ir/Working-Papers/RHUL-PIR-NPCU_Working_Paper-11_Al_Lami_Radicalisation_and_New_Media.pdf.

Al-Lami, M. and O'Loughlin, B. (2009) 'Jihadis try to make friends on Facebook', *Guardian*, 12 January. Available at: www.guardian.co.uk/commentisfree/2009/jan/12/facebook-jihadis.

Allan, S. (2006) *Online News: Journalism and the Internet*, Maidenhead: Open University Press.

Altheide, D. L. (2006) *Terrorism and the Politics of Fear*, Lanham, MD: AltaMira Press.

Altheide, D. L. (2007) 'The mass media and terrorism', *Discourse and Communication*, 1: 287–308.

Altheide, D. L. and Snow, R. P. (1979) *Media Logic*, London: Sage.

Al-Zawahiri, A. (2009) 'Gaza massacre and the seige of traitors', 6 January. Available at: www.al-faloja.info/vb/showthread.php?t=41319.

Amoore, L. (2007) 'Vigilant visualities: The watchful politics of the war on terror', *Security Dialogue*, 38/2: 215–32.

Amoore, L. (2008) 'Response before the event: On forgetting the war on terror', in N. Vaughan-Williams and A. C. Stephens (eds), *Terrorism and the Politics of Response: London in a Time of Terror*, London: Routledge.

Amoore, L. and de Goede, M. (2008) 'Introduction: Governing by risk in the war on terror', in L. Amoore and M. de Goede (eds), *Risk and the War on Terror*, London: Routledge.

Anderson, C. (2007) *The Long Tail: How Endless Choice is Creating Unlimited Demand*, London: Random House Books.

Anderson, M. (2008) 'Mapping digital diasporas', BBC World Service, *World Agenda*. Available at: www.bbc.co.uk/worldservice/specials/1641_wagus08/page5.shtml.

Ansary, A. F. (2008) 'Combating extremism: A brief overview of Saudi Arabia's approach', *Middle East Policy*, 15/2: 111–42.

Appadurai, A. (1996) *Modernity at Large: Cultural Dimensions of Globalization*, Minneapolis: University of Minnesota Press.

Appadurai, A. (2006). *Fear of Small Numbers: An Essay of the Geography of Anger*, Chapel Hill, NC: Duke University Press.

Archetti, C. (2008) '"Unamerican views": Why US-developed models of press–state relations don't apply to the rest of the world', Westminster Papers in Communication and Culture, 5/3: 4–26.

Arquilla, J. (2007) 'Introduction: Thinking about information strategy', in J. Arquilla and D. A. Borer (eds), *Information Strategy and Warfare: A Guide to Theory and Practice*, New York and Abingdon: Palgrave.

Arquilla, J. and Ronfeldt, D. (eds) (2001) *Networks and Netwars: The Future of Terror, Crime and Militancy*, Santa Monica, CA: RAND.

Assman, J. (1995) 'Collective memory and cultural identity', *New German Critique*, 65: 125–33.

Awan, A. N. (2007) 'Virtual Jihadist media: Function, legitimacy, and radicalising efficacy', *European Journal of Cultural Studies*, 10/3: 389–408.

Awan, A. N. and Al-Lami, M. (2009) 'Al-Qa'ida's virtual crisis', *The RUSI Journal*, 154/1: 56–64.

Awan, A. N. et al. (2010) *Media and Radicalisation: Political Violence in the New Media Ecology*, London: Routledge.

Baker, M. (2006) *Translation and Conflict: A Narrative Account*, New York and London: Routledge.

Balibar, E. (2002) *Politics and the Other Scene*, London: Verso.

Ball, M. S. and Smith, G. W. H. (1992) *Analyzing Visual Data*, London: Sage.

Barad, K. M. (2007) *Meeting the Universe Halfway: Quantum Physics and the Entanglement of Matter*, Durham, NC: Duke University Press.

Barber, B. (1995) *Jihad vs. McWorld*, New York: Ballantine Books.

Bardgett, S. (2000) 'The Holocaust Exhibition at the Imperial War Museum', *News of Museums of History*. Available at: http://web.univ-pau.fr/psd/bardgett.pdf (accessed 24 June 2002).

Barnett, C. (2003) *Culture and Democracy: Media, Space and Representation*, Edinburgh: Edinburgh University Press.

Barnett, C. (2005) 'Violence and publicity: Making distinctions, taking responsibility', in D. Gregory and A. Pred (eds), *Spaces of Terror*, London: Routledge.

Barnett, C. (2008a) 'Convening publics: the parasitical spaces of public action', in K. R. Cox, M. Low and J. Robinson (eds), *The Sage Handbook of Political Geography*, London: Sage.

Barnett, C. (2008b) 'Where is public space?'. Available at: www.mediapolis.org.uk/Papers/Clive%20Barnett.pdf.

Baudrillard, J. (1994) *The Illusion of the End*, Cambridge: Polity.

Baudrillard, J. (1995) *The Gulf War Did Not Take Place* (trans. Paul Patton), Sydney: Power Publications.

Bauman, Z. (2000) *Liquid Modernity*, Cambridge: Polity.

Bauman, Z. (2003) *City of Fears, City of Hopes*, London: Goldsmiths College. Available at: www.opa-a2a.org/dissensus/wp-content/uploads/2008/05/bauman_zygmunt_city_of_fears_city_of_hopes.pdf.

Bauman, Z. (2006) *Liquid Fear*, Cambridge: Polity.

Bauman, Z. (2007) *Liquid Life*, Cambridge: Polity.

BBC News (2000) 'Magazine folds after libel bill', 31 March. Available at: http://news.bbc.co.uk/1/hi/uk/696955.stm.

BBC News (2006a) 'Bush and Blair: Key points', 26 May. Available at: http://news.bbc.co.uk/1/hi/world/americas/5018868.stm.

BBC News (2006b) 'Straw's veil comments spark anger', 5 October. Available at: http://news.bbc.co.uk/2/hi/uk_news/politics/5410472.stm.

BBC World Service (2009) *The Forum*, 20 September.

Beer, D. (2009) 'Power through the algorithm? Participatory web cultures and the *technological* unconscious', *New Media & Society*, 11/6: 985–1002.

Beetham, D. (1991) *The Legitimation of Power: Issues in Political Theory*, London: Macmillan.

Bell, M. (1998) 'The journalism of attachment', in M. Kieran (ed.), *Media Ethics*, London: Routledge, pp.15–22.

Bell, M. (2008) 'The death of news', *Media, War & Conflict*, 1/2: 221–31.

Bellamy, A. J. (2005) 'Is the war on terror just?' *International Relations*, 19/3: 275–96.

Ben-Shaul, N. (2007) *A Violent World: TV News Images of Middle Eastern Terror and War*, Lanham, MD: Rowman and Littlefield.

Benjamin, W. (1969) 'On some motifs in Baudelaire', in H. Arendt (ed.), *Illuminations: Essays and Reflections*, New York: Schocken Books, pp. 155–94.

Benkler, Y. (2006) *The Wealth of Networks*, New Haven, CT: Yale University Press.

Bennett, W. L. (1990) 'Towards a theory of press–state relations in the United States', *Journal of Communication*, 10: 103–25.

Bennett, W. L. (2003) 'Communicating global activism: Strengths and vulnerabilities of networked politics', *Information, Communication & Society*, 6/2: 143–68.

Bennett, W. L. and Lawrence, R. G. (1995) 'News icons and the mainstreaming of social change', *Journal of Communication*, 45/3: 20–39.

Bennett, W. L., Lawrence, R. G. and Livingston, S. (2007) *When the Press Fails: Political Power and the News Media from Iraq to Katrina*, Chicago: Chicago University Press.

Bergin, P. et al. (2009) 'Countering Internet radicalisation in Southeast Asia', RSIS–ASPI joint report, March. Available at: http://ctstudies.com/reports/Countering_internet_radicalisation_SEAsia_mar09.pdf.

Bermingham, A., Conway, M., McInerney, L., O'Hare, N. and Smeaton, A. F. (2009) 'Combining social network analysis and sentiment analysis to explore the potential for online radicalisation'. Paper presented at ASONAM 2009 – Advances in Social Networks Analysis and Mining, 20–22 July, Athens, Greece. Available at: http://doras.dcu.ie/4554/.

Bhattacharyya, G. (2008) *Dangerous Brown Men: Exploiting Sex, Violence and Feminism in the War on Terror*, New York: Zed Books.

Biersteker, T. J. and Eckert, S. E. (eds) (2007) *Countering the Financing of Terrorism*, London: Routledge.

Bimber, B. (1998) 'The Internet and political transformation: Populism, community, and accelerated pluralism', *Polity*, 31/1: 133–53.

Blair, T. (2005) 'Press conference with Tony Blair and Afghan President Hamid Karzai', 19 July. Available at: www.pm.gov.uk/output/Page7955.asp.

Blair, T. (2007) 'A battle for global values', *Foreign Affairs*, 86/1: 79–90.

Bobbitt, P. (2008) *Terror and Consent: The Wars for the Twenty-First Century*, London: Penguin.

Boden, D. and Hoskins, A. (1995) 'Time, space and television'. Unpublished paper presented at 2nd Theory, Culture & Society Conference, 'Culture and Identity: City, Nation, World', Berlin, 11 August.

Boden, D. and Molotch, H. L. (1994) 'The compulsion of proximity', in R. Friedland and D. Boden (eds), *NowHere: Space, Time and Modernity*, London: University of California Press, pp. 257–86.

Boltanski, L. (1999) *Distant Suffering: Morality, Media and Politics* (trans. Graham Burchell), Cambridge: Cambridge University Press.

Boltanski, L. and Thévenot, L. (1991/2006) *On Justification: Economies of Worth* (trans. C. Porter), Princeton: Princeton University Press.

Boorstein, M. (2007) 'Eerie souvenirs from the Vietnam War', *Washington Post*, 3 July. Available at: www.washingtonpost.com/wp-dyn/content/article/2007/07/02/AR2007070201710_pf.html (accessed 14 September 2007).

Borowitz, A. (2006) 'Bush demands that Iran halt production of long letters', 12 May. Available at: www.truthdig.com/report/item/20060512_andy_borowitz_iran_letters/.

Bourdieu, P. (1977) *Outline of a Theory of Practice*, Cambridge: Cambridge University Press.

Bourdieu, P. (1990) *The Logic of Practice*, Cambridge: Polity.

Bousquet, A. J. (2009) *The Scientific Way of Warfare: Order and Chaos on the Battlefields of Modernity*, London: Columbia/Hurst.

Bruns, A. (2005) *Gatewatching: Collaborative Online News Production*, New York: Peter Lang.

Bumiller, E. (2002) 'US must act first to battle terror, Bush tells cadets', *New York Times*, 2 June. Available at: www.nytimes.com/2002/06/02/world/us-must-act-first-to-battle-terror-bush-tells-cadets.html.

Burke, J. (2004) *Al-Qaeda: The True Story of Radical Islam*, London: Penguin.

Butler, J. (1990) *Gender Trouble: Feminism and the Subversion of Identity*, London: Routledge.

Butler, J. (1997) *Excitable Speech*, London: Routledge.

Butler, J. (2005) 'Photography, War, Outrage', *PMLA*, 120/3: 822–7.

Butler, J. (2008) 'Sexual politics, torture, and secular time', *The British Journal of Sociology*, 59/1: 1–23.

Butler, J. (2009) *Frames of War: When Is Life Grievable?*, London: Verso.

Buzan, B. (1998) *Security: a new framework for analysis*, Boulder, CO: Lynne Rienner.

Calavita, M. (2005) *Apprehending Politics: News Media and Individual Political Development*, Albany: State University of New York Press.

Caldwell, J. T. (1995) *Televisuality: Style, Crisis, and Authority in American Television*, New Brunswick: Rutgers University Press.

Campbell, D. (1992) *Writing Security: United States Foreign Policy and the Politics of Identity*, Manchester: Manchester University Press.

Campbell, D. (1993) *Politics Without Principle: Sovereignty, Ethics, and the Narratives of the Gulf War*, London: Lynn Reiner.

Campbell, D. (2002a) 'Atrocity, memory, photography: Imaging the concentration camps of Bosnia – the case of ITN versus *Living Marxism*', Part 1, *Journal of Human Rights*, 1/1: 1–33.

Campbell, D. (2002b) 'Atrocity, memory, photography: Imaging the concentration camps of Bosnia – the case of ITN versus *Living Marxism*', Part 3, *Journal of Human Rights*, 1/2: 143–72.

Campbell, D. (2004) *Methods and Nations*, London: Routledge.

Campbell, D. (2007) 'Geopolitics and visuality: Sighting the Darfur conflict', *Political Geography*, 26/1: 357–82.

Carey, J. (1989) *Communications as Culture: Essays on Media and Society*, Winchester: Unwin Hyman.

Carpini, M. X. D. (2009) 'Something's going on here, but we don't know what it is: Measuring citizens' exposure to politically relevant information in the new media environment', in G. King, K. L. Schlozman and N. H. Nie (eds), *The Future of Political Science: 100 Perspectives*, New York and London: Routledge.

Castells, M. (1996) *The Rise of the Network Society: Volume I of the Information Age. Economy, Society and Culture*, Malden, MA: Blackwell.

Cesarani, D. (2005) 'A nation tenderly traces the scars that never fade', *Times Higher Education*, 11 February. Available at: www.timeshighereducation.co.uk/story.asp?storyCode=194047&sectioncode=26, (accessed 26 June 2006).

Chadwick, A. (2007) 'Digital Network Repositories and Organizational Hybridity', *Political Communication*, 24/1: 283–301.

Chakar, T. (2007) 'The impossible war memorial: Is shooting a corpse considered murder', *Memorial to the Iraq War*, London: Institute for Contemporary Arts.

Chong, D. and Druckman, J. N. (2007) 'Framing theory', *Annual Review of Political Science*, 10: 103–26.

Chouliaraki, L. (2005) 'Spectacular Ethics: On the Television Footage of the Iraq War', *Journal of Language and Politics*, 4/1: 43–59.

Chouliaraki, L. (2006) *The Spectatorship of Suffering*, London: Sage.

Chow, R. (2006) *The Age of the World Target: Self-Referentiality in War, Theory, and Comparative Work*, Durham, NC: Duke University Press.

Christensen, C. (2008) 'Uploading dissonance: *YouTube* and the US occupation of Iraq', *Media, War & Conflict*, 1/2: 155–75.

Clark, S. H. and Jones, D. B. (2006) 'Waging terror: The geopolitics of the real', *Political Geography*, 25: 298–314.

Clausewitz, C. von. (1976) *On War*, ed. M. Howard and P. Paret, Princeton, NJ: Princeton University Press.

Closs Stephens, A. (2009) 'Beyond the imaginary geographies of the war on terror?' in A. Pusca (ed.), *Walter Benjamin and the Aesthetics of Change*, Basingstoke: Palgrave.

Cockett, R. B. (1988) '"In wartime every objective reporter should be shot": The experience of British press correspondents in Moscow, 1941–45', *Journal of Contemporary History*, 23/4: 515–30.

Cohen, S. (2001) *States of Denial: Knowing About Atrocities and Suffering*, Cambridge: Polity.

Connelly, M. and Welch, D. (eds) (2004) *War and the Media: Reportage and Propaganda, 1900–2003*, London: I. B. Tauris.

Connerton, P. (2008) 'Seven types of forgetting', *Memory Studies*, 1/1: 59–71.

Conway, M. and McInerney, L. (2008) 'Jihadi video and auto-radicalisation: Evidence from an exploratory YouTube study, EuroISI 2008'. First European Conference on Intelligence and Security Informatics, 3–5 December, Esbjerg, Denmark. Available at: http://doras.dcu.ie/2253/.

Cooper, M. (2006) 'Pre-empting emergence: The biological turn in the war on terror', *Theory, Culture & Society*, 23/4: 113–35.

Cornish, P. (2008) 'Terrorism, radicalisation and the Internet', Chatham House, 31 July. Available at: www.chathamhouse.org.uk/files/12134_0708terrorism_internet.pdf.

Cottle, S. (2006) *Mediatized Conflict: Developments in Media and Conflict Studies*, Maidenhead: Open University Press.

Cox, A. M. (2006) 'The YouTube war', *Time*, 19 July.

Crocker, S. (2007) 'Noises and exceptions: Pure mediality in Serres and Agamben', in

'1000 days of theory', *CTheory*. Available at: www.ctheory.net/articles.aspx?id=574 (accessed January 2008).

Croft, S. (2006) *Culture, Crisis and America's War on Terror*, Cambridge: Cambridge University Press.

Cunningham, B. (2007) 'The rhetoric beat', *Columbia Journalism Review*, November/ December: 36–9.

Curtis, A. (2005) 'Creating Islamist Phantoms', *Guardian*, 30 August. Available at: www.guardian.co.uk/print/0,,5273306–103677,00.html (accessed 18 November 2006).

Danner, M. (2004) *Torture and Truth: America, Abu Ghraib, and the War on Terror*, New York: New York Review of Books.

Danner, M. (2009) 'US torture: Voices from the black sites', *New York Review of Books*, LVI/6 (9 April): 69–77.

Dayan, D. (2005) 'Mothers, midwives and abortionists: Geneology, obstetrics, audiences and publics', in S. Livingstone (ed.), *Audiences and Publics: When Cultural Engagement Matters for the Public Sphere*, Bristol: Intellect Books, pp. 43–76.

Dayan, D. and Katz, E. (1992) *Media Events: The Live Broadcasting of History*, Harvard: Harvard University Press.

Debrix, F. (2008) *Tabloid Terror: War, Culture and Geopolitics*, London: Routledge.

Deichmann, T. (1997) 'The picture that fooled the world', *LM* (February): 24–31. Available at: http://web.archive.org/web/19991110185707/www.informinc.co.uk/LM/LM97/LM97_Bosnia.html.

Der Derian, J. (2009) *Virtuous War: Mapping the Military-Industrial-Media-Entertainment Network* (2nd edn), London: Routledge.

Deuze, M. (2007) *Media Work*, Cambridge: Polity.

Deuze, M. (2008) 'Understanding journalism as newswork: How it changes, and how it remains the same', Westminster Papers in Communication and Culture, 52/2: 4–23.

Devji, F. (2005) *Landscapes of the Jihad: Militancy, Morality and Modernity*, London: C. Hurst & Co.

Devji, F. (2008) *The Terrorist in Search of Humanity: Militant Islam and Global Politics*, London: Hurst.

Dillon, M. (2007) 'Governing terror: The state of emergency in biopolitical emergence', *International Political Sociology*, 1: 7–28.

Dillon, M. (2008) 'Security, race and war', in M. Dillon and A. W. Neal (eds), *Foucault on Politics, Security and War*, Basingstoke: Palgrave.

Dizzard, W. P. (2001) *Digital Diplomacy: US Foreign Policy in the Information Age*, Washington DC: Center for Strategic and International Studies.

Doane, M. A. (2003) *The Emergence of Cinematic Time*, Harvard: Harvard University Press.

Doane, M. A. (2006) 'Real time: Instantaneity and the photographic imaginary', in D. Green and J. Lowry (eds), *Stillness and Time: Photography and the Moving Image*, Brighton: Photoforum and Photoworks, pp. 23–38.

Dodd, V. (2009) 'Anti-terror code "would alienate most Muslims"', *Guardian*, 17 February. Available at: www.guardian.co.uk/politics/2009/feb/17/counterterrorism-strategy-muslims.

Domke, D., Perlmutter, D. and Spratt, M. (2002) 'The primes of our times? An examination of the "power" of visual images', *Journalism*, 3/2: 131–59.

Draaisma, D. (2000) *Metaphors of Memory: A History of Ideas About the Mind* (trans. Paul Vincent), Cambridge: Cambridge University Press.

Dubos, R. (1987 [1959]) *Mirage of Health: Utopias, Progress, and Biological Change*, New Brunswick, NJ, and London: Rutgers University Press.

Durodie, B. (2006) 'We are the enemies within', *Times Higher Education Supplement*, 22 September. Available at: www.durodie.net/articles/THES/20060922enemies.htm.

Durodie, B. (2009) 'Religion, radicalism and terrorism', 23rd Asia-Pacific Roundtable, Sheraton Imperial Kuala Lumpur Hotel, 2 June. Available at: www.isis.org.my/files/apr/23rd%20APR/CS1%20-%20Dr%20Bill%20Durodie.pdf.

Eco, U. (1987) *Travels in Hyperreality*, London: Picador (trans. William Weaver).

Economist, The (2009) 'Unmanned military aircraft: Attack of the drones', 3 September. Available at: www.economist.com/sciencetechnology/tq/displayStory.cfm?story_id=14299496.

Edgerton, G. R. (2001) 'Introduction: Television as historian: A different kind of history altogether', in G. R. Edgerton and P. C. Rollins (eds), *Television Histories: Shaping Collective Memory in the Media Age*, Kentucky: The University Press of Kentucky, pp. 1–16.

Eide, E., Kunelius, R. and Phillips, A. (2008) 'Contrapuntal readings: Transnational media research and the cartoon controversy as a global news event', in E. Eide et al. (eds), *Transnational Media Events*, Gothenburg: Nordicom.

Eisenman, S. F. (2007) *The Abu Ghraib Effect*, London: Reaktion Books Ltd.

Ellis, J. (2002) *Seeing Things: Television in the Age of Uncertainty*, London: I. B. Taurus.

Entman, R. (1993) 'Framing: Towards clarification of a fractured paradigm', *Journal of Communication*, 43/4: 51–8.

Entman, R. M. (2004) *Projections of Power: Framing News, Public Opinion, and US Foreign Policy*, Chicago: University of Chicago Press.

Erll, A. (2008) 'Literature, film, and the mediality of cultural memory', in A. Erll and A. Nünning (eds), (with Sara B. Young), *Cultural Memory Studies: An International and Interdisciplinary Handbook*, Berlin: Walter de Gruyter, pp. 389–98.

Ernst, W. (2004) 'The archive as metaphor', *Open*, 7: 46–3.

Fahmy, S. (2007) *Filling the Frame: Transnational Visual Coverage and News Practitioners' Attitudes Towards the Reporting of War and Terrorism*, Saarbrücken, Germany: VDM Verlag Dr Müller.

Fahmy, S. and Kim, D. (2008) 'Picturing the Iraq War: Constructing the image of war in the British and US press', *International Communication Gazette*, 70/6: 443–62.

Faludi, S. (2007) *The Terror Dream: Fear and Fantasy in Post-9/11 America*, New York: Metropolitan Books.

Featherstone, M. (2009) 'Ubiquitous media: An introduction', *Theory, Culture & Society*, 26/2–3: 1–22.

Felman, S. and Laub, D. (1992) *Testimony: Crises of Witnessing in Literature, Psychoanalysis, and History*, New York: Routledge.

Finkelstein, N. (2000) *The Holocaust Industry: Reflections on the Exploitation of Jewish Suffering*, London: Verso.

Finn, H. (2003) 'The Case for Cultural Diplomacy', *Foreign Affairs*, 82/6: 15–20.

Foucault, M. (2007) *Security, Territory, Population: Lectures at the College de France, 1977–1978* (trans. Grahan Burchell), New York: Picador.

Friedman, T. (2001) 'Foreign affairs: The real war', *New York Times*, 27 November. Available at: www.pulitzer.org/archives/6547.

Friedland, R. and Boden, D. (eds) (1994) *NowHere: Space, Time and Modernity*, London: University of California Press

Friedländer, S. (1992) *Probing the Limits of Representation: Nazism and the 'Final Solution'*, Cambridge, MA: Harvard University Press.

Furedi, F. (2007) *Invitation to Terror: The Expanding Empire of the Unknown*, London: Continuum.

Gamson, W. and Modigliani, A. (1989) 'Media discourse and public opinion on nuclear power: A constructivist approach', *American Journal of Sociology*, 95/1: 1–37.

Garfinkel, H. (1968) 'On the origins of the term "ethnomethodology"', in R. Turner (ed.), *Ethnomethodology: Selected Readings*, Harmondsworth: Penguin, pp. 28–41.

Getachew, M. (2008) 'Compulsive viewing', *New Statesman*, 1 May. Available at: www.newstatesman.com/ideas/2008/05/pornography-war-images.

Giddens, A. (1984) *The Constitution of Society*, Cambridge: Polity.

Giddens, A. (1990) *The Consequences of Modernity*, Cambridge: Polity.

Gilboa, E. (1998) 'Media diplomacy', *The Harvard International Journal of Press/Politics*, 3/3: 56–75.

Gilboa, E. (2001) 'Diplomacy in the media age: Three models of uses and effects', *Diplomacy and Statecraft*, 12/2: 1–28.

Gilboa, E. (2002) 'Global communication and foreign policy', *Journal of Communication*, 52/4: 731–48.

Gilboa, E. (2005) 'Global television news and foreign policy: Debating the CNN effect', *International Studies Perspectives*, 6, 325–41.

Gillespie, M. (2006a) Guest Editor of 'Special Issue: After September 11: Television news and transnational audiences', *Journal of Ethnic and Migration Studies*, 32/6.

Gillespie, M. (ed.) (2006b) *Media Audiences*, Maidenhead: Open University Press.

Gillespie, M. (2006c) 'Security, media, legitimacy: Multi-ethnic media publics and the Iraq War 2003', *International Relations*, 20/4: 467–86.

Gillespie, M., Gow, J. and Hoskins, A. (2010) 'Shifting securities: News cultures, multicultural society and legitimacy', *Ethnopolitics*.

Gilligan, C. and Attanucci, J. (1988) 'Two moral orientations: Gender differences and similarities', *Merrill-Palmer Quarterly*, 34: 223–37.

Gilligan, C. and Wiggins, C. (1988) *The Origins of Morality in Early Childhood Relationships*, Cambridge, MA: Harvard University Press.

Gillmor, D. (2006) *We the Media: Grassroots Journalism By the People, For the People*, O'Reily Media, Inc.

Gilroy, P. (2006) 'Multiculture in times of war: An inaugural lecture given at the London School of Economics', *Critical Quarterly*, 48/4: 27–45.

Giroux, H. (2006) *Stormy Weather: Katrina and the Politics of Disposability*, Boulder: Westview Press.

Gitelman, L. (2006) *Always Already New: Media, History and the Data of Culture*, Cambridge, MA: MIT Press.

Gitlin, T. (1980) *The Whole World is Watching – Mass Media in the Making and Unmaking of the New Left*, London: University of California Press.

Gitlin, T. (1998) 'Public sphere or public sphericules?' in T. Liebes and J. Curran (eds), *Media, Ritual and Identity*, London: Routledge, pp. 168–74.

Gitlin, T. (2001) *Media Unlimited: How the Torrent of Images and Sounds Overwhelms Our Lives*. New York: Metropolitan Books.

Glover, J. (2008) 'Reasons to be cheerful, pt 1', *Guardian*, 24 May. Available at: www.guardian.co.uk/world/2008/may/24/afghanistan.foreignpolicy.

Goddard, P., Robinson, P. and Parry, K. (2008) 'Patriotism meets plurality: Reporting the 2003 Iraq War in the British press', *Media, War & Conflict*, 1/1: 9–30.

Goldsmith, J. and Wu, T. (2006) *Who Controls the Internet? Illusions of a Borderless World*, New York: Oxford.

Goodall, Jr., H. L., Cady, L., Corman, S. R. et al. (2008) 'The Iranian letter to President Bush: Analysis and recommendations', in S. R. Corman, A. Trethewey and H. L. Goodall, Jr. (eds), *Weapons of Mass Persuasion: Strategic Communication to Combat Violent Extremism*, New York: PeterLang.

Gow, J., Paterson, R. and Preston, A. (1996) 'Introduction', in J. Gow et al. (eds), *Bosnia By Television*, London: British Film Institute, pp. 1–8.

Graeber, D. (2006) 'Beyond power/knowledge: An exploration of the relation of power, ignorance and stupidity', Malinowski Memorial Lecture, London School of Economics, 25 May. Available at: www.lse.ac.uk/collections/LSEPublicLecturesAndEvents/pdf/20060525-Graeber.pdf.

Griffin, M. and Lee, J. S. (1995) 'Picturing the Gulf War: Constructing an image of war in *Time*, *Newsweek*, and US news & world report', *Journalism and Mass Communication Quarterly*, 72/4: 813–25.

Grindstaff, D. A. and DeLuca, K. M. (2004) 'The corpus of Daniel Pearl', *Critical Studies in Media Communication*, 21/4: 305–24.

Grusin, R. (2004) 'Premediation', *Criticism*, 46/1: 17–39.

Grusin, R. (2007) 'Publicity, pornography, or everyday media practice? On the Abu Ghraib photographs', *Open:* 13, 46–60.

Grusin, R. (2010) *Premediation*, Basingstoke: Palgrave Macmillan.

Guerin, F. and Hallas, R. (eds) (2007) *The Image and the Witness: Trauma, Memory and Visual Culture*, London: Wallflower Press.

Gul, A. (2008) 'Afghan president escapes assassination attempt', *Voice of America*, 27 April. Available at: www.voanews.com/english/2008-04-27-voa4.cfm.

Hafez, K. (2008) 'Introduction: Arab media: Power and weakness', in K. Hafez (ed.), *Arab Media: Power and Weakeness*, London and New York: Continuum.

Hagopian, P. (2006) 'Vietnam war photography as locus of memory', in A. Kuhn and K. E. McAllister (eds), *Locating Memory: Photographic Acts*, Oxford: Berghahn Books, pp. 210–22.

Hall, S. (2001) 'Out of a clear blue sky', *Soundings*, 19 (Winter): 9–15.

Hallin, Daniel C. (1986) *The 'Uncensored War': The Media and Vietnam*, Oxford: Oxford University Press.

Halpern, Sue (2008) 'The war we don't want to see', *New York Review of Books*, 55/20, 18 December. Available at: www.nybooks.com/articles/22179.

Hamilton, J., and Jenner, E. (2004) 'Redefining Foreign Correspondence', *Journalism*, 5/3: 301–21.

Hammock, J. and Charny, J. (1996) 'Emergency response as morality play: The media, relief agencies and the need for capacity building', in R. Rotberg and T. Weiss (eds), *From Massacres to Genocide*, Washington, DC: The Brookings Institution.

Hansen, L. (2006) *Security as Practice: Discourse Analysis and the Bosnian War*, London: Routledge.

Hanson, E. C. (2008) *The Information Revolution and World Politics*, Lanham: Rowman & Littlefield.

Hassan, R. and Purser, R. E. (eds) (2007) *24/7: Time and Temporality in the Network Society*, Stanford: Stanford University Press.

Held, D. (2006) 'Reframing global governance: Apocalypse soon or reform!', *New Political Economy*, 11/2: 157–76.

Held, D., McGrew, A., Goldblatt, D. and Perraton, J. (1999) *Global Transformations: Politics, Economics and Culture*, Stanford: Stanford University Press.

Henderson, K. (2008) 'Clooney stresses urgency in Darfur intervention', *The State Journal*, 20 February. Available at: www.state-journal.com/news/article/3334121.

Henning, M. (1995) 'Digital encounters: Mythical pasts and electronic presence', in M. Lister (ed.), *The Photographic Image in Digital Culture*, London: Routledge, pp. 217–35.

Henning, M. (2006) *Museums, Media and Cultural Theory*, Maidenhead: Open University Press.

Herman, E. G. and Chomsky, N. (1994) *Manufacturing Consent: The Political Economy of the Mass Media*, London: Vintage.

Hess, S. (1994) 'Crisis, TV and public pressure', *Brookings Review*, 12.

Hewlett, S. (2006) 'The government ban on ITV News is an abuse of power', *Guardian*, Media, 30 October, p. 4.

Hill, A. (2009) *Re-Imagining the War on Terror: Seeing, Waiting, Travelling*, Basingstoke: Palgrave Macmillan.

Hine, C. (2005) (ed.) *Virtual Methods: Issues in Social Research on the Internet*, Oxford: Berg Publishers.

Hirsch, M. (1997) *Family Frames: Photography, Narrative and Postmemory*, Harvard University Press.

Hirsch, M. (2008) 'The generation of postmemory', *Poetics Today*, 29/1: 103–28.

Hjarvard, S. (2004) 'From bricks to bytes: The mediatization of a global toy industry', in I. Bondebjerg and P. Golding (eds), *European Culture and the Media*, Bristol: Intellect Books.

Hjarvard, S. (2008a) 'The mediatization of religion: A theory of the media as agents of religious change', *Northern Lights*, 6: 9–26.

Hjarvard, S. (2008b) 'The mediatization of society: A theory of the media as agents of social and cultural change', *Nordicom Review*, 29/2: 105–34.

Hoijer, B. (2004) 'The discourse of global compassion: The audience and media reporting of human suffering', *Media, Culture and Society*, 26/4: 513–31.

Holland, J. (2009) 'From September 11th, 2001 to 9-11: From void to crisis', *International Political Sociology*, 3: 275–92.

Home Office (2006) *Report of the Official Account of the Bombings in London on 7th July 2005*, London: The Stationery Office (TSO). Available at: www.official-documents. gov.uk/document/hc0506/hc10/1087/1087.pdf.

Hoskins, A. (2001) 'New memory: Mediating history', *The Historical Journal of Film, Radio and Television*, 21/4: 191–211.

Hoskins, A. (2003) 'Signs of the Holocaust: Exhibiting memory in a mediated age', *Media, Culture & Society*, 25/1: 7–22.

Hoskins, A. (2004a) *Televising War: From Vietnam to Iraq*, London: Continuum.

Hoskins, A. (2004b) 'Television and the collapse of memory', *Time & Society*, 13/1: 109–27.

Hoskins, A. (2011) *The Mediatization of Memory: Media and the End of Collective Memory*, Cambridge, MA: MIT Press.

Hoskins, A. and O'Loughlin, B. (2007) *Television and Terror: Conflicting Times and the Crisis of News Discourse*, Basingstoke: Palgrave.

Hoskins, A. and O'Loughlin, B. (2009a) 'Pre-mediating guilt: Radicalisation and mediality in British news', *Critical Terrorism Studies*, 2/1: 1–13.

Hoskins, A. and O'Loughlin, B. (2009b) 'Media and the myth of radicalisation', *Media, War & Conflict*, 2/2: 107–10.

Hughes, K. P. (2007) '"Waging peace": A new paradigm for public diplomacy', *Mediterranean Quarterly*, 18/2: 18–36.

Human Security Brief (2006) *Human Security Brief 2006*, Vancouver: Human Security Center. Available at: www.humansecuritybrief.info/2006/contents/finalversion.pdf.

Huysmans, J. and Buonfino, A. (2008) 'Politics of exception and unease: Immigration, asylum and terrorism in parliamentary debates in the UK', *Political Studies*. Available at: www3.interscience.wiley.com/cgi–bin/fulltext/120121145/pdfstart.

Huyssen, A. (1995) *Twilight Memories: Marking Time in a Culture of Amnesia* London: Routledge.

Huyssen, A. (2000) 'Present pasts: Media, politics, amnesia', *Public Culture*, 12/1: 21–38.

Huyssen, A. (2003) *Present Pasts: Urban Palimpsests and the Politics of Memory*, Stanford: Stanford University Press.

ICSR (2009) *Countering Online Radicalisation: A Strategy For Action*, The International Centre for the Study of Radicalisation and Political Violence (ICSR): London. Available at: www.thecst.org.uk/docs/countering_online_radicalisation1.pdf.

Jackson, R. (2005) *Writing the War on Terror: Language, Politics and Counter-Terrorism*, Manchester: Manchester University Press.

Jameson, F. (1991) *Postmodernism, or the Cultural Logic of Late Capitalism*, London: Verso.

Jansson, A. and Lagerkvist, A. (2009) 'The future gaze: City panoramas as politico-emotive geographies', *Journal of Visual Culture*, 8/1: 25–53.

Jenkins, H. (2008) 'Human rights video in a participatory culture', *MediaShift Idea Lab*, 6 April. Available at: http://www.pbs.org/idealab/2008/04/to-youtube-or-not-to-youtube-h.html.

Jenkins, H. and M. Deuze (2008) 'Convergence culture', *Convergence*, 14/1: 5–12.

Jerslev, A. (2002) *Realism and 'Reality' in Film and Media: Northern Lights Film and Media Studies Yearbook 2002*, Copenhagen: Museum Tusculanum Press.

Johnson, S. (2002) *Emergence: The Connected Lives of Ants, Brains, Cities and Software*, London: Penguin Books Ltd.

Kamalipour, Y. R. and Snow, N. (eds) (2004) *War, Media, and Propaganda: A Global Perspective*, Oxford: Rowman & Littlefield.

Keller, U. (2001) *The Ultimate Spectacle: A Visual History of the Crimean War*, Amsterdam: Gordon and Breach Publishers.

Kennedy, L. (2003) 'Remembering September 11: Photography as cultural diplomacy', *International Affairs*, 79/2: 315–26.

Kennedy, L. and Lucas, S. (2005) 'Enduring freedom: Public diplomacy and US foreign policy', *American Quarterly*, 57/2: 309–33.

Khosrokhavar, F (2005) *Suicide Bombers: Allah's New Martyrs*, London: Pluto Press.

Kieran, M. (1997) *Media Ethics: A Philosophical Approach*, Westport, CT: Praeger.

King, G. (2009) 'The changing evidence base of social science research', in G. King, K. L. Schlozman and N. Nie (eds), *The Future of Political Science: 100 Perspectives*, New York and London: Routledge.

Kitzinger, Jenny (2000) 'Media templates: Key events and the (re)construction of meaning, *Media, Culture and Society*, 22/1: 61–84.

Klein, N. (2007) *The Shock Doctrine: The Rise of Disaster Capitalism*, New York: Metropolitan Books.

Knightley, P. (2003) *The First Casualty: The War Correspondent as Hero, Propagandist and Myth-Maker from the Crimea to Iraq*, London: Andre Deutsch.

Knorr-Cetina, K. (2005) 'Complex global microstructures: The new terrorist societies', *Theory, Culture & Society*, 22/5: 213–34.

Kolstø, P. (ed.) (2009) *Media Discourse and the Yugoslav Conflicts: Representations of Self and Other*, Bristol: Ashgate.

de Koning, M. (2008) 'Identity in transition. Connecting online and offline Internet practices of Moroccan-Dutch Muslim youth', Institute for the Study of European Transformations (ISET) Working Paper No. 9. Available at: www.londonmet.ac.uk/londonmet/library/c52116_3.pdf.

Konstantinidou, C. (2007) 'Death, lamentation and the photographic representation of the Other during the Second Iraq War in Greek newspaper', *International Journal of Cultural Studies*, 10/2, 147–66.

Kristof, N. (2005) 'Back to the brothel', *New York Times*, 22 January.

Kurtz, H. (2003) 'For media after Iraq, a case of shell shock: Battle assessment begins for saturation reporting', *Washington Post*, 27 April. Available at: www.washington-post.com/ac2/wp-dyn/A46401-2003Apr27?language=printer.

Lamont, M. and Thévenot, L. (eds) (2000) *Rethinking Comparative Cultural Sociology: Repertoires of Evaluation in France and the United States*, Cambridge: Cambridge University Press.

Landsberg, A. (2004) *Prosthetic Memory: The Transformation of American Remembrance in the Age of Mass Culture*, Columbia: Columbia University Press.

Lash, S. (2005) 'Intensive Media – Modernity and Algorithm' (draft). Available at: http://roundtable.kein.org/node/125.

Last Tommy, The (2005) BBC 1, 9 August. Archive at: www.bbc.co.uk/history/world-wars/wwone/last_tommy_gallery.shtml.

Latour, B. (1993) *We Have Never Been Modern*, Cambridge, MA: Harvard University Press.

Latour, B. (2004) 'Whose cosmos, which cosmopolitics? Comments on the peace terms of Ulrich Beck', *Common Knowledge*, 10/3: 450–62.

Latour, B. (2005) *Reassembling the Social: An Introduction to Actor-Network-Theory*, Oxford and New York: Oxford University Press.

Layoun, M. N. (2006) 'Visions of security: Impermeable borders, impassable walls, impossible home/lands?' in A. Martin and P. Petro (eds), *ReThinking Global Security: Media, Popular Culture, and the 'War on Terror'*, New Brunswick: Rutgers University Press

Leadbeater, C. (2008) *We-Think: The Power of Mass Creativity*, Profile Books Ltd.

Leman-Langlois, S. and Brodeur, J.-P. (2005) 'Terrorism old and new: Counterterrorism in Canada', *Police Practice and Research*, 6/2: 121–40.

Leonard, M., Amall, A. and Rose, M. (2005) *British Public Diplomacy in the 'Age of Schisms'*, London: The Foreign Policy Centre.

Lessig, L. (2006) *Code: Version 2.0*, Basic Books Inc.

Lewis J. (2005) *Language Wars: The Role of Media and Culture in Global Terror and Political Violence*, London: Pluto Press.

Lewis, J. (2008) 'The role of the media in boosting military spending', *Media War and Conflict*, 1/1.

Lewis, J. and Brookes, R. (2004) 'How British television news represented the case for the war in Iraq', in S. Allan and B. Zelizer (eds), *Reporting War: Journalism in Wartime*, London: Routledge, pp. 283–300.

Livingston, S. (1997) 'Clarifying the CNN effect: An examination of media effects according to type of military intervention', Joan Shorenstein Center, Harvard University, Research Paper R-18.

Livingstone, S. (ed.) (2005) *Audiences and Publics: When Cultural Engagement Matters for the Public Sphere*, Bristol: Intellect Books.

Livingstone, S. (2009) 'On the mediation of everything: ICA presidential address 2008', *Journal of Communication*, 59: 1–18.

Luckhurst, T. (2006) 'Humphrys goes to war', *Independent on Sunday*, Media News, 24 September, pp. 14–15. Available at: www.independent.co.uk/news/media/humphrys-goes-to-war-417250.html.

Luhmann, N. (1989) *Ecological Communication* (trans. J. Bednarz, Jr.), Chicago: Chicago University Press.

Luhmann, N. (2000[1996]) *The Reality of the Mass Media* (trans. Kathleen Cross), Cambridge: Polity.

Lynch, J. (2003) 'Reporting Iraq: What went right? What went wrong?' Reporting the World, Discussion Papers, 15 July. Available at: www.basicint.org/iraqconflict/Pubs/Discussion%20Papers/DS080903.htm.

Lynch, J. and McGoldrick, A. (2005) *Peace Journalism*, Stroud: Hawthorn Press.

Lytle, T. H. (2007) 'A soldier's blog: Balancing service members' personal rights vs.

national security interests', *Federal Communications Law Journal*, 59/3: 593–614. Available at: www.law.indiana.edu/fclj/pubs/v59/no3/12–Lytle.pdf.

Marcus, J. (2007) 'Israel's Syria "raid" remains a mystery', BBC News, 12 August. Available at: http://news.bbc.co.uk/2/hi/middle_east/6991718.stm.

Masco, J. (2002) 'Lie detectors: On secrets and hypersecurity in Los Alamos', *Public Culture*, 14/3: 441–67.

Masco, J. (2006) *The Nuclear Borderlands: The Manhattan Project in Post Cold-War New Mexico*, Princeton: Princeton University Press.

Massing, M. (2008) 'Embedded in Iraq', *The New York Review of Books*, 55/12, 17 July. Available at: www.nybooks.com/articles/21617.

Massumi, B. (2005a) 'Fear (the spectrum said)', *Positions*, 13: 31–48.

Massumi, B. (2005b) 'The future birth of the affective fact', Conference Proceedings: Genealogies of Biopolitics. Available at: www.radicalempiricism.org/biotextes/textes/massumi.pdf (accessed July 2007).

Matheson, D. and Allan, S. (2009) *Digital War Reporting*, Cambridge: Polity.

Mattern, J. B. (2005) *Ordering International Politics: Identity, Crisis and Representational Force*, New York: Routledge.

McCarthy, A. (2001) *Ambient Television: Visual Culture and Public Space*, Durham, NC: Duke University Press.

McNair, B. (2006) *Cultural Chaos: Journalism, News and Power in a Globalised World*, London: Routledge.

Melissen, J. (ed.) (2007) *The New Public Diplomacy*, Basingstoke: Palgrave.

Melissen, J. (2005) 'Wielding soft power: The new public diplomacy', *Netherlands Institute of International Relations*, Clingendael Diplomacy Papers No. 2 (May): 1–31.

Merrin, W. (2005) *Baudrillard and the Media: A Critical Introduction*, Cambridge: Polity.

Merrin, W. (2008) 'Media Studies 2.0'. Available at: http://mediastudies2point0.blog-spot.com/.

Mestrovic, S. G. (2005) *The Trials of Abu Ghraib: An Expert Witness Account of Shame and Honor*, Boulder, CO: Paradigm Publishers.

Michalski, M. and Gow, J. (2007) *War, Image, Legitimacy: Viewing Contemporary Conflict*, London: Routledge.

Miller, D. (2007) 'The propaganda machine', in D. Miller (ed.), *Tell Me Lies: Propaganda and Media Distortion in the Attack on Iraq*, London: Pluto, pp. 80–99.

Mirzoeff, N. (2005) *Watching Babylon: The War in Iraq and Global Visual Culture*, London: Routledge.

Mirzoeff, N. (2006) 'Invisible empire: Visual culture, embodied spectacle, and Abu Ghraib', *Radical History Review*, 95: 21–44.

Mitchell, W. J. T. (2006) 'Networked eyes', in C. A. Jones (ed.), *Sensorium: Embodied Experience, Technology and Contemporary Art*, Cambridge, MA: MIT Press.

Mitchell, W. J. T. (2008a) 'The fog of Abu Ghraib: Errol Morris and the "bad apples"', Harper's Magazine, 316 (1896): 81–6.

Mitchell, W. J. T. (2008b) 'Cloning terror: The war of images, 9/11 to Abu Ghraib'. Available at: http://bezalel.secured.co.il/8/mitchell.htm.

Moeller, S. D. (1999) *Compassion Fatigue: How the Media Sell Disease, Famine, War and Death*, London: Routledge.

Moore, K., Mason, P. and Lewis, J. (2008) 'Images of Islam in the UK: The representation of British Muslims in national print news media, 2000–2008', Cardiff School of Journalism, Media and Cultural Studies (JOMEC), 7 July. Available at: www.caerdydd.ac.uk/jomec/resources/08channel4-dispatches.pdf.

Morrison, D. and Tumber, H. (1988) *Journalists at War: The Dynamics of News Reporting During the Falklands War*, London, Sage.

Moss, G. and O'Loughlin, B. (2008) 'Convincing claims: Representation and democracy in post-9/11 Britain', *Political Studies*, 56/3: 705–24.

Müller, J.-W. (ed.) (2002) *Memory and Power in Post-War Europe: Studies in the Presence of the Past*, Cambridge: Cambridge University Press.

Mulvey, L. (2005) *Death 24x a Second: Stillness and the Moving Image*, London: Reaktion Books Ltd.

Nash, K. (2008) 'Global citizenship as show business: The cultural politics of Make Poverty History', *Media, Culture and Society*, 30/2: 167–81.

Nelson, T. E., Clawson, R. A. and Oxley, Z. M. (1997). 'Media framing of a civil liberties conflict and its effect on tolerance', *American Political Science Review*, 91/3: 567.

Neumann, P. R. (2009) *Old and New Terrorism*, Cambridge: Polity.

Neumann, P. R. and Smith M. L. R. (2008) *The Strategy of Terrorism: How it Works and Why it Fails*, London: Routledge.

Nisbet, E. C., Scheufele, D. A. and Shanahan, J. E. (2004) 'Public diplomacy, television news, and Muslim opinion', *Harvard International Journal of Press/Politics*, 9/11: 11–37.

Nora, P. (1989) 'Between memory and history: *Les lieux de mémoire*', *Representations*, (trans. Marc Roudebush), 26: 7–25.

Nye, J. (2004) 'Soft power and American foreign policy', *Political Science Quarterly*, 119/2: 255–70.

NYPD (2007) *Radicalisation in the West: The Homegrown Threat*, New York: NYPD. Available at: www.nypdshield.org/public/SiteFiles/documents/NYPD_Report-Radicalization_in_the_West.pdf.

Oliver, K. (2007) *Women as Weapons of War: Iraq, Sex, and the Media*, New York: Columbia University Press.

Painter, J. (2007) 'The boom in counter-hegemonic news channels: A case study of Telesur', Working Paper, Reuters Institute for the Study of Journalism, Oxford.

Palmer, J. and Fontan, V. (2007) '"Our ears and eyes": Journalists and fixers in Iraq', *Journalism*, 8/1: 5–24.

Pargeter, A. (2008) *The New Frontiers of Jihad: Radical Islam in Europe*, New York and London: I. B. Taurus.

Paul, C. and Kim, J. J. (2004) *Reporters on the Battlefield: The Embedded Press System in Historical Context*, London: Royal United Services Institute.

Perrone, J. (2003) 'Conflict of interest: The sites you need to see', *Guardian*, 27 March. Available at: www.guardian.co.uk/world/2003/mar/27/iraq.technology.

Peters, J. D. (1999) *Speaking Into the Air: A History of the Idea of Communication*, Chicago and London: The University of Chicago Press.

Peters, J. D. (2001) 'Witnessing', *Media, Culture & Society*, 23/6: 707–23.

Peters, R. (2005) *Jihad in classical and modern Islam: A Reader*, Princeton, NJ: Marcus Wiener.

Petersen, T. (2005) 'Testing visual signals in representative surveys', *International Journal of Public Opinion Research*, 17/4: 456–72.

Pfau, M. et al. (2008) 'The influence of television news depictions of the images of war on viewers', *Journal of Broadcasting & Electronic Media*, 52/2: 303–22.

Philo, G. and Berry, M. (2004) *Bad News From Israel*, London: Pluto Press.

Picard, E. (1993) *The Lebanese Shia and Political Violence*, United Nations Research Institute for Social Development, Discussion Paper 42. Available at: www.isn.ethz.ch/isn/Digital-Library/Publications/Detail/?ots591=0C54E3B3-1E9C-BE1E-2C24-A6A8C7060233&lng=en&id=28964.

Porath, D. (2009) 'Presenting and disseminating memory'. Presentation given as part of the programme for the workshop, 'On Media Memory: The future of mediated collective memory in an age of changing media environments', funded by the Israel Science Foundation, Yad Vashem, Jerusalem, 2 July. Available at: http://on–media–memory.org.il/.

Potter, E. H. (ed.) (2002) *Cyber-Diplomacy: Managing Foreign Policy in the Twenty-First Century*, London: McGill-Queen's University Press.

Price, V., Nir, L. and Cappella, J. N. (2006) 'Normative and informational influences in online political discussions', *Communication Theory*, 16: 47–74.

Rai, S. and Cottle, S. (2007) 'Global mediations: On the changing ecology of satellite television news', *Global Media and Communication*, 3/1: 51–78.

Ramsey, G. (2009) 'Relocating the virtual war', *Defence Against Terrorism Review*, 2/1: 31–50.

Reid, J. (2006) 'Security, freedom, and the protection of our values'. Speech at Demos, 9 August. Available at: www.demos.co.uk/files/johnreidsecurityandfreedom.pdf.

Richards, B. (2007) *Emotional Governance: Power, Media and Terror*, Basingstoke: Palgrave.

Richardson, K. and Corner, J. (1992) 'Reading reception: Mediations and transparency in viewers' reception of a TV programme', in P. Scannell, P. Schlesinger and C. Sparks (eds), *Culture and Power: A Media, Culture and Society Reader*, London: Sage.

Rid, T. and Hecker, M. (2009) *War 2.0: Irregular Warfare in the Information Age*, Westport, Praeger.

Rigney, A. (2004) 'Portable monuments: Literature, cultural memory, and the case of Jeanie Deans', *Poetics Today*, 25/2: 361–96.

Rigney, A. (2005) 'Plenitude, scarcity and the circulation of cultural memory', *Journal of European Studies*, 35/1: 209–26.

Ritchin, F. (2009) *After Photography*, New York: W. W. Norton & Company.

Robin, R. (2005) 'Requiem for Public Diplomacy?', *American Quarterly*, 57/2: 345–53.

Robinson, P. (2002) *The CNN Effect: The Myth of News, Foreign Policy and Intervention*, London and New York: Routledge.

Rose, G. (2007) *Visual Methodologies: An Introduction to the Interpretation of Visual Materials*, London: Sage.

Rose, S. (1993) *The Making of Memory: From Molecules to Mind*, London: Bantam Books.

Rose, S. (2008) 'Memories are made of this', in H. H. Wood and A. S. Byatt (eds), *Memory: An Anthology*, London: Chatto & Windus, pp. 54–67.

Roselle, L. (2006) *Media and the Politics of Failure: Great Powers, Communication Strategies, and Military Defeats*, New York: Palgrave Macmillan.

Rosenau, J. (2003) *Distant Proximities*, Princeton, NJ: Princeton University Press.

Roy, O. (2008) 'Al-Qaeda in the West as a youth movement: The power of a narrative', MICROCON Policy Working Paper 2, Brighton: MICROCON.

Rumford, C. (2008) *Cosmopolitan Spaces: Europe, Globalization, Theory*. London: Routledge.

Sageman, M. (2004) *Understanding Terror Networks*, Philadelphia: University of Pennsylvania Press.

Sageman, M. (2008) *Leaderless Jihad: Terror Networks in the Twenty-First Century*, Philadelphia: University of Pennsylvania Press.

Said, E. W. (1994) *Culture and Imperialism*, London: Vintage.

Samuel, R. (1994) *Theatres of Memory*. Volume 1: *Past and Present in Contemporary Culture*, London: Verso.

Sands, P. (2005) *Lawless World: America and the Making and Breaking of Global Rules*, London: Penguin.

Sassen, S. (2006) *Territory, Authority, Rights: From Medieval to Global Assemblages*, Princeton, NJ: Princeton University Press.

Sassen, S. (2007) *A Sociology of Globalization*, New York and London: W. W. Norton & Co.

Sawyer, R. K. (2005) *Social Emergence: Societies As Complex Systems*, Cambridge: Cambridge University Press.

Scannell, P. (2000) 'For-anyone-as-someone structures', *Media, Culture & Society*, 22/1: 5–24.

Scarry, E. (1985) *The Body in Pain: The Making and Unmaking of the World*, Oxford: Oxford University Press.

Schatzki, T. R., Knorr Cetiina, K. and Savigny, E. von (eds) (2001) *The Practice Turn in Contemporary Theory*, London: Routledge.

Schechter, D. (2003) *When News Lies: Media Complicity and the Iraq War*, New York: Select Books.

Schmeizer, P. (2007) 'Beyond bullets: A top war correspondent on the human side of news', *TC Daily*, 26 November.

Scholte, J. A. (2005) *Globalization: A Critical Introduction* (2nd rev. edn), Basingstoke: Palgrave.

Schudson, M. (1990) 'Ronald Reagan misremembered', in D. Middleton and D. Edwards (eds), *Collective Remembering*, London: Sage, pp.109–19.

Scollon, R. and Scollon, S. W. (2004) *Nexus Analysis: Discourse and the Emerging Internet*, London and New York: Routledge.

Scollon, R. and Scollon, S. W. (2007) 'Nexus analysis: Refocusing ethnography of action', *Journal of Sociolinguistics*, 11/5: 608–25.

Sennett, R. (1974) *The Fall of Public Man*, New York: Norton.

Shandler, J. (1999) *While America Watches: Televising the Holocaust*, New York: Oxford University Press.

Shapiro, M. J. (1997) *Violent Cartographies: Mapping Cultures of War*, London: University of Minnesota Press.

Shaw, M. (2003) *War and Genocide: Organized Killing in Modern Society*, Cambridge: Polity.

Shaw, M. (2005) *The New Western Way of War: Risk-Transfer War and its Crisis in Iraq*, Cambridge: Polity.

Silcock, B. W., Schwalbe, C. B. and Keith, S. (2008) '"Secret" Casualties: Images of Injury and Death in the Iraq War Across Media Platforms', *Journal of Mass Media Ethics*, 23: 36–50.

Silverstone, R. (2002) 'Mediating catastrophe: September 11 and the crisis of the other', *Dossiers de L'Audiovisuel*, 105. Available at: www.lse.ac.uk/collections/media@lse/pdf/mediatingcatastrophe.pdf.

Silverstone, R. (2007) *Media and Morality: On the Rise of the Mediapolis*, Cambridge: Polity.

Simpson, D. (2006) *9/11: The Culture of Commemoration*, Chicago: University of Chicago Press.

Simpson, J. (2001) 'Eyewitness: The liberation of Kabul', *BBC News*, 13 November. Available at: http://news.bbc.co.uk/2/hi/south_asia/1654353.stm.

Singer, P. W. (2009) 'Tactical generals: Leaders, technology, and the perils of battlefield micromanagement', *Air & Space Power Journal*, 1 June.

Sladen, M. (2007) 'Introduction', in *Memorial to the Iraq War* (Accompanying Exhibition Publication), Institute for Contemporary Arts, London.

Slim, H. (2007) *Killing Civilians: Method, Madness and Morality in War*, London: Hurst.

Smith, A. (1976) *The Theory of Moral Sentiments*, Oxford: Clarendon.

Snow, D. A., Burke Rochford, Jr., E., Worden, S. K. and Benford, R. D. (1986) 'Frame alignment processes, micromobilization and movement participation', *American Sociological Review*, 51/4: 464–81.

Sontag, S. (1979/1977) *On Photography*, London: Penguin.

Sontag, S. (2003) *Regarding the Pain of Others*, New York: Farrar, Straus and Giroux.

Sontag, S. (2004) 'Regarding the torture of others', *New York Times*, 23 May. Available at: www.nytimes.com/2004/05/23/magazine/23PRISONS.html (accessed 26 June 2005).

Spence, P. R., Westerman, D., Skalski, P., et al. (2005) 'Proxemic effects on information seeking after the September 11 attacks', *Communication Research Reports*, 22/1: 39–46.

Sreberny, A. (2007) 'War by other means', *The Times Higher*, 12 October: 18–19.

Sreberny, A. (2008) 'A contemporary Persian letter and its global purloining: The shifting spatialities of contemporary communication', in D. Hesmondhalgh and J. Toynbee (eds), *The Media and Social Theory*, London: Routledge.

Sturken, M. (1997) *Tangled Memories: The Vietnam War, the AIDS Epidemic, and the Politics of Remembering*, London: University California Press.

Sturken, M. (2007) *Tourists of History: Memory, Kitsch, and Consumerism from Oklahoma City to Ground Zero*, Durham, NC: Duke University Press.

Suskind, R. (2004) 'Faith, certainty and the presidency of George W. Bush', *New York Times*, 17 October. Available at: www.nytimes.com/2004/10/17/magazine/17BUSH.html.

Taylor, I. (2008) 'Surveying the battlefield: Mapping the different arguments and positions of the Iraq War debate through frame analysis', *Westminster Papers in Communication and Culture*, 5/3: 69–90.

Taylor, J. (1991) *War Photography: Realism in the British Press*, London: Routledge.

Taylor, J. (1998) *Body Horror: Photojournalism, Catastrophe and War*, Manchester: Manchester University Press.

Taylor, P. M. (1998/1992) *War and the Media: Propaganda and Persuasion in the Gulf War*, Manchester: Manchester University Press.

Taylor, P. M. (2003) (3rd edn) *Munitions of the Mind: A History of Propaganda from the Ancient World to the Present Day*, Manchester: Manchester University Press.

Tester, K. (2001) *Compassion, Morality and the Media*, Buckingham: Open University Press.

Tewksbury, D. (2006) 'Exposure to the newer media in a presidential primary campaign', *Political Communication*, 23: 313–32.

Thompson, A. (ed.) (2007) *The Media and the Rwanda Genocide*, London: Pluto Press.

Thompson, A. (2009) 'The genocide video', *Media, War & Conflict*, 2/3: (pages TBA).

Thrift, N. (2004) 'Remembering the technological unconscious by foregrounding knowledges of position', *Environment and Planning D: Society and Space*, 22/1: 175–90.

Tomlinson, J. (2008) 'Global immediacy', in D. Held and H. L. Moore (eds), *Cultural Politics in a Global Age: Uncertainty, Solidarity and Innovation*, Oxford: OneWorld.

Tuchman, G. (1972) 'Objectivity as strategic ritual: An examination of newsmen's notions of objectivity', *The American Journal of Sociology*, 77/4: 660–79.

Tumber, H. (2006) 'The fear of living dangerously: Journalists who report on conflict', *International Relations*, 20/4: 439–551.

Tumber, H. and Palmer. J. (2004) *Media at War: The Iraq Crisis*, London: Sage.

Tumber, H. and Webster, F. (2006) *Journalists Under Fire: Information War and Journalistic Practices*, London: Sage.

Turkle, S. (2008) 'Always-on/always-on-you: The tethered self', in J. E. Katz (ed.), *Mainstreaming Mobiles: Mobile Communication and Social Change*, Cambridge, MA: MIT Press, pp. 121–38.

UN News Centre (2006) 'Annan welcomes extension of African Union mission in Darfur', 21 September. Available at: www.un.org/apps/news/story.asp?News ID=19948&Cr=sudan&Cr1=.

Urry, J. (2003) *Global Complexity*, Cambridge: Polity.

Urry, J. (2005) 'The complexity turn', *Theory, Culture & Society*, 22/5: 1–14.

Urry, J. (2007) *Mobilities*, Cambridge: Polity.

US Department of Homeland Security (2008) *Terminology To Define The Terrorists: Recommendations from American Muslims*, Washington, DC: US Department of Homeland Security. Available at: www.dhs.gov/xlibrary/assets/dhs_crcl_terminology_08-1-08_accessible.pdf.

Van Der Veen, D. (1995) 'Watching for a judgement of real evil', *New York Times*, 12 November.

Vertovec, S. (2006) 'The emergence of superdiversity in Britain'. Centre on Migration, Policy and Society, working paper no. 25, University of Oxford.

Vietnam Notebook (2005) BBC Radio 2, 3 May.

Viner, K. (2009) 'Internet has changed foreign policy for ever, says Gordon Brown', *Guardian*, 19 June. Available at: www.guardian.co.uk/politics/2009/jun/19/gordon-brown-internet-foreign-policy.

Virilio, P. (1986) *Speed and Politics*, New York: Semiotext(e).

Virilio, P. (1989) *War and Cinema: The Logistics of Perception*, London, Verso.

Virilio, P. (1994) *The Vision Machine*, London and Bloomington: British Film Institute and Indiana University Press.

Virilio, P. (1997) *Open Sky*, London: Verso.

Volkmer, I. (2008) 'Conflict-related media events and cultures of proximity', *Media, War & Conflict*, 1/1: 90–8.

Vulliamy, E. (1997) 'I stand by my story', *Observer*, 2 February.

Vulliamy, E. (2007) interviewed by Matt Sepic on KWMU, St. Louis Public Radio, 20 November. Available at: www.publicbroadcasting.net/kwmu/news.newsmain?action=article&ARTICLE_ID=1186123 and http://www.stlpublicradio.org/news/edv.mp3.

Waever, O. (1995) 'Securitization and desecuritization', in R. D. Lipschutz (ed.), *On Security*, New York: Columbia University Press.

Waever, O., Buzan, B., Kelstrup, M. and Lemaitre, P. (1993) *Identity, Migration and the New Security Agenda in Europe*, London: Pinter.

Wall, M. (2005) 'Blogs of War', *Journalism*, 6/2: 153–72.

Wark, M. (1994) *Virtual Geography: Living with Global Media Events*, Bloomington: Indiana University Press.

Warner, M. (2002) 'Publics and Counterpublics', *Public Culture*, 14/1: 49–90.

Weber, S. (2004) 'Target of opportunity: Networks, netwar, and narratives', *Grey Room*, 15: 6–27.

Weinberger, D. (2007) *Everything is Miscellaneous: The Power of the New Digital Disorder*, New York: Times Books.

Weissman, G. (2004) *Fantasies of Witnessing: Postwar Efforts to Experience the Holocaust*, Ithaca: Cornell University Press.

Wertsch, J. W. (2002) *Voices of Collective Remembering*, Cambridge: Cambridge University Press.

Westhead, J. (2006) 'Planning the US "long war" on terror', BBC News, 10 April. Available at: http://news.bbc.co.uk/1/hi/4897786.stm.

Wetherell, M. and Potter, J. (1988) 'Discourse analysis and the identification of interpretive repertoires', in C. Antaki (ed.), *Analysing Everyday Explanation: A Casebook of Methods*, Newbury Park, CA: Sage, pp. 168–83.

White, M. and Schwoch, J. 'History and television'. Available at: www.museum.tv/archives/etv/H/htmlH/historyandt/historyandt.htm (accessed 14 May 2006).

Wiktorowicz, Q (2004) 'Joining the cause: Al-Muhajiroun and radical Islam'. The Roots of Islamic Radicalism Conference, Yale. Available at: http://insct.syr.edu/Projects/islam-ihl/research/Wiktorowicz.Joining%20the%20Cause.pdf.

Williams, R. (1974) *Television: Technology and Cultural Form*, London: Fontana

Williams, R. (1977) 'Structures of feeling', in R. Williams (ed.), *Marxism and Literature*, Oxford: Oxford University Press, pp. 128–35.

Wilton Park (2008) 'Public diplomacy: Meeting new challenges', Report on Wilton Park Conference 902, 6–9 October. Available at: www.wiltonpark.org/documents/conferences/WP902/pdfs/WP902.pdf.

Winter, J. (1995) *Sites of Memory, Sites of Mourning, the Great War in European Cultural History*, Cambridge: Cambridge University Press.

Winter, J. (2006) *Remembering War: The Great War Between Memory and History in the Twentieth Century*, New Haven: Yale University Press.

Wolfsfeld, G. (2004) *Media and the Path to Peace*, Cambridge: Cambridge University Press.

Wood, N. (1999) *Vectors of Memory: Legacies of Trauma in Postwar Europe*, Oxford: Berg.

Wood, J. (2008) *How Fiction Works*, London: Jonathan Cape.

Wright, S. (2009) 'Martyrs and martial imagery: Exploring the volatile link between warfare frames and religious violence', in M. Al-Rasheed and M. Shterin (eds), *Dying for Faith: Religiously Motivated Violence in the Contemporary World*, London and New York: I. B. Taurus, pp. 17–26.

Yehoshua, Y. (2006) 'Re-education of extremists in Saudi Arabia', Middle East Media Research Institute (MEMRI), *Inquiry and Analysis*, 260 (18 January). Available at: www.memri.org/bin/articles.cgi?Page=archives&Area=ia&ID=IA26006#_ednref10.

Žarkov, D. (2007) *The Body of War: Media, Ethnicity, and Gender in the Break-up of Yugoslavia*, Durham, NC: Duke University Press.

Zelizer, B. (1998) *Remembering to Forget: Holocaust Memory Through the Camera's Eye*, Chicago: University of Chicago Press.

Zelizer, B. and Allan, S. (eds) (2002) *Journalism After September 11*, London: Routledge.

Zhang, X. (2009) 'From propaganda to international communication: China's promotion of soft power in the age of information and communication technologies', in X. Zhang and Y. Zheng (eds), *China's Information and Communications Technology Revolution: Social Changes and State Responses*, London: Routledge, pp. 103–21.

Zimmermann, P. R. (2007) 'Public domains: Engaging Iraq through experimental digitalities', *Framework: The Journal of Cinema & Media*, 48/2: 66–83.

FURTHER READING

Gowing, N. (2009) '"Skyful of lies" and black swans: The new tyranny of shifting information power in crises', Reuters Institute for the Study of Journalism, University of Oxford.

Hagopian, P. (2009) *The Vietnam War in American Memory: Veterans, Memorials, and the Politics of Healing*, Amherst: University of Massachusetts Press.

Hamilton, J. (2009) *Journalism's Roving Eye: A History of American Foreign Reporting*, Baton Rouge: Louisiana State University Press.

Lynch, M. (2008) 'Political opportunity structures: Effects of Arab media', in K. Hafez (ed.), *Arab Media: Power and Weakness*, New York: Continuum.

Maltby, S. and Keeble, R. (eds) (2007) *Communicating War: Memory, Media and Military*, Suffolk: Arima Publishing.

Mitchell, W. J. T. (2005) 'There are no visual media', *Journal of Visual Culture*, 4/2: 257–66.

Seaton, J. (2005) *Carnage and the Media: The Making and Breaking of News About Violence*, London: Allen Lane.

Seib, P. (2004) *Beyond the Front Lines: How the News Media Cover a World Shaped By War*, Basingstoke: Palgrave Macmillan.

Seib, P. (2008) *The Al-Jazeera Effect: How the New Global Media Are Reshaping World Politics*, Washington, DC: Potomac Books Inc.

Taylor, P. M. (2007) '"Munitions of the mind": A brief history of military psychological operations', *Place Branding and Public Diplomacy*, 3/3: 196–204.

NAME INDEX

SUBJECT INDEX